The Architecture of the Visible

TECHNOLOGIES:
STUDIES IN CULTURE & THEORY

Editors: Gary Hall, Middlesex University, and Chris Hables Gray, University of Great Falls

CONSULTANT EDITORS
Parveen Adams, Keith Ansell Pearson, Jim Falk, Steve Graham, Donna Haraway, Deborah Heath, Manuel DeLanda, Paul Patton, Constance Penley, Kevin Robins, Avital Ronell, Andrew Ross, Allucquere Rosanne Stone

Technologies is a series dedicated to publishing innovative and provocative work on both 'new' and 'established' technologies: their history, contemporary issues and future frontiers. Bringing together theorists and practitioners in cultural studies, critical theory and Continental philosophy, the series will explore areas as diverse as cyberspace, the city, cybernetics, nanotechnology, the cosmos, AI, prosthetics, genetics and other medical advances, as well as specific technologies such as the gun, telephone, Internet and digital TV.

BOOKS IN THE SERIES

THE ARCHITECTURE OF THE VISIBLE

GRAHAM MACPHEE

continuum
LONDON • NEW YORK

CONTINUUM

The Tower Building, 11 York Road, London SE1 7NX

370 Lexington Avenue, New York, NY 10017-6503

www.continuumboooks.com

First published 2002

British Library Cataloguing-in-Publication Data
A catalogue record for this book is available from the British Library.
    ISBN 0-8264-5925-0 (hardback)
    ISBN 0-8264-5926-9 (paperback)

Library of Congress Cataloging-in-Publication Data
CIP data is available from the Library of Congress

Typeset by CentraServe Ltd, Saffron Walden, Essex
Printed and bound in Great Britain by
Biddles Ltd, Guildford and King's Lynn

Contents

Acknowledgements

This book grew out of an earlier, quite different project, but I would like to take this opportunity to thank again all those who offered advice and insights, especially Peter Nicholls, Drew Milne, Andrew Crozier, Bob Perelman, and Marjorie Welish. The last section of chapter three appeared in an earlier form in Magdalena Zaborowska (ed.) *Other Americans, Other Americas* (Aarhus, 1998), and I am grateful to Aarhus University Press for permission to use it here.

The book would not have assumed its current form without the prompting of a number of friends and colleagues over the years, and I would like to thank in particular Desmond Bailey, David Johnson, Simon Morgan-Wortham, and Prem Poddar. I am indebted to Charles Silver at the Museum of Modern Art, New York, and to Ulla Spittler for her painstaking and thoughtful translation. I have benefited greatly from the judicious insights offered by Gary Hall, and I am grateful to him for generosity and tact. I would also like to thank Howard Caygill for his encouragement and interest in the project.

I owe a longer-term debt of thanks to Anne MacPhee, who has done so much over the years to educate my eye. However, my greatest debt is to Sally Eberhardt for helping me to orientate my vision. This book is dedicated to her with love.

Introduction

> It was not reason but a man-made instrument, the tele-
> scope, which actually changed the physical world view; it
> was not contemplation, observation, and speculation which
> led to the new knowledge, but the active stepping in of
> *homo faber*, of making and fabricating.
>
> Hannah Arendt, *The Human Condition*

Soon after the launch of the first Sputnik in 1957, Hannah Arendt
observed in *The Human Condition* that for the first time 'an earth-born
object made by man . . . moved in the proximity of the heavenly
bodies as though it had been admitted tentatively to their sublime
company', an event which she described as 'second in importance to
no other, not even the splitting of the atom' (1989, p. 1). For Arendt,
the significance of Sputnik was as much to do with the reaction it
provoked as with the 'uncomfortable military and political circumstances attending it', a response which she noted was not one of
triumph, but of relief – relief, in the words of one American
newspaper, that we might at last 'escape' from our 'imprisonment [on]
the earth' (*ibid.*). 'The banality of this statement', she writes, 'should
not make us overlook how extraordinary in fact it was'; for notwithstanding the Christian longing for other-worldly salvation, according
to Arendt 'nobody in the history of mankind has ever conceived of the
earth as a prison for men's bodies or shown such eagerness to go
literally from here to the moon' (*ibid.*, p. 2). The broader significance
of this drive to escape the earth is understood by Arendt in terms of a
fundamental rearrangement of human vision. With space flight, the
human eye is able to occupy a completely new viewpoint, one which

is no longer anchored on the earth, but looks down on it from an Archimedean point beyond the limits of the world and of human experience. This new vantage point marks a profound change in the ways in which humanity has experienced its inextricable involvement in the world, an involvement which Arendt calls simply 'the human condition'. Space flight enables a vision of the world which is no longer bound to earthly experience, and in securing this new viewpoint, technology is no longer directed towards humanity's ongoing engagement with the world, but towards the dream of escaping the 'human condition' itself.

At first sight, Arendt's reflections on Sputnik and the modern Archimedean viewpoint may seem, quite literally, a million miles away from contemporary visual culture, but her remarks can be brought back down to earth by considering the subsequent discussion of the telescope in *The Human Condition*. Although the successful launch of Sputnik 1 marks the moment when a new viewpoint becomes possible, for Arendt this perspective was not unprecedented, but had been anticipated by the discovery of the telescope. While we still gaze at the stars from our location on earth, the telescope destroys the certainty of the senses, which tell us that it is the sun that moves and not the earth; thus, from the heliocentric perspective which it opens up, we see 'nature from a point in the universe outside of the earth'. 'Without actually standing where Archimedes wished to stand', Arendt observes, 'we have found a way to act on the earth and within terrestrial nature as though we dispose of it from outside, from the Archimedean point' (*ibid.*, p. 262). The power of the telescope lies in the fact that its challenge to the senses occurs not simply at the level of cognition – which would only have reinforced the old opposition between mind and body – but at the level of sensory experience; the telescope not only allows the world to be thought of differently, it also allows it to be *experienced* differently. Consequently, its ramifications are far-reaching and contradictory. In an immediate sense, the telescope enhances the resolution and range of vision, and with it the power of the perceiving consciousness that peers through it to survey the world and the cosmos. Yet ultimately, the telescope's Archimedean viewpoint demolishes the very possibility not simply of a subjective or 'human', but also of an *earth-bound* point of view. From

2

INTRODUCTION

the Archimedean vantage point implied by the telescope, human existence is no longer unique or exceptional; 'watched from a sufficiently removed vantage point in the universe', notes Arendt, the constant striving of human history 'would appear like a process of biological mutation' comparable to 'the mutation that now goes on before our eyes in the small living organisms which we [fight] with antibiotics' (*ibid.*, pp. 322–3). And while the telescope's discovery of a geometrically ordered world initially privileges vision as a model for consciousness, in the long run it implies the failure of vision to provide such a model. For as Arendt observes, the Archimedean viewpoint requires 'the entirely un-Platonic subjection of geometry to algebraic treatment', a subjection that frees scientific thought from spatiality, and thus from 'the shackles of earth-bound experience' (*ibid.*, p. 265). The impact of the telescope is therefore radically contradictory: while it provides the conditions for the perceiving consciousness to experience its own power and the freedom to range over a world apprehended through sensation, ultimately it undermines the very possibility of any such subjective vantage point, and indeed of vision's very locatedness in the world.

The trajectory that Arendt describes in her discussion of the telescope dramatizes many of the central concerns of this study. The penetration of visual culture by technology – from the emergence of photography in the nineteenth century, through film and video to the new digital information technologies – has come to be understood as one of the central features of Western modernity. Visual technologies permeate the main forms of mass-mediated popular culture, and have played a crucial role in the development of modern mass societies and the subsequent emergence of what might be described – however problematically – as a new global cultural space. Equally, their proliferation has also had a powerful influence on modes of representation and meaning that do not appear to be directly dependent on technology, as is perhaps most evident in the case of modernism and postmodernism in literature and the visual arts. The complex changes associated with these developments have demanded new paradigms of cultural, social and political explanation, and as such they have increasingly come to be seen as undermining the most basic assumptions of modern philosophy and critical thought. The far-reaching

3

nature of this impact, and the perception of its cumulative power over an extended period, has contributed powerfully to the sense of a radical historical discontinuity between our own social, cultural and political situation and those which preceded it. Indeed, for a number of theorists – perhaps most prominently Guy Debord, Jean Baudrillard, Paul Virilio, and Frederic Jameson – the technological organization of vision and the visible defines the fundamental character of our contemporary condition. What unites the different positions developed by these writers is the view that the perceptual parameters of the modern subject become redundant within the technological image-space of post-war, Western culture, which is therefore understood as marking the collapse of the broader conceptual frameworks developed by modern thought. Rather than confirming the unity and spontaneity of the modern subject, the new condition of technological appearance is seen either to mark the failure of such a subject to assimilate this new sensory world, or as final proof of this subject's propensity to violence and domination. From this perspective, what defines our contemporary condition is precisely the inapplicability of modern paradigms of representation, meaning, action and politics, paradigms that are understood as irretrievably bound up with the model of an isolated and self-sufficient perceiving consciousness.

The contention that animates the present study, and sets it apart from most existing approaches, is that the new technological condition of visual culture cannot simply be understood as marking the breakdown of our inherited conceptions of vision and the perceiving subject, conceived of as settled or complete. Rather, this book argues that in forcing us to rethink the very terms of visual experience, this new condition requires that we rediscover and reinvent the traditions of thinking bequeathed by modern culture. Implicit in this approach is a line of argument that is in fact shared by a number of the central thinkers discussed in the book: namely that the retroactive power of the present does not only work to demonstrate the insufficiency of past paradigms, so revealing the limits of their conceptual parameters; it also works to reinvent those parameters, allowing us to discover possibilities that, in a sense, were *not already there*, but which become available only in retrospect. At the broadest level, the present study is concerned with the ways in which the technological reformulation of visual culture has shaped contemporary understandings of cultural production and meaning, visual and literary representation, social agency, and political judgement. However, given the range of issues involved, it locates its analysis within the more restricted focus provided by the most prominent and influential theoretical accounts of the new technological condition of visual culture – namely those developed by Debord, Baudrillard, Virilio, and Jameson. This location reflects an assessment of the significance of these four critics that extends beyond linear notions of influence, intellectual development and disciplinary definition, since their work is understood to encapsulate many of the central tensions, anxieties, dilemmas, and contradictions that figure in a much broader context of intellectual inquiry.

The wider significance of this strand of cultural criticism lies in the perceived affinity between its own assessment of the collapse of modern conceptions of vision in contemporary culture and the broader questioning of the modern subject associated with a range of intellectual projects, from Michel Foucault's critique of theoretical humanism to the deconstruction of metaphysics associated with Martin Heidegger and Jacques Derrida. The perception of this affinity depends on an increasing awareness of the role played by vision as an organizing principle within modern thought, which institutes a separation between the determinate and visible world of experience, and an invisible or supersensible world which nonetheless frames and organizes it. Once the unseen truths of revealed religion began to disintegrate in early modern Europe, the eye assumed a powerful new role in defining experience and the activity of consciousness. However, the subsequent history of modernity has made intellectuals increasingly suspicious of the faith placed in sight, which is now often understood to involve a dangerous circularity that amounts to little more than blindness. Because the very power of the eye seems to presuppose its own self-evidence and certainty, vision has increasingly been criticized for implying an underlying – and so invisible – structure of consciousness that is self-sufficient and in certain possession both of itself and the world it confronts. In its most emphatic form, this suspicion views Kant's apperceptive subject, the pivot of the 'Copernican turn' taken by modern thought, as bearing out the prejudices involved in the everyday act of seeing, where we experience what we see as certain, and where we forget the particularity of our own perspective and its part in shaping what is seen. In these terms, the Kantian subject replicates the illusions of sense perception by setting itself in opposition to a visible world of objects whose presence is clear and certain, so assuming its own *invisible* unity and spontaneity.

A sense of the political and ethical consequences widely identified with modern thought's reliance on notions of vision can be seen in Richard Beardsworth's *Derrida and the Political* (1996). Beardsworth argues persuasively that the division between the visible and the invisible is a profoundly political question for modern thought. Kant's understanding of freedom as something counter to or outside of spatio-temporal experience casts it as invisible, and so unknowable; but by placing freedom beyond spatio-temporal experience, Beardsworth argues that Kant occludes the partiality of his rational morality, and limits it to a negative freedom of restriction. Kant's location of the moral nature of the subject in the supersensible can therefore be seen to lie at the root of the Enlightenment's blindness to its own suppressions and acts of violence.

This understanding of the political stakes involved in the division between the visible and the invisible is consistent with the central modern critique of Kant developed by Hegel, which significantly turns on the issue of *recognition*. Hegel connects the question of social and political invisibility – for example, the marginalization of poverty in modern bourgeois society, or its exporting of violence to the unseen colonial periphery – with Kant's occlusion of the conceptual suppressions involved in his negative notion of freedom. For Hegel, Kant's conception of the spontaneity of the moral law already presupposes the prior condition of legality or lawfulness, and its failure to acknowledge this presupposition is identified by Hegel as *misrecognition*. Equally, this structure of misrecognition is discernible in the failure of modern society to acknowledge the social violence of poverty and political marginalization, or the military violence of colonialism. Hegel's thought therefore seeks to re-inhabit or 're-cognize' the history of Western philosophy, and its apogee in Kant and the Enlightenment, in order to bring to visibility such invisible suppressions; that is, it seeks to reorientate the terms of modernity's self-understanding by recognizing the history of modern thought's misrecognitions. Yet according to Beardsworth, however powerful Hegel's critique of Kant may be, it fails to free itself from the very logic of visibility that ensnares Kant and Enlightenment thought. The central problem for Beardsworth is that Hegel's approach locates each moment of violence at a particular site in space and time, instead of understanding violence as the generalized condition of location or siting. As a result, according to Beardsworth, Hegel assumes precisely the scene of visibility and presence which had earlier been presupposed by Kant. 'Violence is repressed', writes Beardsworth, 'precisely by being placed in a site', so that the demand for 'visibility' or recognition 'ends up being blind'. The dynamic of recognition is 'blind', according to Beardsworth, 'because it is unable to see beyond the law of visibility, that is, the law of contradiction' (*ibid.*, p. 94). Within these terms, visibility appears to involve an inescapable commitment to presence, and modern thought's perennial faith in the dream of an absolute visibility dooms it to political failure and the exponential intensification of violence.

This suspicion of vision and the visible finds a powerful echo in recent cultural criticism, which has increasingly assumed a necessary connection between visibility and presence. Indeed, for Debord, Baudrillard, Virilio, and Jameson, the historical development of con- temporary visual culture provides a kind of dramatic confirmation or realization of the wider critical reassessment of modern thought. In these terms, the self-evidence of unaided vision is seen as analogous to the Enlightenment faith in the clarity and certainty of the visible, while technology's increasing penetration of visual culture is seen as under- mining such a certainty in a way that matches the theoretical decon- struction of the claim to presence. Where rational consciousness was once modelled on the self-directing character of the perceiving subject, the coherence of visual experience is now no longer seen as a function of the subject's activity, but rather as a function of the technologies that organize the gaze and the image-world it surveys. Thus, where philosophical critique identifies the failure of the modern subject's vision, so technology is understood as actualizing this failure, so making it the condition of contemporary experience. The significance of technologically mediated visual culture is therefore seen to lie in its disruption or overcoming of the perceptual parameters assumed by modern thought. From this perspective, as Jonathan Crary has recently argued, our contemporary cultural condition presages 'an unmistakable historical discontinuity' between contemporary visual experience and 'the notions of apperception that were important . . . to Leibniz and Kant' (1999, p. 19).

Yet if recent accounts of the technological condition of visual culture claim a broader significance in these terms, in doing so they raise a number of important theoretical questions. In regarding contemporary visual experience as irretrievably inert, disorientating or worthless, recent cultural criticism implies an inescapable hostility towards both vision and technology. However, it is by no means clear that the critique of metaphysics and presence necessarily involves such an absolute rejection of the visual experience of technological modernity. Indeed, as Heidegger remarks in 'What are Poets For?' (1946), 'an eye that looks out upon the integral whole of beings will receive a hint from the phenomena of rising technology', a hint that directs 'it towards those realms from which there could perhaps emerge a surpassing of the technical' (1975, p. 112). Equally, however we choose to understand this broader questioning of vision and of the modern subject, the assumption of an absolute discontinuity between modern thought and contemporary experience poses a particular conundrum when it comes to supply the parameters for cultural analysis: for the very conceptual categories which criticism has at its disposal to describe visual experience are precisely those which this same experience renders obsolete. In this situation, contemporary theory risks painting itself into a corner, for if the technological organization of vision is understood as marking the irretrievable collapse of our inherited paradigms of understanding and meaning, then the visual experience it gives rise to can only ever be understood in terms of disorientation and loss. As a consequence, the new modes of seeing made possible by the extraordinary technological developments of the last century and a half are ultimately conceived as empty and worthless. And however much critics may seek to view this situation with a dialectical equanimity or a joyous, Nietzschean resolve, by emptying visual experience of all value, their positions necessarily imply the collapse of political agency, and a passive, rather than an active, nihilism.

This book aims to identify conceptual resources for moving beyond this impasse by asking whether the experience of technological modernity might allow us to rethink the very nature of 'vision' and 'visibility'. However, it does not claim to offer a comprehensive account of all the complex intellectual histories involved, nor to present a 'representative' survey. Instead it examines the conceptual assumptions underlying a number of the most influential theoretical accounts of contemporary culture by placing them in relation to broader tendencies within modern thought and pivotal moments in the reformulation of visual experience in modernity. In doing so, this study pursues three related lines of inquiry.

The first is suggested by Arendt's characterization of the impact of the telescope, and the claims she makes for the significance of 'the active stepping in of *homo faber*, of making and fabricating' (*op. cit..*, p. 274). While Arendt's statement of the importance of the telescope might appear to exhibit a naïve technological determinism, within the context of her argument it can instead be understood as a reminder that, from the outset, modern thought was not divorced from technology, but was in a profound sense already 'technological'. Therefore, not only must assumptions about the 'pure' or 'natural' status of modern conceptions of vision be questioned, but the role which these retrospective claims may play within recent accounts also needs to be addressed. And once modern conceptions of vision are understood as being bound up in the emergence of 'global technology' in the widest sense, then even if our experience is fundamentally separated from them, these older paradigms may yet offer a means for assessing the nature of our own situation and for identifying different possible conceptions of visual experience.

The second line of inquiry addresses technology's impact in terms of the transformation of the spatio-temporal co-ordinates of experience. While this question extends to other modes of experience, this study argues that visual culture is particularly revealing in that the traces of this transformation become apparent – or are made *visible* – through distortion, disharmony and irresolution. It therefore asks how vision's foregrounding of the space and time of experience might offer particular insights into technology, and how technology's capacity to reorganize the co-ordinates of experience might offer ways of rethinking vision.

9

The third line of inquiry broadens the terms of discussion by examining the wider intellectual context within which the analysis of technology and visual culture takes place. In questioning assumptions about the necessarily metaphysical nature of vision, this book seeks to reopen discussion of the transcendental conditions of perceptual experience – or what we might call the invisible architecture of the visible. But it does so in the light of technology's animation of the visual world, and of the complex re-examination of the transcendental that has been such a feature of recent critical thought. Taken together, these different lines of questioning identify possibilities for rethinking the conceptual parameters of vision, from notions of intentionality and memory to questions of form and the temporality of the visible itself.

In pursing these lines of inquiry, this book concentrates on particular moments in modern thought and culture which register or respond to the new modes of experience made possible by the telescope, photography and film, and more broadly by the dynamic visual context of urban modernity. By exploring these moments, it seeks to draw out some of the wider implications of the technological transformation of visual experience for cultural analysis, visual and literary representation, social agency, and the critical reassessment of modern thought. The first chapter looks at the very different approaches offered by the theoretical philosophy of René Descartes and the art criticism of Charles Baudelaire, and examines their respective reactions to the telescope and the camera. In arguing that technology plays a vital role in modern accounts of visual experience, whether understood in cognitive or aesthetic terms, this chapter concludes by briefly considering the place of perception in Kant's critical philosophy. This discussion provides an important context for chapter two, which looks at the work of Debord, Baudrillard, Virilio, and Jameson, and seeks to assess their respective relationships to the earlier conceptions of vision which they judge to have been rendered obsolete. This chapter identifies a number of significant problems in their different understandings of visual experience, and consequently it asks whether this term might be thought differently. The third chapter turns to the broader intellectual context within which contemporary approaches to vision and visual culture take place. It centres on Derrida's critical engagement with phenomenology, an engagement that has powerfully influenced contemporary understandings of meaning, subjectivity, and the relationship between language and visual experience. The reading offered here stresses the productive potential which Derrida sees in phenomenology alongside his deconstruction of many of its central assumptions and claims, and attempts to draw out the significance for cultural criticism of this more equivocal and nuanced assessment. The last chapter pursues some of the implications of Derrida's questioning of the role of vision in modern thought by examining an important attempt to re-articulate this tradition, namely that developed by the Weimar philosopher and critic, Walter Benjamin. It draws on the recent reinterpretation of Benjamin's work by Howard Caygill, who argues that Benjamin's thinking offers a complex engagement with visual experience that has until now been neglected.

The closing discussion of Benjamin brings into sharp focus the conceptual dilemmas or aporias posed by technology's transformation of visual culture, dilemmas which lend a much wider significance to the conjunction of vision and technology examined here. One of the central arguments of this book is that any investigation of vision and the visible must engage with the conditions that make perceptual experience possible – or with what we have called the invisible architecture of the visible. However, the lesson that emerges most clearly from the extraordinary impact of technology in modernity is that visual experience is not self-identical or fully present, and therefore any consideration of its conditions cannot assume a static and universal transcendental structure. As such, technology poses particular problems for critical analysis, since in generating new and unprecedented modes of perceptual experience it questions the very possibility of a subjective, 'human', or even earth-bound point of view. As we have seen, for Hannah Arendt this situation is anticipated by the contradictory potentials encapsulated in the telescope: for if the telescope enhances the subject's vision and places it at the centre of a visual field reaching into the cosmos, it also pulls away the very ground underlying the subject's privileged point of view. This book argues that the importance of Benjamin's approach lies in the fact that it seeks to resist 'solving' this aporia – for example, by bringing technology's animation of the visible to order under the steady gaze of a self-possessed subject, or by dissolving the specificity of visual experience into the autonomous logics of an unknowable technology. Rather than privileging either term, Benjamin instead looks to technology itself to discover ways of reinventing the very terms in which we might think the dynamic and constantly changing architecture of the visible.

CHAPTER 1

Visions of Modernity

... all shapes speak to us, and nothing is indifferent or
unnecessary ...

Friedrich Nietzsche, *The Birth of Tragedy*

VARIETIES OF PERCEPTION

One of the most striking features of recent theoretical accounts of
contemporary culture has been the pervasive concern with the impact
of technology on vision and the visual. Since the 1960s, a range of
critics, including most prominently Guy Debord, Jean Baudrillard, Paul
Virilio, and Frederic Jameson, have argued that technology not only
reinvents visual culture, but that the new predominance of the visual
changes the nature of culture itself. Technology's capacity to reproduce
and circulate images is seen to mesh with the larger dynamics of post-
war consumer society, and to anticipate broader patterns of social,
economic, and cultural change. The unprecedented ubiquity and autonomy of the reproduced image comes to describe the condition of
cultural meaning in the widest sense, and its lustre and power is
understood to overwhelm the perceiving subject and to exceed its
capacity for recognition, orientation, and judgement. Technology's
impact is therefore understood to extend far beyond immediate questions of sensory apprehension, for in providing the new conditions of
cultural meaning, technologically mediated images colonize the subject
and reorganize the terms of its cognitive and political engagement with
the world. Thus these accounts are iconoclastic in a double sense: first,
they see the loss of an older visual condition and the emergence of a
new one; and second, they see the collapse of the modern subject and
the epistemological and political frameworks it was understood to entail.

The aim of this chapter is to provide a context for assessing these accounts by returning to key moments in the formulation of the modern paradigm of vision, but it does so in the light of this renewed sense of technology's significance. By focusing on the technological reinvention of the visual, recent approaches ask why vision should have come to provide such a ubiquitous model for modern thought rather than another of the senses, and what this model might involve. Unlike touch, vision can operate at long range; unlike smell, it allows the complex of sensory data to be distinguished, differentiated, and allotted a discrete source or origin; unlike hearing, it is able to adjust and direct its own receptivity; and unlike taste, it allows us to put out of our minds – at least for some of the time – the role of our bodies in the experience of sensation, so obscuring the partiality and specificity of our own sensory experience. Thus understood, vision offers a model of engagement with the world which Michel Foucault has described as *representation*, a paradoxically immaterial grasping of the world, whose rendering of the substantiality of things claims to be uncorrupted by material transmission or the experiential specificity of the human organism (1970, ch. 3). For many modern intellectuals and artists, such an understanding of vision has offered a powerful new model for envisaging the exercise of human capacities in relation to the sensible world; yet, at the same time, it has raised for others difficult questions about the relationship between consciousness and perception, and between the subject and the sensible world. In recalling the history of modern conceptions of vision it is therefore important to bear in mind the problematic status of vision within modern culture, and the very different ways in which it was understood.

Within modern European culture, vision has been valued in two distinct senses: first, in terms of knowledge or epistemology; and second, in terms of the aesthetic, or its role in the experience of beauty. For many modern thinkers, especially those concerned with the natural sciences, the significance of vision was seen to lie primarily in enabling the rational understanding of the world. In these terms, vision is conceived of as a detached gaze which weighs its judgements against the evidence of observation, rather than the dictates of faith, tradition, or a predetermined order of nature. Associated with evidence and rational inquiry, such a conception of vision implies a particular paradigm of the subject's relation to the world, within which the disinterested and rational subject confronts a world of objects which become progressively knowable for human thought. Thus for the philosopher, geometer, and physicist René Descartes, vision offered a powerful instrument for mastering the sensible world by extending the reach and scope of knowledge. In choosing to open his *Optics* of 1637 with a robust affirmation of the practical potential of lens manufacture, and particularly of the telescope, Descartes identifies the importance of vision in terms of its instrumental utility: 'the conduct of our life', he observes, 'depends entirely on our senses, and since sight is the noblest and most comprehensive of the senses, inventions which serve to increase its power are undoubtedly among the most useful there can be' (1988, p. 57). But for others, vision was valued not for its role in the service of cognition, but in terms of its own sensuous qualities. From this perspective, vision is understood in terms of the sensory apprehension of appearances through which the subject's gaze discovers a proportion or harmony which points to a meaningful-ness beyond its own limits. Again, such a conception of vision also implies a particular paradigm of the subject and its relationship to the world, within which the spontaneity of the perceiving subject in harmonizing the flux of appearances confirms its inner unity and freedom. The poet and critic Charles Baudelaire, for example, cele-brated the modern heroism of the artist by imaging the artist as an optical instrument: the artist for Baudelaire is 'a kaleidoscope endowed with consciousness, which with every one of its movements presents a pattern of life, in all its multiplicity, and the flowing grace of all the elements that go to compose life' (1972, p. 400).

However, if modern culture has celebrated vision in both episte-mological and aesthetic terms, it has also questioned the value of such visual knowledge and of the harmony of beautiful appearance. For important strands within modern culture, the epistemological and aesthetic claims summarized here were not only unsatisfactory, but also self-deluding, arrogant, and even potentially dangerous. In terms of its epistemological value, questions were quickly raised about the unlocated and idealized relationship of subject and object implied by this conception of vision. The world as object of the gaze is conceived of as discrete and uniformly visible, a vista which presents to the perceiving subject the fullness and clarity of its appearance. The activity of perception does not touch or distort this world, nor add its imprint to the visual data it receives, since it does not inhabit the world; and because unlocated, vision does not suffer from the vagaries of vantage point or perspective, nor from limits to its resolution or scope. However, the critical or scientific credentials of such an understanding of the visible quickly come unstuck, in that its assumption of the visibility of the world presupposes what it should find out, and its knowledge of the world is built on its prior assumptions about its nature. What is more, in assuming the clarity of and coherence of appearances, such a conception of vision excludes any kind of visual experience which does not occur in these terms, casting it as aberrant, distorted, and illusory. Equally, in terms of the aesthetic value of vision, questions were soon raised about the nature of beauty and its harmonizing of the visible world. If the meaningfulness or coherence of appearances is produced by the subject in framing or forming the matter of sensation, the question immediately arises as to the source of this frame. If the subject is understood as isolated and self-enclosed, this frame must presumably emerge spontaneously from within; but in that case, the claims made for such a harmonious apprehension of the world ring rather hollow. For although beauty is meant to attest to the freedom and spontaneity of the subject's perception of the world, its freedom is bought at the cost of the enslavement of things, which are viewed not in terms of their own specificity, but through the visual framework of the subject. The harmony so 'discovered' would then be worthless, since, if what is seen is simply the projection of the subject, then the coherence of appearances would be at best an irrelevance, and at worst a mistaken 'confirmation' of the subject's harmony with the world.

These kinds of objections can be found in the writing of Hume, Kant, and Hegel, but they are perhaps most economically encapsulated in the opening discussion of appearance in Friedrich Nietzsche's *The Birth of Tragedy* (1872). Here Nietzsche questions the notion of visual coherence which he sees as underlying both aesthetic and cognitive accounts of vision, and he does this by introducing music, an artistic medium which depends on a quite different notion of 'harmony'. According to Nietzsche, European thought has since Plato tended to limit the possibilities of visual experience by organizing it according to a restricted conception of coherence, in which 'all shapes speak to us, and nothing is indifferent and unnecessary' (1993, p. 15). Nietzsche questions the status of such visual coherence by locating it in a world racked by the 'dread that grips man when he suddenly loses his way amidst the cognitive forms of appearance, because the principle of sufficient reason . . . seems suspended' (ibid., p. 16). Within such a world, we might well ask whether the static harmony of appearances is not as much a function of the subject's desire for stability and security, as it is a reflection of the coherence of the world or the unity of the subject. In these terms, the force of Nietzsche's statement of the meaningfulness of appearance lies in the gap it identifies between the terms of visual coherence and a universe which is indifferent to human conceptions of relation, causality, and meaning. However, there is another sense in which Nietzsche's questioning of coherence asks to be read, one which comes to the fore when the example of music is brought to mind. Vision has come to imply a paradigm of meaningfulness based on clarity and coherence, against which alternative forms of experience are cast as aberrant, incoherent, and false. Yet a quite different notion of 'harmony' is offered by music, one which is not static but occurs in the variable temporal patterning of rhythms. Such an alternative notion of harmony in turn suggests that the coherence underlying epistemological and aesthetic accounts of vision provides only one possible model of patterning or 'harmony'. In these terms, Nietzsche's comparison between music and visual art can be understood as diagnostic rather than simply antagonistic, and does not imply a hostility to all forms of patterning, nor constitute a demand for an absolute incoherence to set against the unity of visual form. Rather, it challenges us to think beyond the static character of visual form, and instead envisage different models of patterning, rhythm, or spatio-temporal arrangement. In this light, we might read Nietzsche's statement more literally, as raising the possibility of a meaningfulness that exceeds the limits of modern accounts of aesthetic and cognitive vision. It may be that 'all shapes' do indeed 'speak to us', although not only in terms of a clarity and coherence that is fully present, right there and just now; but also through distortion, visual ambiguity, blurring, and dissonance. In this sense, Nietzsche asks how our inherited conceptions of vision might narrow the possibilities of visual experience, and in so doing he raises the prospect of different possible configurations of vision.

If modern European culture has celebrated vision for both its cognitive and aesthetic potential, it has also developed ways of critically questioning the terms through which these claims are articulated. The value of the critical approach developed by Nietzsche, among others, is that it allows a return to the traditions of modern aesthetic and epistemological thought which is diagnostic, rather than simply antagonistic. In this spirit, this chapter charts the development of modern understandings of vision by looking first at the role of vision in Descartes' theoretical philosophy, and then at the exploration of urban visual experience in Baudelaire's art criticism. In examining these accounts, particular attention is paid to the role of technology, which can be seen to function in two different ways. On the one hand, by enhancing the reach and clarity of vision, technology throws back to the perceiving subject an image-world that seems to match all the more exactly the rational clarity of its own cognition; but, on the other, it provides an image of the world that jars with the expectations of the eye, so challenging the terms of visual coherence and threatening the perceiving subject's priority in visual experience. Descartes and Baudelaire both offer accounts of vision which engage with the impact of technology, and in each case technology plays a pivotal role in their understandings of visual clarity and coherence. But in the light of modern culture's own questioning of the clarity and coherence of vision signalled here by Nietzsche, this chapter also asks how technology poses questions for their respective accounts of vision, and how it contributes to the growing awareness of the limits of modern vision.

CERTAINTY AND DOUBT

Cartesian philosophy has come to be understood as an inaugural moment within modern conceptions of vision, and yet the status of this location may seem equivocal. For Martin Jay, Descartes stands as a pivotal figure within a tradition of 'ocularcentrism', against which much recent French thought has directed its criticism; but for Maurice Merleau-Ponty and an earlier moment of twentieth-century French thought, Cartesian philosophy is most notable for its hostility to vision and the visual (Merleau-Ponty, 1964A, pp. 159–92; Jay, 1993, ch. 1). Underlying this apparently divergent reception is a certain ambivalence to vision in Cartesian thought: on the one hand it ties vision to the service of cognition while, on the other hand, it makes a fundamental distinction between knowledge and visual experience. Yet in fact this ambivalence makes possible its singular achievements. Descartes' aim was to escape the world of analogies, equivocations, and assertions that characterized medieval Scholasticism, and to discover instead a point that is certain and free from doubt in order to ground knowledge. His thinking of vision takes place within this project, and is organized around its central terms, certainty and doubt. The fundamental dynamic which drives Descartes' thinking of vision is a refusal to equate vision directly with knowledge, and this refusal opens the way for a characteristically modern conception of vision, in which sensory experience is distinguished from the cognitive framing or forming of sensation by consciousness. And it is only because visual experience cannot directly give rise to knowledge that vision becomes a cultural and philosophical issue for modernity, rather than a problem only for optics or neuropsychology.

If vision plays an important role in Cartesian thought, technology provides the conceptual mechanism which allows it this function. The scientific investigation of vision, and the new optical technologies to which it gave rise, embodied within visual experience a broader anxiety over the security of knowledge that was prevalent in early modern Europe. Economic and political transformations within the borders of Europe, coupled with military and commercial expansion beyond, saw the emergence of alternative explanatory models and new contexts of experience which left traditional assertions of certainty looking increasingly limited and arbitrary. For many of Descartes' contemporaries, the achievement of certainty involved forgoing the security of appeals to tradition and revealed religion, and the subjection of knowledge of the world to the test of empirical observation. But for Descartes, this wider uncertainty also emerges within empirical perception itself, given the epistemological questions raised by early modern science, by new instruments like the telescope, and by the representational techniques of Renaissance and Baroque art. If

Descartes joins his contemporaries in refusing the convenience of appeals to tradition or faith, he also rules out the most obvious alternative for establishing such a point of certainty, namely the self-evidence of empirical perception. For Descartes, just as much as religion, empiricism is also understood to involve a series of leaps of faith: one must have faith in the visual distinctness and availability of objects, in their willingness as it were to show themselves as they really are; one must have faith that visual data are communicated accurately to the eye and in a way that resembles the sensible world; one must have faith that the bodily reception and transmission of sensory data are not subject to distortion; and one must have faith that consciousness reproduces the visual world in all its richness and complexity.

Descartes' awareness of the uncertain nature of visual experience grew out of a sustained interest in vision and the emergent science of optics: he conducted optical research, speculated on lens design, and wrote on optics and light not only in his *Optics*, but also in his ambitious account of the physical universe, *The World*, written between 1629 and 1633 (1998). As such, Descartes' thought is informed by the broader reconceptualization of vision occurring in seventeenth-century thought.[1] The first effective telescope, developed by Galileo Galilei and announced in his *Sidereal Messenger* of 1610, led to a series of discoveries which bore out the astronomical models of Copernicus and subsequently Kepler.[2] The observation of Jupiter's satellites, Saturn's rings, the mountainous surface of the moon, sunspots, and a multitude of stars previously too small to see with the naked eye, all proved difficult to explain within the existing Aristotelian accounts of the cosmos. In terms of natural philosophy, the heliocentric planetary system revealed by the telescope pointed to a universe operating according to mathematical laws which could be calculated and predicted. In particular, the advances made by Kepler in calculating elliptical orbits encouraged a style of inquiry which depended on mathematical proofs and prediction, rather than the authority of the ancients or reference to the Bible. Kepler's extension of this mathematical approach to the telescope itself in his *Dioptrics* (1611) included

[1] For an account of this interaction, see Garber, 2001.
[2] For an account of this history, see Park, 1997, ch. 6.

light and the action of lenses within this mathematically organized and predictable world. However, the reformulation of the visible world on mathematical principles was not unequivocally comforting, nor did it necessarily lead to a renewed faith in the certainty and self-evidence of vision. Rather, the extension of geometrical and mathematical models to the behaviour of the observable world and to the action of light pointed to the necessity of supplementing visual experience with modes of investigation and understanding which are not given in visual experience, but which involve a distinctly non-visual, conceptual cognition. This unsettling effect was replicated at the level of visual experience by the telescope itself, which introduced an alternative image-world with its own parameters of scale and resolution, an effect heightened by the spherical and chromatic aberration inherent in optical lenses.

The impact of the telescope and the new sciences of astronomy and optics on existing understandings of vision was further complicated by developments in the representational techniques of visual art. Just as the art of lens manufacture upset the contemplative stance of natural philosophy by pointing to a world of mathematical principles underly-ing sensory experience, so other arts also contributed to this process, not least painting. Leon Battista Alberti's *On Painting* (1435) offers a practical methodology for single-point perspective, based on the vanishing point as the organizing principle of the picture plane.[3] While Alberti's text is more concerned to offer a practical guide than a mathematical exposition, and while he famously claimed that the artist is concerned only with what is directly available in visual experience, his method depends on an initial geometrical organization of the picture plane which, although subsequently effaced, underpins the resulting representation. The visual self-evidence of the perspectival image thus rests on an invisible armature constructed according to the principles of Euclidean geometry. Once again, the identification of a mathematical form underlying appearances raises questions about the credibility of visual experience, rather than straightforwardly reinforcing it. After all, single-point perspective allowed painters to

[3] For an account of the impact of single-point perspective on understandings of vision, see Park, 1997, ch. 5.

render an image of a three-dimensional world upon a plane which existed in only two, an achievement which points more to the gullibility of the eye than to its reliability as a guide to empirical truth. As much as furthering claims to a certain 'realism' in visual art, single-point perspective raised all the more urgently the question of illusion and the propensity of vision to mistake illusion for truth; perhaps not surprisingly, the dissemination of perspectivalism in the Renaissance and Baroque was accompanied by a renewal of interest in *trompe-l'oeil*, anamorphosis, the distorting effect of mirrors, and the *camera obscura*.

The doubts concerning sensory perception raised by representational techniques, optical technologies, and the new science, play a crucial role in Descartes' theoretical philosophy, underpinning its understanding of vision. In the *Meditations on the First Philosophy* (1641), for example, the disparity between the image of the sun seen by the naked eye and the knowledge derived from the rational calculations of astronomy is seen to indicate the inherent uncertainty of sensory experience: this disparity demonstrates 'that the idea which seems to have emanated most directly from the sun itself has in fact no resemblance to it at all' (1988, p. 90). Such uncertainty, however, is not restricted to the heavens nor provoked only by the telescope. In the Second Meditation, Descartes offers the more everyday scenario of looking out of a window across a square where men are passing. While accepting that we 'normally say that [we] see the men themselves', Descartes asks what exactly we do see, above and beyond 'hats and coats which could conceal automatons'. The point here for Descartes is that what we take for immediate perception 'is in fact grasped solely by the faculty of judgement which is in [the] mind'; we do not see the men in all their substantial reality, but rather we register certain images through which we '*judge* that they are men' (*ibid.*, p. 85). What emerges here is the way in which the technological manipulation of the visible world, whether through optical instruments like the telescope, or through more down-to-earth mechanical devices and tricks, points to a fundamental division between visual data on the one hand, and the operation of the thinking consciousness on the other. In the *Optics* this role can therefore be extended to include not only the technology of visual reproduction in the form of engraving, but also the technique of single-point perspective. Descartes points out that although engravings consist 'simply of a little ink placed here and there on a piece of paper, they represent to us forests, towns, even battles and storms'. Again, the disparity between the minimal visible marks of an engraving and the 'countless different qualities' which they evoke for consciousness is emphasized by the technique of single-point perspective, where circles are represented by ellipses and squares by rhombuses: 'it often happens', Descartes observes, 'that in order to be more perfect as an image and to represent an object better, an engraving ought not to resemble it' (1988, pp. 62–3).

The central issue here for Descartes is not to decry the distortions of optical instruments or the misrecognitions thrown up by city life, nor to denounce single-point perspective as an especially illusionistic technique, or engraving as a particularly distorting technology of reproduction – all projects which tend to imply the necessity of rediscovering an immediate and direct mode of visual perception uncontaminated by technology or technique. Rather, Descartes deploys instances of technologically and technically mediated images in order to exemplify the working of vision *per se*: as he says of the example of the engraving, 'we must think of the images formed in our brain in just the same way' (*ibid.*, p. 63). Descartes' allusion to technologically mediated vision is not merely rhetorical, nor does it simply provide a convenient metaphorical device to drive his argument at particular moments. On the contrary, technology plays an important role in illuminating the nature of visual experience and its relationship to cognition. For Descartes, new lens technologies like the telescope, and illusionistic techniques such as anamorphosis or single-point perspective, reveal something which was already there in 'normal' or 'everyday' vision: namely, the difference between the mental act of perception and the mechanical processes involved in the transmission of light and of sense data in the nervous system. The importance of technology and technique, therefore, is that they crystallize out this mechanical operation, forcing us to acknowledge the mathematical ordering underlying visual experience. For Descartes, there is no opposition between technologically mediated and 'pure' vision, because *all vision* is 'technological' in a very direct and immediate sense.

This understanding returns us to the topos of doubt, and begins to indicate why vision plays such an important role in charting or defining the very nature of doubt. The Cartesian understanding of visual experience as mechanical or 'technological' undermines empirical sense certainty, demonstrating that we do not immediately perceive the world as it 'really is'; therefore we cannot locate sensible perception as a point of certainty, because when taken in isolation it is inherently subject to uncertainty and doubt. However, Cartesian philosophy attempts to harness the disruptive potential of this doubt, employing it as a kind of homeopathic cure for epistemological uncertainty. Thus in the first person narrative of the *Meditations*, doubt is not an involuntary state inadvertently suffered by Descartes, but a consciously chosen method through which certainty is to be achieved, the necessary and indispensable first step for proceeding towards certain knowledge. In order to identify what is truly certain and indubitable, Descartes proposes that first he must suppose 'that everything I see is spurious', that 'body, shape, extension, movement and place are chimeras', that 'I have no senses', and therefore that 'my memory tells me lies, and that none of the things that it reports have ever happened' (*ibid.*, p. 80). The fundamentally illusory nature of sensory experience is presented most memorably in the First Meditation's fiction of the malicious demon, a hypothetical entity 'of the utmost power and cunning' who has 'employed all his energy and power to deceive'. The point of this fiction is to encapsulate economically the conception of vision emerging from Descartes' optical studies and his understanding of visual art; its effect is to block contemporary accounts of the self-evidence of sensory experience, whether based on the teleology of divine creation or the certainty of empirical perception. At a stroke Descartes has lost the sensible world in all its richness and complexity, and must assume 'that the sky, the air, the earth, colours, shapes, sounds and all external things are merely the delusions of dreams which he has devised to ensnare my judgement' (*ibid.*, p. 79).

However, despite its apparently all-encompassing nature, Descartes' radical doubt has very definite limits, and it is precisely the demarcation of these limits which allows him to establish certainty. For if we cannot be certain that the ideas which fill our consciousness correspond to objects existing 'out there' in the world – they might after all be dream images, which provide the same experiential intensity as waking perception even though our eyes are closed – we can at least be certain that we are thinking them. Even if what I am thinking is illusory, argues Descartes, the fact that I am thinking is certain and indubitable. This inner certainty establishes a fundamental opposition between thinking substance (*res cogitans*), understood as soul and mind, and extended substance (*res extensa*), the corporeal world which comprises not only inanimate but also animate nature. This distinction reposes the question of knowledge and its relationship to visual experience by bracketing the question of vision, or the sensory perception of extended substance, and focusing attention on the operation and nature of consciousness instead. The activity of the *cogito* is described throughout the *Meditations* in terms of an *internal* self-perception or inner vision: 'when the mind understands' we learn in the Sixth Meditation, 'it in some way turns towards itself and inspects one of its ideas which are within it' (*ibid.*, p. 111). Mental perceptions which are perceived both clearly and distinctly are taken by Descartes to be certain and indubitable, and so the self-certainty of the *cogito* arises from the clarity and distinctness of its mental self-perception revealed in the 'natural light' of thinking. The *cogito*'s own act of self-perception allows Descartes to establish the existence of the 'I' as thinking substance, and that of a perfect and infinite entity underlying it, namely God.

If the initial separation and opposition of thinking and extended substance makes possible the *cogito*'s self-certainty, it also implies an analogous division and hierarchy within consciousness itself between the clear and distinct ideas of pure understanding and the more confused ideas derived from sensory perception. The issue of know-ledge thus becomes a question of the degree of clarity and distinctness of particular mental perceptions, and once the notions of number and duration have been secured as innate and indubitable, their application to sensory perception allows the inherent clarity of extension, shape, position, and movement to be derived – that is, the basic mathematical co-ordinates of mechanics and Euclidean geometry. Given that the existence of extended substance is understood to be guaranteed by God, Descartes is now able to return to sensory experience a measure of certainty, albeit in very narrowly defined terms. Corporeal things 'may not all exist in the way that exactly corresponds with my sensory grasp of them', concedes the Sixth Meditation, 'since in many cases my grasp of them is very obscure and confused'; yet crucially they must 'possess all the properties which I clearly and distinctly understand', namely 'all those which, viewed in general terms, are comprised within the subject-matter of pure mathematics' (*ibid.*, p. 116). Cartesian thought loses the world only to re-establish it once again, but it does so on a new footing which, notwithstanding its reliance on the residues of Scholasticism, is recognizably modern. However, it does so at a cost. Notoriously, Cartesian rationality excludes the body and its inhabitation of the world from cognition, and reduces the co-ordinates of visual experience to the fixed three-dimensional space of Euclidean geometry and the linear causality of mechanics.

The particular significance of Descartes' 'technological' understanding of vision lies in its role in redrawing the relationship between visual experience and knowledge, so making possible the separation which underpins the Cartesian subject and its epistemological certainty. This role becomes clearer when Cartesian vision is set against the Scholastic conceptions of sensible forms and empiricist conceptions of the receptivity of the senses. Within medieval Scholasticism, vision was understood to occur through the migration of 'intentional' or 'sensible' forms – in Latin *species* or *simulacra*, in Greek *eidola*. These *species* are understood as fixed images that peel off from substances and fly through the air into the perceiver's soul by way of the sense organs (see Park, 1997, pp. 100–7). From a Cartesian perspective, a certain homology emerges here between Scholastic tradition and the emergent empiricism: however different their conceptions of vision might be, what they both share at the very least is a certain conception of transmission or resemblance. For Scholasticism, substances emanate *species* which migrate to the eye, directly transferring the sensible form of the object to the perceiver's soul; for empiricism, the form of the object impresses itself upon the perceiver's mind through the senses. In each case, the mental image produced resembles or directly reproduces some quality or aspect of the object or substance, however conceived. The reason why instances of technologically mediated sight best exemplify the working of vision for Descartes is that they interrupt both empiricist and Scholastic accounts of resemblance by dramatizing the difference between the mechanical operation of light and the eye on the one hand, and the operation of the soul or thinking substance on the other. This conception of the relationship of knowledge and vision is fleshed out in the example of the engraving offered at the beginning of the *Optics*. The engraved image is formed in terms of the representational conventions of artistic technique, and cannot be said to embody the form of the object itself; equally, as a discrete and artificial object, it cannot be said to emanate the *species* or sensible forms of the substances which it represents. That we nonetheless recognize the image produced indicates to Descartes that the 'problem' is not how mental images 'resemble' objects, but 'how they can enable the soul to have sensory awareness of all the various qualities of the objects to which they correspond' (*ibid.*, p. 63). Light, which is conceived of by Descartes as an excitation of extended substance, produces a corresponding excitation in thinking substance, or the soul, by way of the mediation of the pineal gland, which provides the linkage between these otherwise incompatible substantial realms. Mental perception is therefore to be thought of as an excitation within thinking substance which corresponds *in its own terms* to a quite different mode of excitation in the fundamentally incompatible realm of extended substance (1998, pp. 124–39). Cartesian vision might be thought of as an act of translation or transcription from one quite distinct mode or 'language' into another, in which no direct transmission or transference takes place. In terms of Michel Foucault's typology in *The Order of Things* (1970), this redrawing of the relationship between vision and knowledge marks the movement from a conception of knowledge based on resemblance to one based on representation.

Perhaps the most forthright expression of Descartes' new conception of the relationship between knowledge and visual experience is offered in the opening pages of the first part of *The World*, entitled 'The Treatise on Light', where vision is described by way of an analogy with speech. Descartes' analogy of sight and speech is both distinct from Rousseau's later conception of speech and in certain senses close to post-Saussurian conceptions of linguistic signification. Like visible rays, speech is conceived of by Descartes as an excitation within extended substance – as vibrations in the air – and thus the relationship between words, as extended substance, and their meaning, as thinking substance, is *arbitrary* or conventional, a point reinforced by the existence of different languages. If a jump is possible in the case of speech between arbitrary patterns of sounds waves and mental perceptions which clearly bear no resemblance to them, Descartes argues that such a jump must also be plausible in the case of vision:

> Now if words, which signify something only through human convention, are sufficient to make us think of things to which they bear no resemblance, why could not Nature also have established some sign which would make us have the sensation of light, even if that sign had in it nothing that resembled this sensation? And is it not thus that Nature has established laughter and tears, to make us read joy and sorrow in the face of men (*ibid.*, p. 4).

Although the talk here of a providential nature sits uneasily alongside Cartesian claims to explain the physical world in terms of efficient rather than final causes, the subsequent account of light and corporeal substance in both *The World* and the *Optics* describes a universe of inert, extended matter explainable through mechanical action; that is, precisely the mathematically predictable world implied by single-point perspective and early modern science. Notwithstanding its baroque expression, the model of vision enabled here by analogy with the conventional nature of linguistic signification does not involve the resemblance of mental images to physical objects, in the sense of a direct transference of the object's form to consciousness; instead, vision is to be understood not as resemblance, but as formal correspondence. And indeed, the terms of this formal correspondence are already in place: the self-inspection of consciousness identifies reason in terms of the clarity and distinctness of pure mathematics, while the world of extended matter is understood in terms of geometrical space and mechanical causality. Without such an a priori and transcendent notion of form, however, this analogy would simply beg the question as to why excitations in extended substance should give rise to mental perceptions which in some way correspond to them, rather than just producing random effects.

EYE AND MIND

What makes Descartes' understanding of vision modern in the broadest sense is not so much the securing of a mathematically predictable world – indeed, such a world will prove anathema to certain strands within modern thought and culture – but the separation of the rational operation of consciousness and visual experience. For Descartes, the question of knowledge and the question of vision may be related, but they are not the same; that is, knowledge cannot be directly extrapolated from visual experience, but must be thought of primarily in terms of the operation of consciousness and its activity in ordering and disposing mental perceptions derived from sensory experience. How this operation or activity is to be understood, and how this frame might stand in relation to sensory experience, will subsequently become central questions for modern thought; and consequently vision becomes an important issue in modernity, although indirectly and to the extent that it relates to broader questions about the nature of the subject. Vision will now take part in an expanded conceptual topography which involves plotting the subject's activity in its framing of the sensible world; but it does so at a certain remove, for these larger questions are no longer reducible to vision *per se* but exceed its terms. Indeed, once separated from knowledge, questions of sensory perception increasingly come to be thought of as constituting their own particular realm of inquiry – the aesthetic. And although the relationship of this realm to knowledge and moral action will subsequently prove to be a major concern for modern thought, the experience of modernity tends to pull them apart.

However, Descartes himself does not pursue these issues, although they are implicit in his thinking, but instead attempts to close them down. The question of form is already 'solved' for Cartesian thought, in that form is located as prior to both visual experience and the activity of consciousness: form does not emerge in the activity of consciousness and its apprehension of the sensible world but occurs a priori, as the prior proportionality of being and consciousness; or in the terms of the *Meditations*, form is neither given nor produced in experience, but exists prior to experience in God. Of course, Descartes' a priori form emerges in the convenient symmetry between the mathematical nature of the *res cogitans* and the corporeal world: that the form of thinking and extended substance should correspond is already implicit in the characterization of rationality as pure mathematics, and of extended substance as the geometrical world of extension and mechanical motion. These fixed co-ordinates circumscribe visual experience, making it subservient to the imperatives of knowledge and restricting the kinds of visual experience which are to be understood as valuable or of interest. Visual experience becomes simply a matter of collecting or registering sensory data, whose meaningfulness is to be found elsewhere, in cognition's activity of inspecting the mental perceptions to which it gives rise, and evaluating their compatibility with its own rational co-ordinates: any visual experience which does not correspond to the three-dimensional space and objective duration of Cartesian rationality can now safely be dismissed as illusion. Such a conception of visual experience qualifies the nature of Descartes' enthusiasm for the telescope and for the representational techniques he alludes to in developing his account of vision. Optical technologies and representational techniques may reveal something about the nature of vision, but what they reveal is already there, and in this sense they do alter or affect the nature of visual experience. Indeed, what they reveal is that the activity involved in perception occurs only within consciousness, in the *cogito*'s rational self-inspection, and is therefore not a matter of sensory but of mental perception. While this allows Descartes to differentiate between different kinds of visual experience, as more or less clear, it renders all visual experience as secondary and derivative, and inherently prone to error and uncertainty. Equally, it means that visual experience has no lessons to offer to the eye, since neither the eye nor the visible world are actively involved in perception. Optical technologies and representational techniques cannot fundamentally change the nature of visual experience because the co-ordinates of visibility are already fixed, in the mathematical time and space of Cartesian rationality. And so Cartesian vision implies a tightly circumscribed visual experience exemplified by the telescope, where the object becomes clear and precisely resolved, yet it remains beyond the viewer's reach. The world thus becomes clearly visible and available for knowledge, but the eye can only register an inert vista which unfolds within an invariable configuration of space and time. And while the subject can at last be certain of its vision, this sight offers it only the comfortless confirmation of its own rationality, rather than a sense of its inhabitation and involvement in contexts of experience that stretch beyond it.

The paradoxes that emerge from this account allow us to return to the apparently polarized reception of Descartes in twentieth-century French thought, and see that it is not so polarized after all. Indeed, Merleau-Ponty's critique of the Cartesian hostility towards vision already anticipates the subsequent critiques of his privileging of vision identified by Martin Jay in the discourse of 'anti-ocularcentrism'. Merleau-Ponty captures the paradoxical nature of Descartes' attitude to vision nicely in his late essay 'Eye and Mind', where he characterizes the Cartesian enterprise as 'a thought that wants no longer to abide in the visible and so decides to construct the visible according to a model-in-thought' (1964A, p. 169). What Merleau-Ponty so elegantly articulates here is the contradiction between Descartes' explicit separation of cognition and vision, and their implicit conflation through their a priori formal identity. Descartes separates vision from the rational structure of consciousness, but only in order to organize them in the same terms, so that his model of the visible mirrors his conception of rationality, while his conception of rationality mirrors his model of the visible. As we have seen, the operation of consciousness occurs as an inner vision which inspects ideas under the 'natural light' of reason, and its criteria for certainty – clarity and distinctness – are avowedly visual criteria, even though this activity takes place entirely within consciousness where nothing is in fact 'seen' at all. Thus, for more recent French thought, Cartesian rationality privileges the model of vision, or at least a model of vision; while as Merleau-Ponty maintains, Cartesian thought represents a reduction and restriction of vision within an a priori conception of form.

However, Merleau-Ponty's essay offers other insights by questioning the separation of consciousness and the visible world which underlies Descartes' restricted notion of visual experience. Although the variability of representational technique may reveal something about the nature of vision for Descartes, what it reveals is the fundamental gap between cognition and the visible, a gap which necessitates the latter's subordination. In contrast, Merleau-Ponty discovers a quite different lesson in the historical variability of aesthetic technique, one which sees visual experience as the site of interaction between consciousness and the visible world. For Merleau-Ponty, the range of styles evident in art history, and particularly in modern art, provides evidence of the dynamic nature of visual experience. The renewal of aesthetic technique is understood to result from the modification of the gaze as it responds to the shifting contours of the visible: thus, the historical variability of aesthetic technique provides a testament to the active nature of sight and its responsiveness to the visible. Painting involves a recognition 'that vision happens among, or is caught in things' because it is itself located 'in that place where there persists . . . the undividedness of the sensing and the sensed' (ibid., pp. 162–3). The responsiveness of the eye is therefore understood to provide a sense of the subject's involvement within larger contexts of experience; vision is a mapping that 'radiates from a self', in which 'everything I see . . . is marked upon the map of "I can"' (ibid., p. 162). Yet vision's activity is not to be thought of as self-involved: citing Paul Klee, Merleau-Ponty argues that although it is the eye that is active, its responsiveness amounts to a reversal of the gaze, in that the visibility of the world is imprinted or traced in the active reorganization of vision. The activity of vision allows a kind of return in the gaze, since the aesthetic image produced registers the contribution of things in giving the conditions of appearance. For Merleau-Ponty then, vision should not be understood as simply a means for enabling knowledge, since its responsivity allows a kind of awareness that is not available to cognition. And significantly it is art that offers the place where this kind of awareness becomes possible.

BEAUTIFUL APPEARANCE

To move from Descartes to Baudelaire is not only to jump two centuries of intellectual, social, economic, and intellectual development, but also to encounter a profound change of heart. Baudelaire's understanding of vision reflects the dissatisfaction felt by many artists and intellectuals with the nineteenth century's optimism in scientific and technological progress, an optimism prefigured by Descartes' enthusiasm for the telescope.[4] While Descartes sought to generalize the technologically mediated sight of the telescope as the theoretical model for all vision, Baudelaire had to contend with the technological organization of appearances in urban modernity. And when generalized as the condition of vision in the modern metropolis, technology proved much harder to restrain within fixed and prescribed limits than Descartes had supposed. Baudelaire's Paris was perhaps the greatest urban centre of Europe, a city of intense industrial and commercial activity, which by the mid-nineteenth century had outgrown its medieval centre and was sprawling westwards. Like other urban centres, the city streets of Paris offered a visual scene which constantly reinvented itself, with new shop fronts, apartment buildings, dioramas, arcades, and streets signs appearing and disappearing according to the quickening rhythms of urban life. But the appearance of Paris was also being reinvented in a unique and singular way, and in the second half of the century it was systematically and deliberately recreated around the grand designs of the new prefect, Baron Haussmann. Even before Haussmann had entered the prefecture, Paris was undergoing a building boom, so that contemporaries complained that the city resembled a building site (Clark, 1973, pp. 32–5). The Flowers of Evil, Baudelaire's central poetic work, was written in a city whose appearance was in the process of being recreated, with large areas transformed into wastelands of mud, debris, and construction materials: by 1858, the year after its first publication, the Rue de Rivoli and the Boulevard Saint-Michel, the first of Haussmann's great web of avenues and boulevards, had been completed. The reconstruction of Paris revealed the nature of technology in a new and unprecedented way, as the capacity not simply to enhance visual definition or range, but to reorganize the visible world.

Just as for Descartes two hundred years earlier, for Baudelaire technology necessitated the rethinking of vision by breaking the immediate link between appearance and the image perceived; but for Baudelaire, unlike Descartes, the breaking of the self-evidence of vision

---

[4] Significantly, the connection between scepticism towards scientific progress and the rethinking of vision found in Baudelaire is also central to Nietzsche's Birth of Tragedy, 1993, pp. 4–5.

occurred at the level of visual experience rather than being restricted to cognition. In terms of experience, vision comes to involve not just questions of certainty and clarity, but also questions of recognition, orientation, and memory. Because of their incremental construction over the centuries, great medieval cities like Paris, with their narrow streets and closely packed buildings, offered a network of familiar locations within which personal and public associations and meanings were embedded. The appearance of the city was itself a storehouse of popular memory and public history, upon which public and personal experience were etched and entwined. The familiar face of the city therefore offered to its inhabitants not only a means of geographical orientation, but also a cartography of tradition, a semantic topography within which their own social, economic, and personal location was set within larger historical co-ordinates. With the destruction and rebuilding of Paris, the face of the city no longer bore the complex of urban histories embedded in the old city, but rather its appearance was formed by external dictates. The appearance of the city increasingly became ordered according to the imperatives of official memorialization and state grandeur, the commercial requirements of the new consumer society, and the changing dynamics of architectural and aesthetic fashion; but these imperatives played themselves out in a space organized by the eminently political designs of Napoleon III and Baron Haussmann. In the wake of the revolutionary street fighting of 1848, the long, wide boulevards which Haussmann drove through the working-class districts were designed to clear their populations from the centre of the city, provide speedy transit for troops, and make the erection of barricades impossible (Berman, 1983, pp. 150–2). For Baudelaire, the reconstruction of Paris meant quite literally the disappearance of tradition, in that the technological reorganization of the city obliterated the traditional meaningfulness of its appearance. But while this experience was lamented by Baudelaire, he also grasped the insights it offered into the condition of vision. In 'The Swan', for example, the lyric 'I' famously begins by lamenting that 'the form a city takes / More quickly shifts, alas, than does the mortal heart'; but while lamentation may appear uppermost here, the force of the poem lies in its exploration of the temporal complexity of vision and the activity of the subject in framing appearances (1993, p. 175). The emergence of a disparity between the appearance of the city – 'the form a city takes' – and the framing of appearances by the associations, memories, and desires of 'the mortal heart', makes palpable the active contribution of the subject's perception to visual experience. It is only when appearances no longer mesh so easily with their framing by the subject that the frame itself becomes manifest, although it does so as distortion, disorientation, and loss.

Baudelaire's sensitivity to the distinction between appearance and its subjective framing was sharpened by another important nineteenth-century technological development, photography. Using the older technology of the *camera obscura* alongside new chemical processes, fixed photographic images were produced from at least the late 1830s by, among others, the French collaborators Daguerre and Niepce, and the Englishman William Fox Talbot. Initial reactions to photography were divided, and generated debates about its status as art or science, about the relationship between them, and about the nature of visual and artistic truth (see Scharf, 1974 and Freund, 1980). However, what was common to both photography's proponents and its detractors was an awareness of the difference between the photographic image and the traditional representational techniques of visual art.[5] This obser-vation was made as early as 1840 by Arthur Parsey in the second edition of his work *The Science of Vision*: Parsey pointed out that the extremes in perspectival scale which are often involved in photographic images – for example, the apparently disproportionate enlargement of foreground objects or the exaggerated foreshortening of extended objects – appeared to a contemporary audience as distortions because they jarred with their visual expectations (Scharf, 1974, p. 193). This observation was echoed as a criticism by a number of artists, who added to it their disapproval of the camera's lack of selectivity within its visual field and blanket reproduction of visual detail, which seemed quite alien to the tenets of aesthetic tradition (*ibid.*, p. 147). Baudelaire was a passionate contributor to these debates as we shall see, but while he was hostile to the intrusion of photography onto the terrain of the

[5] However, as Peter Galassi has argued, this difference needs to be qualified given the extensive role of the *camera obscura* in painting prior to the development of photography; see his *Before Photography*, 1981.

fine arts, he also saw important lessons for thinking vision in the gap that emerged between them. For Baudelaire, the difference between the photographic and the aesthetic image testified to the fact that vision was not a matter of the blank duplication of appearances or the passive recording of the visible world, but involved the active framing or construction of appearances in visual experience.

This active conception of vision as the production of form in visual experience lies at the heart of Baudelaire's famous essay 'The Painter of Modern Life', written towards the end of 1859 or early in 1860 (1972, pp. 390–435). Here he offers a description of the visual processes underlying the aesthetic practice of the illustrator Constantin Guys which stresses the agency of vision in terms of the active role of memory in the recognition and production of form. According to Baudelaire, 'all true draughtsmen draw from the image imprinted in their brain and not from nature', a shift that makes perception itself a productive act, rather than a passive registering of external stimuli. The raw material of Guys' practice is not a more or less accurate mental reproduction of the visual scene, but a pattern of 'impressions' which already isolate and select *in* 'the culminating features or highlights of an object', while selecting *out* those of lesser significance; and in turn, these features may themselves be exaggerated or enhanced according to their associative meaningfulness in memory. Yet if the essay recognizes the activity of aesthetic perception, it also ascribes a dynamism to the visible world, so recognizing its contribution to visual experience. In a striking passage, the urban scene is animated as a 'riot of details', so animated in fact that they press their demands on the perceiving eye, 'demanding justice, with the fury of a mob in love with absolute equality'. The visible world of modernity becomes dynamic, and is itself no longer the passive object of observation, but an active participant in visual experience which draws the eye and demands attention. Having said this, the essay also makes it clear that the visible world is not an equal partner: as the Hobbesian tone of the passage indicates, the animation of the visible is understood as a threat to the sovereignty of aesthetic perception. According to this logic, to accede to the demands of the mob would be to revert to the state of nature and its war of all against all, where 'any form of justice is inevitably infringed, any harmony sacrificed', where 'a multitude of trivialities are magnified', and where 'a multitude of little things become usurpers of attention' (*ibid.*, p. 407). If aesthetic perception is able to recognize the dynamism of the urban scene, it holds to itself the sovereign right to legislate form to the riot of visual detail, since the coherence and harmony of the image cannot emerge from within, but must be supplied by the form-giving imagination. Paradoxically, despite their apparent animation, the riot of details are in another sense dead, in that they are without inherent significance or relation. They must therefore await the messianic power of the artist, whose 'resurrecting and evocative memory', in the words of the essay, 'says to every object: 'Lazarus, arise' (*ibid.*, p. 408).

Bound up in Baudelaire's art criticism, then, is a conception of vision which registers the dynamic nature of visual experience in modernity. The vista of the city is animated and enlivened by its condensation of time and space, a condition within which the scene of appearance and the time of apprehension are constantly renewed. The visible world is no longer inert but creates new contexts for visual experience, producing transformations and combinations which demand attention and force new juxtapositions upon the viewer. In turn, vision is conceived of as an active process of selection and synthesis, which forms and organizes visual experience in terms of the spatial and temporal co-ordinates of human meaning. But, significantly, such a conception of vision is only possible for Baudelaire within the limits of art – as aesthetic perception – and this limitation of the activity of perception has a number of profound consequences. Most obviously it leads to a radical distinction between two different kinds of seeing: between an aesthetic vision which masters the animated vista of the visible world on the one hand; and on the other, a utilitarian or instrumental vision which fixes its gaze on the incoherence of objects, at once turning them to use while at the same time succumbing to their disconnection and meaninglessness. This first kind of seeing is identified with those who are removed from the immediate concerns of practical industry and social action, and who are therefore able to adopt a mode of perception freed from the contingent imperatives of immediacy: with the distracted gaze of the *flâneur*, whose leisurely perambulations discover vital moments of perception in the city's disconsolate appearance; with the individualistic eye of the dandy, whose aristocratic sensibility expresses itself as sartorial distinction; and of course, pre-eminently with the artist, whose technique has a singular ability to render or actualize aesthetic perception in the beautiful image. The second kind of sight is identified in this essay with the 'strict utility' of the businessman's gaze, and elsewhere in Baudelaire's art criticism with photography, and is understood as a mode of perception in which 'the fantastic reality of life becomes strangely blunted' (*ibid.*, p. 406). Driven by the pursuit of profit, the businessman sees the world as a disparate series of objects available for manipulation, exploitation, and exchange, but which therefore lack any intrinsic significance or connection. Within such a regime of perception, vision is trapped in the contingency of things, endlessly registering the shifting intensities of the visible but unable to discover a proportion or unity from within the endless flux of visual experience.

Vision is thus split into an aesthetic perception which promises transcendence, and a utilitarian gaze which remains locked in contingency. And in turn, this division points at another level to a more deep-seated ambivalence towards the visible and towards its role in visual experience. For while the visible contributes actively to visual experience in aesthetic perception, generating new contexts for the perceiving subject to master and bring to order, the goal of aesthetic perception is to triumph over the very accelerations and variations of intensity that constitute modern, urban experience. Baudelaire's aesthetic thus energetically throws itself into the swirl of appearances in the modern city, but only in order to master and so escape it. On the other hand, the utilitarian vision which abides within the contingency of visual experience only ever reproduces the contingency it confronts, and so its passive reproduction of appearance remains bereft of meaning or coherence. The dynamism of the visible is thus at once the condition of aesthetic vision, what makes its transcendence possible, but also precisely that which is to be transcended. The bifurcation between aesthetic and utilitarian vision is a manifestation of this ambivalence: Baudelaire wants to ascribe an agency to perception, but he also wants to circumscribe the contribution made by the visible to visual experience, because he understands it to threaten the coherence and unity of the subject's perception. Consequently, he restricts visual agency to aesthetic perception because he understands beauty to figure a meaningfulness or harmony which is fundamentally artificial or humanly produced, rather than deriving from the appearance of things. As we shall see, this ambivalence towards the visible, and the splitting of vision in which it results, produces a series of oppositions and contradictions in Baudelaire's art criticism; however, it is important to realize that it is this conception of the aesthetic which allows Baudelaire to reinvent visual experience. While there are certainly problems involved, Baudelaire's opposition between utilitarian and aesthetic perception is not simply capricious or arbitrary, but signals a significant reformulation of the conceptual terrain marked out by Cartesian vision.

The central conceptual shift underlying Baudelaire's notion of aesthetic perception is its insistence on the production of form: rather than locating form prior to experience, Baudelaire envisages its production *within* visual experience, so locating the configuration of form within historical time. This shift involves a reconceptualization of the temporality of both visual experience and the image, but in a broader sense it also implies a reconceptualization of the nature of human meaning and of historical time. This broader dimension is best illustrated through a comparison with Cartesian vision and its understanding of the providential teleology underlying the certainty of rational form. Visual experience becomes certain for Descartes because of the correspondence between the rational form of mental perception and that of the visible world, a correspondence which precedes visual experience and which is guaranteed by God. Thus, although Descartes claims to evacuate sensible nature of final causes, in a larger sense the Cartesian universe is providential and is ruled over by a benevolent deity, and not by a malevolent demon. In 'The Painter of Modern Life' Baudelaire demonstrates a keen awareness of the relationship between Enlightenment conceptions of providential nature and the model of representation which such conceptions of nature imply. As the 'source and prototype of all possible forms of good and beauty', providential nature demands 'truth to nature', and so installs verisimilitude as the paradigm of representation. Baudelaire refuses to accept the primacy of verisimilitude, but in doing so he argues we must also replace the providential nature underlying it, complaining that is was 'the rejection of original sin [that was] responsible for the general blindness' of the Enlightenment. What is at stake here is much more than a difference in taste or the arbitrary preference for one stylistic mode over another, but the derivation of form and therefore of the spatio-temporal co-ordinates of vision. Because of this larger framework, the essay's rejection of verisimilitude is articulated primarily in theological rather than aesthetic terms: the Enlightenment's providential nature is replaced by an idiosyncratic doctrine of original sin whose conception of a fallen and broken cosmos is bereft of intrinsic significance or unity. In this light, verisimilitude's 'truth to nature' becomes a misplaced subservience to nature which misrecognizes it both morally and aesthetically: as the essay argues, it is crime that is natural while 'virtue . . . is artificial', and it is 'evil [that] is done without effort, *naturally*' while 'good is always the product of an art' (*ibid.*, p. 425).

Baudelaire's rejection of the providential nature underlying verisimilitude involves a rejection of its temporal structuring of vision as an infinite series of discrete and integral moments. The formal unity of Cartesian vision is not subject to variation according to the contingency of circumstance, but is always already present in cognition, identically and without variation. It is therefore static, in the sense that each moment of mental perception is conceived of as self-present and discrete, as the instantaneous apprehension of a frozen world of extension under the unvarying co-ordinates of rational cognition. Time is external to the moment of perception, simply providing a linear trajectory as the framework for an endless and infinitely repeatable succession of such moments, which are otherwise indifferent to and unaffected by it. This is why Cartesian vision is principally concerned with the three-dimensional spatial relations of Euclidean geometry, which brackets time and its potentially disruptive contamination of pure space. For all its idiosyncrasy, Baudelaire's theology of fallen nature robs perception of its temporal homogeneity because it locates the question of form within the contingency of visual experience. In conceiving nature as irretrievably sinful and broken, Baudelaire must confront a creation which has been abandoned by God and from which the divine guarantee of form has been withdrawn, and so this premodern theological setting underlies his aesthetic modernism. While the ultimate destination of Baudelaire's aesthetic theory will be the traditional goal of the harmonious proportion of beauty, his radical insistence on the activity of aesthetic perception and the production of form invests his conception of the aesthetic image with a particular temporal complexity. Without a fixed configuration of form prior to experience, form must be produced within experience; and this relocation in turn reinvents the conditions of formal correspondence. On the one hand, the subjective framing of visual experience is no longer temporally isolated and self-present, but is haunted by the memory of other moments of vision which evoke myriad associations and meanings. And on the other, the scene which confronts the subject is no longer a discrete field of appearance, but is shot through with the resonance of other times and places, its unity ruined by the discordant mêlée of resemblance. For Baudelaire, visual experience can no longer be imagined as the simple synchronicity of a self-present subject confronting a temporally unified space, but occurs as the coincidence of nonsynchronous moments within which the achievement of unity or meaningfulness becomes a fraught, and even unlikely, prospect.

Baudelaire's conception of vision is rooted in this understanding of its temporal dividedness and heterogeneity, but at the same time his theology of the Fall casts this disunity as sinful and lacking grace, and demands that it be redeemed by an ordering or arrangement which is not natural but humanly created. This dynamic underlies the description of the aesthetic image provided by his salon review of 1859, which combines Baudelaire's theological and aesthetic conceptions of creation (1972, pp. 285–324). The review explains that 'the whole visible universe is nothing but a storehouse of images and signs, to which man's imagination will assign a place and a relative value' (ibid., p. 306). Consequently, 'a good picture must be created like a world' and not ordered according to the tenets of verisimilitude, which would simply be the blank replication of the purely contingent spatial arrangement of heterogeneous appearances. The first task of aesthetic creation is to disrupt the arbitrary simultaneity of appearance, while the act of recomposition that follows in its wake effects a rearrangement that is temporal as well as spatial, so that 'the creation we see is the result of several creations, the earlier ones being completed by the later'. The beautiful image is therefore not an immediate unity, but 'a series of superimposed pictures' with 'each fresh surface giving reality to the dream, and raising it one degree towards perfection' (ibid.,

p. 305). Its beauty is not a function of the contingent arrangements that might occur within arbitrary acts of superimposition, but lies in the arrangement of the contingent debris of the visible 'according to rules whose origins can be found only in the deepest recesses of the human soul'. The beautiful image thus integrates temporally heterogeneous moments within a spatial arrangement, whose simultaneity orders the disconsolate appearance of fallen nature within the terms of human perception and its patterns of association, resemblance, relation, and unity. The aesthetic image does not capture a unity or truth lying in nature, but 'creates a new world', or at least 'the sensation of something new' (*ibid.*, p. 299).

Baudelaire's aesthetic theory liberates aesthetic technique from its subservience to nature, whether understood in terms of a neo-classical aesthetics of verisimilitude and 'truth to nature', or in terms of the Romantic impulse to discover the unity of consciousness and nature. And in so doing, it reinvents the temporality of aesthetic perception by redescribing the kind of return which it offers. Underlying verisimilitude is a conception of vision as the passive registering of nature's order and meaning; in Romanticism, however, vision is ascribed an active role, and so the gaze can be thought of as a projection which discovers in the scene that confronts it a sensuous arrangement which corresponds to its own patterns of perception. Romantic vision thus describes a return which confirms the perceiving subject's harmony with the world, through its discovery of a formal proportion in nature that anticipates the configuration of its own perception. For Baudelaire, this kind of return is no longer possible because nature has no inherent order or meaning: the eye looks out onto a vista that is broken and without intrinsic form, and which can only return the arbitrariness and contingency of its fallen state. His aesthetics must therefore radicalize the active element of Romantic vision by conceiving of aesthetic perception as a transformation: the aesthetic gaze reorders the scattered and empty 'images and symbols' of nature according to a properly human configuration of form, so that the image reflects back to the perceiving subject a coherence or meaningfulness which anticipates the terms of its own gaze. This unity is of course not cognitive, since it does not grasp a 'reality' or meaning which exists in the external world; nor does it provide the subject with a sense of its affinity with a larger universe or order of meaning, for what is returned is a humanly derived form. What it does offer, though, is an experience of the creative power of the imagination, which underlies the possibility of meaningfulness by ordering the inert and arbitrary space and time of sensuous matter within properly human co-ordinates.

The radical implications of this conception of vision for aesthetic technique are perhaps most clearly articulated by Baudelaire in another critical essay from about the same time, 'Richard Wagner and *Tannhäuser* in Paris' (1972, pp. 325–57). Although not directed primarily at the visual, this essay is particularly relevant in this context because of its celebration of the spatio-temporal unification of the *Gesamtkunstwerk*, or integrated work of art. Wagner's aesthetics are understood by Baudelaire to match his own, and thus to transcribe his conception of the activity of vision into a broader account of human meaning in the face of an indifferent universe. Just as his own art criticism understands the beautiful image in terms of a spatio-temporal unity, Baudelaire sees this conception of beauty underling Wagner's description of legend or myth, which the essay quotes at some length. 'Whatever the epoch or nation it belongs to', writes Wagner,

> legend has the advantage of incorporating exclusively what is purely human in the given epoch or nation, and of presenting it in an original and very striking form, thus intelligible at the first glance. A ballad, a popular refrain, are enough to evoke this character for you in the twinkling of an eye, in the most clear cut and arresting form . . . The nature of the scene and the whole tone of the legend combine to transport the mind to a dream-state that quickly carries it on to a perfect clairvoyance, and the mind discovers a different concatenation of phenomena, which the eyes could not perceive in the normal state of waking (*ibid.*, pp. 339–40).

Crucially for Baudelaire, myth is not the articulation of the inherent meaningfulness of nature or the cosmos, but 'an allegory created by a people', a work of artifice which subsumes nature under the Ideal. Baudelaire's essay thus translates Wagnerian legend into his own theology of fallen nature: 'just as sin is everywhere', it notes, 'so is redemption everywhere, so is myth everywhere'. Myth is the

43

redemptive transformation of fallen nature into the unified spatio-temporal co-ordinates of human meaningfulness; just as his own conception of beauty transforms the scattered and transient moments of the visible into a unity, so Wagner's legend transforms the broken historical world into 'the sign of a common origin, the proof of the irrefragable relationship, provided we look for that original exclusively in the ultimate source and common origin of all being' (*ibid.*, p. 348). Aesthetic technique is therefore granted an activity inconceivable in the terms of neo-classical or even Romantic thought, but its transformative activity is ordered according to the pure interiority of the imagination, which is described as the 'source' and 'origin' of 'all being'. And this pure interiority orders technique according to a telos in the Ideal that lies in opposition to the world, and which must violently suppress and order the world. The telos of the Ideal is here quite nakedly 'despotic', for 'every single detail must concur to a total effect', and every technical means must be directed to 'this imperious ideal' (*ibid.*, p. 337).

When translated back into visual terms, Baudelaire's conception of the aesthetic explains the ambivalent conception of visual experience we have already identified. While it grants to vision an active role which contrasts markedly with Cartesian thought and its inert conception of visual experience, it also necessitates a hostility to the visible as inherently tied to the meaninglessness and contingency of fallen nature. This hostility underlies the Hobbesian tone of the description of Guys in 'The Painter of Modern Life', a tone which is itself revealing. For what it indicates is that the essay's conception of beauty is not one of unforced harmony, but of the suppression of contingency under the despotic ordering of the Ideal. Baudelaire's aesthetic vision has a political dimension, which is attested to by the essay's glorification of Napoleon III and French colonial militarism. Both aesthetically and politically, Baudelaire betrays his more radical insights in the search for a sovereign subject who will bring the world to order. Yet at the same time, his understanding of vision also suggests a much more complex account of the visible, one which in many ways anticipates recent accounts of its animation within the technological conditions of contemporary culture. For Baudelaire the image is not an immediate unity, but is inhabited by resemblances which allude to other moments of vision and other scenes of appearance. Therefore, it is to be conceived as being composed of temporally heterogeneous moments, like inscribed but transparent leaves superimposed one on top of the other. And in turn, the apprehension of the image is seen to involve memory, so that the activity of vision becomes a process of recognition inhabited by associations and memories that recall earlier moments of visual experience. Yet if Baudelaire could find this temporal complexity and perceptual activity in the aesthetic image, his understanding of the purely integral and interior nature of the imagination led him to see the image-making capacity of the camera as a threat, since in his eyes it offered a mode of visual experience that is inherently non-human. But what makes Baudelaire's writing on photography interesting is that, despite his hostility, his account of the photographic image can be understood as qualifying and extending this conception of visual experience. Despite his ostensible aims, Baudelaire's account of the technologically mediated image of photography comes to ascribe an agency to the visible which is unavailable both within the co-ordinates of Cartesianism, and within his own conception of aesthetic vision.

PHOTOGRAPHY AND ORIGINAL SIN

The extraordinary enthusiasm for photography in the mid-nineteenth century provoked heated debates over the nature of art and the aesthetic and cognitive potential of technology, debates which tended either to counterpose or equate the camera's ability to replicate appearances with a conception of artistic truth (Scharf, 1974, pp. 127–42). However, Baudelaire's intervention in these debates needs to be differentiated both from positions which argued for, and those which argued against, the aesthetic merits of photography on the basis of the camera's 'realism' or objectivity. Baudelaire's polemic against photography in the review of the Salon of 1859 quite deliberately distinguishes his approach from either celebrations or denunciations of the 'objectivity' or 'realism' of the camera, and thus from the transposition of such claims to the fine arts. Indeed, the review undercuts the notion of realism itself by lampooning the sensibility that wants 'a chamber pot, for example, or a skeleton, to be excluded' from a canon of realist representation: this satire draws attention to the fact that claims to objective representation in fact depend on an implicit selectivity. In the case of photography, the camera is directed and thus objects are always 'arranged' before it, and so like the artist's eye, the camera also frames appearances. Underlying Baudelaire's account of photography is a refusal to accept that the photographic image escapes from the direction of aesthetic technique because of its production by a technological apparatus; the central issue for Baudelaire is rather the kind of relationship that is possible in photography between technology and technique. In Baudelaire's view, the technologies of engraving or lithography – just like the technical activities of drawing and painting – can be subordinated to the ends of technique, and so the image is formed by aesthetic technique according to the goal of beauty. But this is not possible in the case of photography, because of its blanket reproduction of the scene which confronts it. To whatever extent the photographic image is constructed according to the imperatives of aesthetic technique, Baudelaire argues that because of the nature of the technological apparatus, there are always residual elements of contingency within the photographic image which interrupt the spatio-temporal unity of beauty. Consequently, he claims that beauty can only be realized by the fine arts.

This understanding of the relationship between technique and technology explains why the target of his vitriol in the review of the Salon of 1859 is not 'realistic' photography, such as portraits in contemporary dress or urban scenes, but the artistically posed photography which had become so popular over the preceding decade, and which was championed by the Société française de Photographie. In these photographic images the imprint of technique is clear and unmistakable: objects are selected and arranged as in the tradition of still-life painting, while human figures are dressed in Classical or traditional costume, posed in the characteristic attitudes of portrait painting, and placed among suitable props. It was against this 'artistic photography' that the review directs its ire, ridiculing the belief that by 'posing a pack of rascals . . . dressed up like carnival-time butchers and washerwomen, and in persuading these "heroes" to "hold" their improvised grimaces for as long as the photographic process requires' that 'the tragic and charming scenes of ancient history' could be represented (Baudelaire, 1972, p. 295). Notwithstanding its vituperative tone and social snobbery, Baudelaire's assessment of the failure of photography is neither a result of the social status of the models nor of the imperfect mastery of technique on the part of individual photographers. Nor does he claim that such pictures fail to represent Classical Greece or Rome as they once 'really were', a cognitive aim whose aesthetic value Baudelaire would not have recognized. Rather, Baudelaire sees the failure of photography as inherent within the technological apparatus, whose blanket reproduction of the scene is unable to transform the contingency of the present into the meaningful unity which Classical scenes achieved in fine art, without some kind of residue or remainder. Or, in the terms of the review, such technologically mediated images fail because they are unable to invest the scenes of the present with the integral 'tragedy', 'charm', or 'heroism' of the Classical ideal. Photography is therefore narcissistic according to Baudelaire, because the photographic image reflects back to the broken and contingent world of fallen nature an image of contingency and incoherence. Its failure is not its lack of historical truth – its status as 'illusion' – nor does it arise from an 'objectivity' that makes it artless and alien to technique. Photography fails precisely in pursuing the goals of aesthetic technique, because it inevitably introduces traces of contingency which mar the spatio-temporal unity of beauty.

Baudelaire's distinction between photography and fine art may at first appear familiar enough, but because of the temporally complex conception of vision underlying its approach, its conception of the photographic image remains suggestive – whether or not we accept its evaluations. Significantly, Baudelaire does not see the photographic image as static and temporally homogenous, and thus as fixing appearances within a rigid unity, but rather the reverse. It fails to achieve the harmony of the beautiful image because it inserts traces of contingency, and so disrupts the spatio-temporal unity of appearances. But what is interesting here is that Baudelaire's hostility nonetheless registers a kind of return here, although not of course the harmonious anticipation of the subject's gaze promised by beauty. The invocation of 'carnival-time butchers and washerwomen' that so offends Baudelaire does so because it provokes associations that jar with the anticipated meaningfulness of the scene. But despite Baudelaire's claim that the appearance of fallen nature irretrievably lacks the meaningfulness of humanly produced form, these contingent elements do have a significance which is recognizable within the terms of human meaning. The example of photography is employed by Baudelaire to emphasize the primacy of humanly derived technique over and against the contribution of the visible to visual experience; but this primacy is qualified by the meaningfulness located in aspects of the image which, as technologically derived, escape the direction of technique. This instance lends a particular significance to the description of the visible world later in the review, as 'nothing but a storehouse of images and signs' (*ibid.*, p. 306). Although this description aims to confirm the primary role of technique in visual experience, it nonetheless concedes that appearances are already in some sense conformable to the terms of human perception, or that they are in some sense already 'formed': the visible does not simply produce a haze of formless stimuli, but appears in the form of 'images and signs' which prompt or provide a context for their active recognition and synthesis in human perception. Further, the discordant resemblances offered by the photographic image reveal something about the anticipation which animates the viewer's gaze, precisely because they jump out at the eye and interrupt the expectations of the gaze. These associations are dissonant because they cut across the gaze's expectation of an image that would embody 'charm', 'tragedy', and 'heroism'; but in doing so they reveal what is excluded from the regime of recognition that orders perception, and so they point to the semantic topography underlying this viewer's gaze. This account of the photographic image in fact questions the inert nature of technological reproduction, not least by illuminating the terms of aesthetic vision and its organization of technique.

Baudelaire's hostility to the camera takes us a long way from Descartes' enthusiastic embrace of the telescope and its practical potential not only for knowledge, but also for commercial and military adventure. And yet it would be wrong to see here simply a neat reversal in their responses to new and powerful optical instruments, from a technological optimism – exemplified by the telescope and its enhancement of vision's reach and power – to a technological pessimism – exemplified by the camera's blank replication of the disconsolate scene of urban modernity. In Cartesian thought, the technological mediation of vision by the telescope is employed to exemplify the fundamental and unbridgeable distinction between cognition and vision, and the inherently illusory nature of visual experience: the disparity between the image seen by the naked eye, and that seen through the telescope, points to the variable and therefore illusory nature of visual experience. The inherent unreliability of visual experience must be overcome by the activity of the rational consciousness, whose perception is purely mental and so unencumbered by the vagaries of visual experience. The telescope, just like representational techniques such as single-point perspective or anamorphosis, serves to exemplify this process: in both technology and technique, the uncertainty of visual experience is resolved within the mathematical co-ordinates of an optical geometry that matches the rational form of consciousness. For Descartes, then, technology reveals the inert and passive nature of visual experience and the necessity of its subordination to cognition, and this is ultimately why technology and technique can be equated.

The conceptions of technique and technology developed by Baudelaire's aesthetic theory emerge out of a fundamentally different understanding of visual experience. The experience of urban modernity makes it impossible to ignore either the agency of perception – rather than cognition – in organizing visual experience, or the active role of the phenomenal world in determining the conditions of appearance. What this meant for Baudelaire was the collapse of the Cartesian notion of form as prior to experience, and he responded by developing a productive notion of form. And yet his understanding of the productivity of form in visual experience is limited by his reliance on a theology of original sin. Although Baudelaire can recognize the dynamic and productive nature of visual experience, he insists that the telos which orders the configuration of form must be derived from a purely human and invariable imagination, because to recognize the involvement of the visible in producing the terms of vision would be to accept the inherence of contingency, ruin, and decay as the very condition of human meaning. Baudelaire's opposition between human meaning and contingency produces a series of subsequent oppositions, between unity and dispersal, between aesthetic and utilitarian vision, and between technique and technology. In order to ensure that the configuration of form is uncontaminated by the contingency of the fallen world, he obscures the involvement of the visible in visual experience, and orders aesthetic perception according to the telos of the Ideal, which is fixed in the spatio-temporal unity of beauty. This is why Baudelaire stresses the agency of aesthetic over the passivity of utilitarian vision, and why he opposes aesthetic technique to techno-logical reproduction. For Baudelaire, the agency of visual experience must be securely located within human interiority and, while it legislates the unity of the riot of visual details, it cannot accede to or negotiate their demands.

However, Baudelaire's art criticism registers a sense of the difficulty of these straightforward oppositions. Baudelaire was by no means unaware of the ample evidence of the historical and cultural variability of conceptions of beauty and aesthetic technique, as is evident in his critical writing. In order to accommodate this variation while maintain-ing the constancy of the human imagination, Baudelaire sought to articulate the eternal and the transient together within a conception of beauty that allowed a measure of variability, but only within the clear trajectory ordered by the telos of the Ideal: thus, his famous description of the double nature of beauty in 'The Painter of Modern Life' as combining 'a relative circumstantial element, which we may like to call . . . contemporaneity, fashion, morality, passion' and the 'eternal and invariable' (ibid., p. 392). However, such a conception of beauty risks making the clear separation of the human imagination and the contingency of circumstance equivocal, and the significance of Baude-laire's polemic against photography can be located as an attempt to draw a clear line of separation that restores the unequivocal nature of this opposition. From this perspective, what photography reveals is that, while this dual conception of beauty recognizes the involvement of both the eternal and the transient, ultimately the responsibility for beauty lies with an invariable and constant operation of human perception, identified with the interiority of the imagination. The technological reproduction of photography is thus understood to demonstrate the recalcitrance of the visible to the goals pursued by aesthetic technique. And so, while technique and appearances may seem to coexist harmoniously in fine art, the photographic image reveals that their relationship is really one of enmity and conflict.

Yet, as we have indicated, Baudelaire's account of the photographic image can be read quite differently. Even though Baudelaire aims to demonstrate the inert nature of the photographic image, by breaking the Cartesian identification of technology and technique he grants to technology an agency and effectivity which is fundamentally different from the terms of human perception. And while he may complain about the dissonance of the photographic image, his complaint nonetheless ascribes to the photograph a certain power. Baudelaire claims that the photographic image is 'narcissistic' in the sense that it returns to the contingent gaze an image of its own temporal disunity; but although the photograph fails to return an image which confirms the unity of the imagination, its return is not meaningless or formless, but determinate and meaningful in relation to the gaze's anticipation of form. The significance of this return lies in the fact that it qualifies Baudelaire's account of aesthetic perception by allowing its figuring of the temporality of vision to be read differently. If the image is composed of superimposed layers, their heterogeneity must be overcome by the aesthetic gaze, which orders them through its anticipation of their unity. But although Baudelaire wants to locate the source of this unity in the uncontaminated interiority of the soul, and thus to see it as invariable and purely human, his account of aesthetic vision establishes a role for memory in providing the terms of recognition. The introduction of memory is, however, troubling, because it suggests that the terms of recognition emerge out of prior moments of visual experience, and therefore out of the histories of the gaze's confrontation with the visible world. The involvement of memory implies that the visible must in some sense contribute to the configuration of vision, since it has shaped the parameters of visual experience, and so the very terms of vision are implicated in or contaminated by the contingency of history.

Baudelaire can ignore these problems in the case of aesthetic perception, because here visual experience appears simply to confirm the transcendent co-ordinates of the imagination's unity; but in the case of the photograph, these problems cannot be ignored, since what is returned is an image of what has been excluded in the formation of the gaze. What jumps out from the photographic image and strikes Baudelaire's eye is not an undifferentiated incoherence, but particular moments of contingency that are dissonant precisely because they cut across the gaze's expectation of spatio-temporal unity. That is, the photograph captures or makes visible what cannot be integrated within this configuration of form, and so has been excluded in order to constitute the terms of the gaze. The dissonance of the image therefore alludes to or registers the prior moments of recognition and exclusion which underlie the gaze and provide its conditions of visibility, but which are of course now absent and so cannot appear. In this sense, the photographic image offers a return which is not simply narcissistic, since it reveals to the eye something of its own structuring of vision by bringing to appearance what is excluded by the gaze in its anticipation of form. Yet equally, this return is time-bound, for what appears as dissonant does so because it is excluded from this particular regime of vision and its anticipation of a particular configuration of form. Paradoxically then, the frozen appearance of the photograph reveals something of the histories of visual experience which are involved in the constitution of the gaze, but which are unavailable in the apparent immediacy and vitality of aesthetic vision. By identifying the capacity of technological reproduction to offer an image which interrupts the anticipation of the aesthetic gaze, Baudelaire makes it possible to question the inviolability and pure interiority of form. And consequently, the photographic image questions the oppositions which we have identified as underlying Baudelaire's conception of vision. Yet while Baudelaire's art criticism cannot articulate this questioning, it emerges nonetheless in the divergence between its account of aesthetic technique and his own poetic practice.

Perhaps the strongest statement of the invariable character of the imagination is provided by Baudelaire's defence of Wagner in 'Richard Wagner and *Tannhäuser* in Paris', which offers the most sustained account of technique's ability to encompass the eternal and the transient. The ballads and popular refrains employed by Wagner, along with the legend cycles that provide their narrative unity, are recognized by Baudelaire to have emerged historically, but because they have entered popular tradition they are understood to be no longer tied to a particular time or place. In becoming the common inheritance of the collective, these motifs and narrative paradigms are conceived of as transcending any single age or set of circumstances, and so according to Baudelaire they constitute 'an allegory created by a people'; but, at the same time, Wagner's deployment reinvents them in order to offer a response to the particular circumstances of the age. Baudelaire thus understands Wagner's opera as an exemplar of modern epic, which demonstrates how the development of aesthetic technique nonetheless confirms the transhistorical nature of human meaning. But in this light, what is most striking about Baudelaire's own poetic practice in *The Flowers of Evil* is that it does not employ the linguistic resources of Parisian street language or popular song, nor the folk stories and urban tales of its inhabitants; and rather than aspiring to the condition of modern epic, it employs the self-consciously artistic technique of lyric poetry. As we are reminded in 'The Albatross', included as the second poem in the 1861 edition, lyric does not transcend the limits of a particular time and place, but is tied very specifically to its life in the Classical world: only then could it claim a place in popular tradition, while now it appears increasingly out of sympathy with the times, becoming the preserve of individual poets and their isolated readers. Rather than testifying to the invariability of the imagination, then, the unhappy fate of lyric in modernity emphasizes the historical location of aesthetic technique and its immersion in the changing circumstances of historical time. And there is a further irony here. In modernity, lyric embodies the contingency of the isolated subject, not the collective experience of popular tradition; consequently the finality that Baudelaire's poetry locates in its discovery of the allegorical meaning of the city's sights proves to be the endpoint of only one 'I's' investment in a particular time and place, and thus as only one possible allegorical meaning among others. Baudelaire's poetic practice does not so much elevate the contingency of its objects into the spatio-temporal unity of myth, as direct our attention back to the historically specific limits of lyric as a poetic technique. And in the dissonance between its technique and the tenor of the age, its aesthetic framing of the disconsolate appearance of Paris points back to the contingency of the frame. Against the claims made by Baudelaire in defence of Wagner, *The Flowers of Evil* questions the capacity of aesthetic technique to transcend its location within historical time without some kind of residue or return, and so it suggests that the aesthetic gaze remains dependent on the contingency of time and place. By extension, then, Baudelaire's poetic practice points to the involvement of vision in the very contingency which it claims to master under the integrated appearance of beauty.

THE CONDITIONS OF VISION

The difficulties and inconsistencies that arise in Baudelaire's account of vision makes it hard to draw a simple and straightforward trajectory from Descartes to the conception of visual experience underlying aesthetic modernism. Consequently, we should be wary of thinking in terms of a single, enduring paradigm of modern vision which we are now capable of moving beyond. And yet, if we take Baudelaire's aesthetic theory at face value, there are clearly aspects which resemble Cartesian vision. Descartes' conception of the inherent unreliability of visual experience presents an unequivocal statement of the priority of human cognition over the phenomenal world: by casting visual experience as passive and dependent on the activity of the *cogito*, it reduces the visible world to an array of objects available for human manipulation and use. While Baudelaire's theology of original sin allows him to develop a more complex understanding of vision, at the same time it leads him to suppress the contribution of the visible to the framework of perception, because he wants to maintain its purity against the fallen state of the world. Consequently, Baudelaire disavows the imbrication of vision within the contingency of the visible, and so orders aesthetic technique according to a telos located in the Ideal. A certain symmetry arises here between Descartes and Baudelaire in their respective understandings of subjectivity and its relation to the visible world. Baudelaire breaks the Cartesian conception of providential nature by replacing it with the broken and disconsolate creation of the Fall, and yet such a theological framework ultimately only replaces the beneficent deity of the *Meditations* with its malevolent demon. Baudelaire is thus led back into the world of Cartesian dualisms, because by understanding the visible world as demonic, he must oppose the inviolable interiority of human meaning to its contingency and meaninglessness.

Despite Baudelaire's rejection of providential nature, his dethroning of cognition as the arbiter of visual experience, and his recognition of the production of form within visual experience, his conception of the relationship between the perceiving subject and the visible world still somehow resembles that of Cartesian rationality. Notwithstanding all their differences, for both Descartes and Baudelaire vision describes the priority of the subject over the phenomenal world, a hierarchy which implies that human perception, cognition and action should be orientated to the subordination of the world and its forming in purely human terms. In at least this sense their conceptions of vision can be identified as operating within a shared paradigm, a paradigm that has been described within contemporary French theory as 'ocularcentric'. On the one hand, vision comes to supervise a fixed and knowable world of inert objects, anchored within three-dimensional geometrical space and mechanical causality; on the other, vision becomes the instrument of the sovereign subject locked in a heroic struggle against dead nature, to which it alone can bring the appearance of meaningfulness and harmony. In each case, vision fixes the relationship between subject and object, enthroning the subject as master of a disenchanted world: in Descartes' case, the subject's mastery is flamboyantly disavowed in the apparently disinterested pursuit of knowledge, while in Baudelaire's, it is flamboyantly displayed in the brittle heroism of the dandy.

Yet if Descartes and Baudelaire both share a certain hostility to the visual world, the trajectory that runs between them is not as straightforward as this convergence may suggest. While the priority of the perceiving subject in Baudelaire may in some sense resemble the Cartesian *cogito*'s mastery of extended substance, there are also important differences, and significantly these differences are revealed in their respective conceptions of technology. Descartes' a priori conception of form implies a fixed and homogenous configuration of space and time within which technology and technique are equated. But Baudelaire's recognition of the production of form in visual experience means that the sovereignty of the perceiving subject can only be secured by the radical separation of the form-giving activity of perception on the one hand, and the dynamic but formless contingency of the visible world on the other; as a consequence, Baudelaire is led to oppose technique and technology. Aesthetic technique is to be guided by the pure interiority of the imagination which, as he explains in his review of the Salon of 1859, directs technique 'according to rules whose origins can be found only in the deepest recesses of the human soul' (*ibid.*, p. 392). Technique is therefore ordered according to what Baudelaire understands as the eternal and invariable structure of human meaningfulness, and which he designates as the Ideal because it is independent of, and so uncorrupted by, the particular circumstances of time and place. However, Baudelaire's figuring of photographic reproduction questions the inviolability of this opposition, while his own poetic practice points to the contingency of technique. The problems that emerge in Baudelaire's account of the activity of perception begin to suggest different possibilities for figuring the relationship of subjectivity and the phenomenal world, and therefore different possible conceptions of vision and visual experience.

The importance of attending to the differences, as well as the continuities, between Descartes and Baudelaire lies in the opportunity it provides for generating a much more differentiated understanding of modern conceptions of vision. While the characterization of modern thought as 'ocularcentric' captures the role vision has played in reducing being to the categories of the subject, such a blanket description is less attentive to the alternative possibilities which it may offer. The problems which arise for Baudelaire in seeking to develop a productive notion of form are valuable in understanding the development of post-Cartesian accounts of vision, and in particular they provide a context for identifying the significance of Immanuel Kant's transcendental philosophy. While Descartes' separation of consciousness from the corporeal world allowed a recognition of its activity in constructing objects in cognition, it did so at the cost of reducing visual experience to an inert and passive registering of external stimuli. And although Baudelaire's recognition of the dynamic nature of visual experience allowed him to ascribe an active role to perception itself, it also required him to identify a faculty underlying sensory perception which orders and disposes sensation. Baudelaire identified this faculty as the imagination, but as we have seen, he conceives of it in terms of the pure interiority of the soul, a position that results in a hostility to the visible which in at least some sense resembles Cartesianism. Kant's transcendental analysis attempts to think these terms differently, and as such it offers an important vantage point for reassessing the potential of modern accounts of vision.

The significance of Kant's critical philosophy in the present context is twofold. First, Kant insists on a commitment to the human experience of space and time, and so outside of his practical philosophy he refuses any direct access to a ground or principle prior to experience; consequently, he rejects Descartes' inner certainty of God and the a priori conception of form which it underlies. Second, if Kant demonstrates a new commitment to experience, he also extends analysis beyond experience to the conditions which make it possible. He therefore anticipates Baudelaire in recognizing the active nature of visual experience, although his understanding of this activity is very different from Baudelaire's.[6] Kant realizes that simply to dismantle the a priori framework of Cartesianism leaves empirical perception subordinate to the contingent configuration of the sensory world. It would replace an a priori conception of form with an a posteriori conception, in which experience is once again passive, but now ordered according to the changing arrangement of the sensory world. Therefore, in order to establish the activity of the subject without appealing to a transcendent notion of form, Kant seeks to identify the subjective conditions which are necessary to account for the kind of experience which humans have. From this perspective, experience is not simply immediate but implies the productive activity of consciousness, an activity which can be distinguished from the contents of experience, but which is not unrelated or opposed to experience in the manner of Cartesianism. This insight enables Kant to make an important change of methodological focus: instead of starting with an account of the subject's activity, whether located in the rational *cogito* or the imagination, and then proceeding to relate it to experience – approaches we have identified in Baudelaire and Descartes – Kant starts with experience and then seeks to describe the conditions which make it possible. He calls this kind of approach a 'transcendental' inquiry, because rather than attempting to describe the substantial world which the subject would reconstruct from the broken fragments of sensory experience, it seeks to specify the conditions which make experience possible in the first place. Kant identifies these conditions as the agreement of the forms of intuition, namely space and time, and the categorical organization of the understanding. The forms of intuition are understood as the basic intuitive co-ordinates through which representations are ordered for consciousness; the twelve categories, which Kant tabulates

---

[6] For a comparative discussion of Kant and Baudelaire, see Pippin, ch. 2.

under the headings of Quantity, Quality, Relation, and Modality, are the basic concepts that organize the understanding, so comprising a kind of conceptual grammar. Kant thus conceives of the activity of consciousness in terms of judgement, understood as the unification of intuitive representations under the concepts of the understanding. His transcendental approach supplements the investigation of perception with an analysis of what he terms 'apperception', or the subjective conditions necessary for perceptions to be cognizable.

The importance of this shift can be identified through a comparison with Descartes' approach. Cartesianism can take for granted the mechanical operation of empirical perception because it locates a *transcendent* configuration of form as prior to and unconnected with experience; that is, the Cartesian reduction of visual experience goes hand in hand with its bifurcated focus, which is split between the purely mental activity of the *cogito* and a purely mechanical conception of sensory perception. In contrast, Kant's *transcendental* perspective does not presuppose a transcendent configuration of form, but seeks to identify the conditions which make formal coherence possible. This shift has enormous consequences, but in the present context its significance can be identified in terms of Kant's reconceptualization of space and time. In the 'Transcendental Aesthetic' of the *Critique of Pure Reason* (1781/1787), Kant rejects the Cartesian conception of time as the duration of substances, and of space as the objective relations between them. He does so by conceiving of space and time as the subjective conditions of appearance, and so reformulates their a priori status. Space is identified as the 'form of all outer intuition', while time is identified as 'the formal condition of inner intuition' and so provides 'the a priori condition of all appearances whatsoever' (Kant, 1929, A34/B50). Rather than providing an external and objective framework, space and time are understood as the forms of intuition within which objects appear in human experience, and are a priori in this strict sense. Consequently, the coherence of appearances is not fixed in an objective configuration of form, but is to be discovered or produced in the negotiation of the understanding and the imagination, which forms sensation according to the co-ordinates of space and time and brings them under the concepts of the understanding. Yet because these co-ordinates are integral to human intuition, they are understood to be compatible with the understanding, and Kant regards them as necessary and universal.

This conception of intuition circumvents the Cartesian bifurcation between thinking and extended substance, and so qualifies the penetrating power of the *cogito*'s rational cognition and the illusory character of empirical experience. For Kant, intuition is neither purely a matter of sensation, nor purely a product of cognition, but is both sensible and intelligible: its receptivity to sensation differentiates it from cognition, while its intelligible form makes it compatible with the categorical organization of the understanding. In this sense, appearances are not the static surfaces of things which might be seen through or around, and therefore Kant rejects the Cartesian renunciation of the sensible world and its denunciation as inherently illusory. Appearance (*Erscheinung*) is not illusion (*Schein*), since appearances are not inert and arbitrary, awaiting their truth in the rational *cogito*, but are already ordered according to the forms of space and time. The corollary of this rejection of the illusory nature of appearances is Kant's reformulation of the nature of knowledge. The Cartesian claim to grasp the substantial reality lying *behind* appearances now becomes unsustainable, since objects can only be known *in* appearance. Because objects can only appear within the forms of intuition, then knowledge cannot claim to be free of the limits of human experience or grasp things as they are 'in themselves'. Thus, while Descartes aims to lay hold of the substantial reality of objects unencumbered by the particular conditions of experience, for Kant, knowledge cannot be opposed to experience, but is only possible within its limits.

A comparison with Baudelaire's understanding of vision is also revealing. If Descartes subordinates perception to cognition, Baudelaire wants to rescue it and restore its agency and productivity. However, as we have seen, Baudelaire's attitude to perception is coloured by an anxiety over the contribution of the visible world to visual experience, or the role of sensation. This anxiety leads him to separate the activity of aesthetic perception from the receptivity of utilitarian or cognitive vision, because the latter is seen as ensnared in the inert and formless world of things, while the former is identified with the pure interiority of the imagination. Baudelaire's understanding of beauty therefore envisages it as the triumph of the imagination over the sensory world, and as such it marks aesthetic perception's transcendence of the contingency of experience. But for Kant, the intuition is both receptive and productive, in that it both receives *and forms* the matter of sensation so that it can be brought under the concepts of the understanding. Thus, rather than subordinating perception to cognition or opposing them in the pursuit of the Ideal, he attempts to describe the relationship between them which must obtain for experience to be possible. Consequently, imagination is not opposed to experience, and nor is the apprehension of beauty placed in another realm to the 'everyday' or 'utilitarian' apprehension of cognition, although they are distinguished. The experience of beauty is understood to offer a particular mode of the imagination's unification of intuition which Kant calls reflective judgement, and which he differentiates from the determinate judgement of cognition in the first and second introductions to the *Critique of Judgement*. While in determinate judgement intuitions are ordered or unified by the imagination under the concepts of the understanding, in the apprehension of beauty, intuitions anticipate the terms of their unification without the application of an external unity or law. Thus the aesthetic judgement of taste instances 'a lawfulness without a law', within which there is 'a subjective harmony of the imagination with the understanding without an objective harmony', an agreement which is experienced as the sensation of pleasure (Kant, 1987, p. 92). Thus if Kant distinguishes between aesthetic judgement and the determinate judgement of cognition, this distinction is not understood to oppose 'utilitarian' and 'aesthetic' perception, nor to testify to the triumph of the pure interiority of the imagination over the riot of sensation. Rather, reflective judgement reveals the proportionality of intuition to its unification, so indicating that the forms of intuition are conformable to the categorical structure of the understanding. The feeling of pleasure which Kant identifies in beauty thus provides an indication from within experience of the conformity of intuition and understanding, a conformity that underlies our perceptual experience, and which Kant calls 'the transcendental unity of apperception'. But if this unity is necessary for experience, it cannot be an object of experience or be grasped in concepts as knowledge.

Although Kant's critical philosophy may appear to mark a shift of attention away from perception to transcendental apperception, by inquiring beyond the immediate limits of visibility Kant's approach suggests ways of revaluing visual experience.[7] By extending the terms of inquiry, from the Cartesian *cogito* that frames perception to the conditions of possibility which underlie this act of framing, Kant fundamentally reformulates the opposition between knowledge and appearance that structures Cartesianism, and which persists within Baudelaire's art criticism as the opposition between utilitarian and aesthetic vision. For Descartes, the images we perceive constitute an illusory realm that must be seen through, so that what consciousness aims at in knowledge is something that ultimately lies outside or beyond visual experience. By understanding intuitions as both intelligible and sensible, Kant redefines appearance as the site of knowledge, rather than the perennial scene of illusion. But equally, his understanding of the intuition as both receptive and productive avoids Baudelaire's later hostility to the visible, which fears that the riot of sensation might escape the direction of the imagination. In contrast, Kant sees in reflective judgement a mode of apprehension in which intuitions order themselves, so that the productivity of the imagination is envisaged as the negotiation of differences, rather than the despotic imposition of form. In these terms, perceptual experience takes on a new importance: it is no longer to be thought of as simply a reservoir of inert raw material to be processed in consciousness, nor as a riot of details awaiting form, but becomes the site where understanding and sensibility meet, and where the claims of each might be recognized and negotiated.

This being the case, serious objections were soon raised concerning Kant's methodology, and significantly Baudelaire's vexed confrontation with the photograph dramatizes some of the main issues at stake. Many of the charges levelled at Kant by his nineteenth-century critics revolve around his claim that the forms of intuition and the categories of the understanding described by the critical philosophy provide the transcendental conditions for all possible experience. For Hegel and Nietzsche, this claim was belied by Kant's own methodology, since its

---

[7] For a lucid account of Kant's revaluation of experience and its broader implications, see Cassirer, 1981, pp. 169–71.

description of these conditions was tied to a particular, historically specific configuration of experience, one centred on the unity of the isolated apperceptive subject. Therefore, while Kant's approach was understood by both Hegel and Nietzsche as valuable in raising the question of the conditions that make experience possible, its methodology was seen as inevitably leading to a fixed and invariable conception of the transcendental. Notwithstanding their differences, both Hegel and Nietzsche consequently sought to extend the terms of Kant's approach by tracing the historical formation or genealogy of different configurations of experience, thereby identifying alternative ways of conceiving the transcendental.[8] The problem identified here at a theoretical level can be seen at the level of experience in Baudelaire's hostile reaction to photography. For just as Kant's critics complained that his conception of the apperceptive subject was limited to one particular condition of experience, so Baudelaire's hostility to photography lies in its dependence on a particular conception of the subject, which feels that the sovereignty of its imagination is threatened by the new experiential contexts opened up by the camera. Yet for critics of Kant such as Hegel and Nietzsche, the perceived limitations of the critical philosophy did not render its insights irretrievably worthless or redundant. In revaluing experience and extending the terms of analysis from perception to apperception, Kant's transcendental philosophy was seen to discover new avenues for approaching vision, avenues whose direction remained open.

[8] For accounts of Hegel and Nietzsche in these terms, see Rose, 1979 and Owen, 1995.

CHAPTER 2

The Disappearance of the World

I will now shut my eyes, stop my ears, and withdraw all
my senses. I will eliminate from my thoughts all images of
bodily things, or rather, since this is hardly possible, I will
regard all such images as vacuous, false and worthless.

René Descartes, *Meditations on First Philosophy*

THE AUTONOMY OF APPEARANCE

The impact of technology on vision has been a widely shared concern
for artists and intellectuals since Baudelaire, but the current sense of a
new visual condition of culture is generally associated with the
particular intellectual and cultural environment of post-war France.
Within this context, the broader interest in the technological reproduction of images and the organization of sight by optical technologies
takes on its own tenor and inflection, and not only in purely visual
terms. While this context has been described by Martin Jay as 'anti-
ocularcentric', it is important not to lose sight of the ways in which
accounts of the visual also take part in a more wide-ranging reassessment of modern thought (for accounts of this broader context, see
Jay, 1993 and Descombes, 1980). For prominent strands within recent
French theory, the new visual condition of culture is understood to
presage a fundamental break with the conditions of experience in
modernity, and therefore with modern rationality and the modern
subject. This connection between vision and a wider reformulation of
modernity can be seen emerging from the 1960s, initially in the
writing of Guy Debord, and then more recognizably in the work of
Jean Baudrillard and Paul Virilio. In turn, the transposition of these
intellectual developments to the United States, and thus to the English-

speaking academy, can be identified with Frederic Jameson's well-known account of postmodernism, which draws extensively on Debord and Baudrillard. And although Jameson's transposition of these currents involves important differences, his redeployment of their terms within the broader notion of 'postmodernism' retains their sense of a fundamental recasting of modernity.

While Debord, Baudrillard, Virilio, and Jameson each offers a different account of the new condition of the visual, within the terms of their shared reassessment of modernity it is possible to see certain common features or tendencies. Centrally, where modern thought is understood to stress the autonomy of the perceiving subject, this new cultural condition is understood to presage the autonomy of the visual. This shift rewrites the paradigm of vision bequeathed by modern culture, reformulating both the condition of appearance and the activity of the subject in perception. In terms of appearances, the mass reproduction and dissemination of images is seen to have penetrated and formed the sensible world in a new and unprecedented sense, so that where modern culture came to see in visual experience the difficult task of discovering or producing form, appearances are now understood to have already been organized or 'pre-formed'. In terms of the subject, technology is understood to colonize the conscious and unconscious processes through which the subject senses, desires, and understands the sensible world. Consequently, technologically reproduced images and optical instruments are understood themselves to supply the aesthetic, libidinous, or cognitive frames through which the subject orders visual experience and makes it meaningful. The image-world that confronts the subject in perception does not depend on the subject's activity in framing or forming appearance, but is already formed; and so in a sense all sights have already been seen prior to the contingency of visual experience. Equally, technology withdraws from objects their ability to throw back to the subject a sense of its own involvement in the configuration of appearances, since the technological replication and dissemination of appearances means that the contours and textures of appearance no longer figure the specificity of the object world, draining objects of their uniqueness and spatio-temporal location. Appearances no longer provide the secure context for the subject's mastery of the world, but mutate and replicate according to technological logics which exceed the categories of the subject. This condition is understood to have profound consequences for the nature and effectivity of cultural artefacts, for the dynamics of vision, and for the figuring of the subject's capacities for agency, judgement, and knowledge.

Recent cultural theory registers the scope and power of technology's impact on vision in a way that had been resisted by Descartes' theoretical philosophy and Baudelaire's aesthetic theory, and its significance lies not least in embedding representation's idealized conception of vision within the physical – although not necessarily tangible – world of refraction, reproduction, photochemical transformation, and digital information flow. And yet, paradoxically, Debord, Baudrillard, Jameson, and Virilio all articulate this shift in terms of 'the loss of the real' or the 'de-realization' of the world, casting the impact of technology as the separation of the visual from its immersion in the contingency of time and place. Because appearances no longer provide a secure context for the subject's spatial and temporal inhabitation of the world, these critics see the new image landscape as having been freed from the economic, social, and political imperatives which were understood to have once stood 'behind' the appearance of modernity. It is this loss which is understood to mark a fundamental break with modernity and modern thought, and therefore to define and demarcate the contemporary condition. And it is also here that a deep-seated pessimism emerges, whether or not this new condition is ostensibly denounced, celebrated, or contemplated under the equanimity of the historicizing gaze. Notoriously, these critics envisage dystopic scenarios of disempowerment and total control, which see technology driven by autonomous and inescapable logics removed from social action. Within these terms, the fate of visual experience is cast as ineluctable, resolving itself either as an absolutely blank seeing, or as an inescapable disorientation and incoherence.

However, if announcements of 'the loss of the real' have sought to define contemporary culture in terms of a fundamental break with modernity and the predicaments of modern thought, what is striking is that each of these four critics sees this new visual condition as the actualization of modern thought and its conception of vision. In each case, the autonomy of the image-world of technology is understood to have fulfilled the claims of modern vision, and so to have achieved the harmony or proportionality which Descartes and Baudelaire had looked for in visual experience; but in doing so, technology is understood to create a condition that is quite different from that which modern thought had desired or intended. According to Debord, social experience is now dominated by the 'spectacle', which 'inherits all the weaknesses of the Western philosophical project which undertook to comprehend activity in terms of the categories of seeing' (1983, para. 19). Equally, for Baudrillard 'all the repressive and reductive strategies of [the] power systems' which emerge from the social, economic, and political histories of modernity 'are already present in the internal logic of the sign' (1981, p. 163). For Virilio, the 'omnivoyance' realized in the technological 'vision machine' is identical with 'Western Europe's totalitarian ambition', as exemplified by the modern state and its sphere of public right (1994, p. 33). And for Jameson, the image-saturated space of postmodernism is the ironic actualization of Hegel's 'end of art', in that all 'social life . . . can be said to have become "cultural" in some original yet untheorized sense' (1991, pp. xvii, 48). For each of these critics, technology's organization of the visible and of the formative activity of perception actualizes the visual coherence that modern thought had hoped for, but only to produce an integrated image-world in which appearances are illusory and the subject's gaze is fixed and preordained. The irony thus lies in the fact that the 'harmony' of such integrated appearance neither confirms the compatibility of reason and extended substance, nor the spontaneity and agency of the subject, and so produces neither knowledge nor beauty, but the reverse. In seeing only the pre-formed images of technological reproduction, the subject is locked into fixed and inert configurations of experience, while the phenomenal world appears either as the blank repetition of sights already seen, or as a flux of visual intensities which overwhelms the categories of the perceiving subject.

The particular combination of difference and repetition here points to a more complex kind of relationship between contemporary and modern conceptions of vision than is often acknowledged. The contemporary visual condition is understood to mark a fundamental break with modern culture, yet at the same time its specificity is defined in terms of its ironic actualization of the terms of modern vision. This relationship itself provides an analytical frame for assessing the iconoclasm of recent accounts, since rather than placing recent theoretical approaches in opposition to modern vision, it identifies them as formulations of its fate. From this perspective, recent accounts can be judged in terms of the processes of theoretical translation and reformulation involved in their figuring of the fate of modern conceptions of vision. By setting them alongside modern conceptions of vision, it becomes possible to identify those possibilities which are recognized and worked through, and those which are misrecognized or occluded. The point here is not to denounce recent accounts for deviating from modern conceptions of vision, but rather to attend to the specific ways in which the possibilities and restrictions offered by modern conceptions of vision are rearticulated within contemporary theory. Such an approach does not constitute a historicism which blunts critical evaluation by according a time to everything, nor does it order its evaluation around the self-satisfaction of either present or past, as progress or decline. Instead, it seeks to mobilize the differences and continuities between past and present in order to gauge the extent to which recent accounts work through the past and become different to it, and the extent to which they fail to be so different.

This chapter pursues this approach by focusing on the concept of visual experience, which has provided the central site for rethinking approaches to vision and the visual. For Descartes and Baudelaire, it was the moment of clarity or harmony found in visual experience which sustained the promise of knowledge or beauty, and which thereby testified to the autonomy of the subject and its mastery of the phenomenal world. In contrast, recent cultural theory stresses the ways in which the image landscape of contemporary culture exceeds the capacities of the subject, so rendering visual experience as ineluctably blank, inert, or disorientating. For Debord and Baudrillard, the mechanism which underlies this reformulation is the extension of the commodity form to visual experience, which is described as the 'reification' of vision; consequently, their positions are examined in relation to Lukács' initial development of the term. While Jameson also employs this term, his stress on the disorientating nature of visual experience and his more extended consideration of modern thought and culture places him in certain ways closer to Virilio, who focuses on the historical transformation of perception. Consequently, these two critics are examined in relation to their recasting of the dynamics of visual experience and the interplay between visual technique and technology.

However, if the interchange between earlier and more recent accounts of vision provides a framework for addressing contemporary theoretical developments, this interchange does not only work one way. In sharpening our awareness of the restrictions involved in modern conceptions of vision, and of the continuities and differences which emerge with regard to more recent approaches, this interchange also allows us to identify possibilities that were latent within modern culture, but which were not recognized or could not be articulated within the terms of its own self-understanding. In the light of more recent accounts of the technological organization of appearance, Baudelaire's awareness of the role of memory, association, and similarity in vision begins to describe visual experience in terms which exceed his own opposition of technique and technology, and which therefore suggests different trajectories for the fate of modern vision. Within this broader framework, the elements of visual ambiguity, distortion, and contingency which Baudelaire's aesthetic theory aimed to over-come, but which figure so strongly in his poetry, might point to different ways of thinking visual experience in urban modernity. This chapter therefore concludes by returning to Baudelaire by way of his poetic practice, in order to examine the possibilities for thinking vision which appear there with hindsight.

THE TRIUMPH OF THE SPECTACLE

Guy Debord, a filmmaker and leading member of the Situationist International, is perhaps now best known for his polemical account of the power of the image in *Society of the Spectacle* (1967). The account of the new visual condition of social experience which Debord develops here revolves around the concept of 'the spectacle', which describes the absolute autonomy of the image in consumer society. But despite the impression given by the illustrations added in the English transla-tions, it is not primarily concerned with technology since, according to Debord the spectacle is to be understood in terms of 'social relations among people' rather then 'the techniques of the mass dissemination of images' (1983, paras. 4, 5). Consequently, the term becomes an extension of the concept of 'reification' initially introduced by the Hungarian philosopher Georg Lukács, and Debord's understanding of the autonomy of the image assumes a broader influence and applicability; used interchangeably with the term 'commodification' it has become one of the central terms employed in defining the relationship of technology and visual experience. Thus, while reification was initially seen by Debord to offer an alternative to what he perceived as technological determinism, for Baudrillard and Jameson the term comes to designate the very mechanism through which technology is understood to organize appearance and to colonize the frameworks of perception. Given this larger contribution to contemporary understandings of visual experience, it is worth examining Lukács' term and its subsequent redeployment in *Society of the Spectacle*.

The organizing premise of *Society of the Spectacle* is presented in its opening paragraph as the opposition between integrated 'experience' and its fragmentation or 'separation' in the spectacle: 'Everything that was directly lived', Debord argues, 'has moved away into representation' (*ibid.*, para.1). Experience 'proper' is thus opposed to visual experience, which is understood as inherently fragmented and fragmenting; or, to use Debord's terms, it is understood as 'image' as opposed to the 'reality' of an experience that is 'really lived' (*ibid.*, para. 7). The fundamental nature of this opposition is made explicit in the comparison of vision and touch in the first chapter, a comparison that ascribes to the human sensorium a static and unalterable character. The spectacle, Debord argues, 'naturally finds vision to be the privileged human sense' because 'it is the most abstract, the most mystifiable sense'; in contrast, touch is exempt from the 'various specialized mediations' of vision, which is why it had once allowed the world to be 'grasped directly', so providing the sensory basis for a full and integrated experience (*ibid.*, para. 18). Notwithstanding this nominally historical scheme, both touch and vision emerge here as fixed sensory capacities which imply rigid configurations of experience: the spectacle is presented as a function of the historical development of modernity, but only after this development is identified with a 'seeing' that is conceived as a configuration of experience unaffected by the process of historical change. As experience proper is identified with the given capacities of touch, so the fragmented experience of the spectacle is identified with vision *per se*, which in turn allows the spectacle to be identified with a rationality conceived of as antithetical to integrated experience: thus, according to Debord, the 'spectacle inherits all the weaknesses of the Western philosophical project which undertook to comprehend activity in terms of the categories of seeing' (*ibid.*, para. 19).

It is in these terms that Debord presents his account of the spectacle as an extension of the concept of reification developed by Georg Lukács in 'Reification and the Consciousness of the Proletariat', the central essay of *History and Class Consciousness* ([1923] 1971, pp. 83–222). Lukács' essay, which is often identified as the founding document of 'Western Marxism', in fact sought to draw together a broad dissatisfaction with the intellectual and institutional hegemony of neo-Kantianism within the German-speaking world. This dissatisfaction was shared by a number of currents within post-Kantian thought; Lukács' own thinking was influenced by such diverse figures as Hegel, Nietzsche, Kierkegaard, Marx, Simmel, and Weber. Lukács was aware that a straightforward rejection of the current intellectual orthodoxy would lead either to resignation or to new forms of mysticism and self-assertion, rather than providing a critical context for engaging with a Europe torn apart by the First World War. Consequently, his essay sought to provide a reassessment of the opportunities and restrictions offered by Kant's legacy, by placing it within the specific historical configuration of European modernity. The essay does this by developing the problematic of reification (*Verdinglichung*), and the term translates a broad range of accounts of modernity, including Marx's account of the commodity form, into a critical framework for addressing Kant's transcendental viewpoint. However, this translation does not directly relate to vision or visual experience, but to Kant's analysis of the conditions underlying the agreement of perception and cognition in transcendental apperception.[1]

Lukács saw Kantian rationality as torn between the demands of

[1] For a fuller account of Lukács' intellectual context and development, see Bernstein, 1984.

necessity and of freedom. But rather than being simply a 'mistake', he understood this tension as offering an important insight into the condition of neo-Kantian thought, which offered one way of developing Kant's legacy. For Lukács, the 'antinomies', or aporias, of neo-Kantian thought reveal its indebtedness to a restricted conception of experience which 'reduces space and time to a common denominator and degrades time to a dimension of space' (1971, p. 89). These antinomies are thus understood as the distortions thrown up by modern thought's attempts to systematize contingency and render experience within the static co-ordinates of a rigid and inflexible rationality. In turn, Lukács saw that these distortions could be mapped onto the various critical accounts of modernity, which describe modern social and economic forms in terms of an analogous spatio-temporal restriction. Thus, in the Marxian vocabulary that is most evident in the essay, the suppression of the contingency of social experience in neo-Kantian social theory can be seen as analogous to the suppression of the sensuous quality of objects in exchange. Within the terms of the essay, reification provides a way of reading between the development of modern thought and the historical conditions of modernity, not by seeing the one as a 'reflection' or 'expression' of the other, but by identifying how the modes of suppression particular to each require an analogous restriction of the spatio-temporal co-ordinates of reason and experience.

Two points are worth emphasizing briefly before moving on to Debord's deployment of reification and assessing its contribution to the analysis of the image-world of consumer society. First, Lukács is not offering an account of perception or visual experience *per se*, but an examination of the conflicts between cognitive and perceptual experience on the one hand, and their transcendental conditions on the other. Or to put it another way, Lukács seeks to identify the disparity between modern thought's systematic rationalization and the contingency of experience, and to draw out its consequences for social thought and experience. He describes these consequences in terms of a violent disjunction between the rational systematization of social institutions and the forms of social experience developing in modernity. Lukács does not, therefore, counterpose rationality and experience as fixed and unrelated entities, which is why he is careful to locate his analysis within different historical formations of rationality and different configurations of experience; yet, at the same time, he understands reason and experience to be nonidentical or different. Second, and as a consequence, his methodology does not involve imputing a systematic character to either reason or experience; rather, it takes the claims of neo-Kantian thought to systematic coherence and subjects them to immanent critique. For Lukács, the suppression of the contingency of social forms in neo-Kantian social theory leads it to view their historical development in terms of 'natural laws', as the progressive unfolding of rational social life. He observes that despite the allegedly 'iron' nature of such 'laws', social change does not conform to their prescriptions; instead it increasingly challenges the stable social hierarchies which they are designed to explain and underwrite. However, from the systematic and progressive viewpoint of neo-Kantian social theory, social change which does not conform to these 'natural laws' can only be understood as the eruption of irrational contingency within the rational development of social life, and therefore must be violently suppressed. Thus for Lukács, the claims to rationality and systematic coherence underlying such accounts are internally contradictory, since they depend on a non-systematic and arbitrary 'state of emergency' within which the legality of reason must be suspended in order to maintain the condition of its legality. As these terms suggest, his critique was designed to identify the theoretical conditions of the conservatism of the 'critical' German social thought of his time, which he saw anticipating and justifying the events of the First World War and its immediate aftermath. This paradoxical combination is identified in the essay most closely with German social democracy, which is understood by Lukács as justifying state and paramilitary violence at home and aggression abroad through its acceptance of the suspension of national and international legality in the very name of law, rationality, and progress.

Debord's account of the spectacle offers itself as an extension of Lukács' conception of reification to the realm of visual experience, but when set against the conceptual dynamic of Lukács' essay such an 'extension' is not an extension at all. Lukács' term depends on its movement between the transcendental and the empirical: its critical force derives from the fact that, in respecting the transcendental distinction between the intelligible and the sensible, it nonetheless finds an analogous restriction in both rationality and social experience, a discovery which in turn questions the fixing of the transcendental co-ordinates of reason and experience. In transposing Lukács' terminology from its location 'between' apperception and perception to the realm of perception, Debord unwittingly collapses its critical potential by erasing the distinction which its immanent critique inhabits and questions. The implications of this transposition can be seen most readily in terms of the different methodological standpoints involved. As we have indicated, Lukács takes the claims of modern thought and modern social institutions to systematic coherence as the starting point for immanent critique, and so does not impute a systematic coherence to modern rationality or to modern experience. Debord's approach, however, wholly identifies spectacular vision with 'the incessant spread of the precise technical rationality' of modern thought, and so assumes that spectacular experience and modern rationality are inherently systematic (1983, para. 19). In Lukács' terms, Debord's approach would not offer a critique of the reification of modern thought, but an example of it: like neo-Kantianism, Debord's central term, 'the spectacle', replicates the claims of modern social institutions to constitute an enclosed system which proceeds according to logics, or 'iron laws', which wholly determine social experience.

The corollary of this shift is perhaps less evident, but by no means less significant. In misrecognizing Lukács' methodological approach, Debord misrecognizes the nature of the conflict between systematiza-tion and contingency which lies at the heart of Lukács' account of reification. For Lukács, the drive to systematization shared by modern thought and modern social institutions must constantly come into conflict with the very contingency which it excludes and opposes to itself; that is, the contingency which interrupts systematization is itself produced or constructed by the drive to systematic coherence, as the 'irrational' implied by 'rationality'. Much of the essay is involved in arguing for a response orientated towards 'the standpoint of the proletariat', but however the essay's response is judged, what is more significant in the present context is the nature of the terms of this conflict. Lukács does not counterpose a 'real' or 'authentic' experience to the systematic drive of modernity, since the contingency that interrupts this drive is itself a function of it. Rather, he seeks to identify the aporetic nature of this 'rational' systematization, which can only recognize divergent configurations of experience as the irrational and the purely contingent. This is why Lukács' statement that 'reification is . . . the necessary, immediate reality of every person living in capitalist society' in not a description of totalitarian control, nor the reduction of all visual experience to a single grid or framework (1971, p. 197). Indeed, the one instance of visual experience which Lukács discusses in the essay – the example of landscape painting borrowed from Ernst Bloch – is employed as an illustration of the way in which the apparently autonomous image generates different modes of perception according to the different experiential configurations within which it is viewed. The point of this illustration is not that reification occurs in the image's imposition of a fixed mode of perception on all viewers, but that it occurs in the image's assumption of an autonomy which is belied by its apprehension across different contexts of experience (*ibid.*, pp. 157–8).

In identifying visual experience with the systematic unity of modern thought, Debord not only accepts modern thought's claims to unity and coherence, but also drastically reduces the possibilities for critique. Debord can only counter such claims by an appeal to a unified or 'real' experience which must stand outside the unstable conflict between modern rationality and the emergent configurations of modern experience. Although Debord implies that this integrated experience is situated in some unidentified moment in the past, it is perhaps better understood as a function of his deployment of Lukács' vocabulary of 'separation' and 'fragmentation'. Because Debord mistakes reification for a description of the inescapable systematization of empirical perception he can only view the fragmentation of experience one-sidedly, as marking the triumph of systematization, rather than as simultaneously providing evidence of its failure. The moments of incoherence that Lukács saw as the opportunity for developing immanent critique are misrecognized by Debord as the necessary and unavoidable condition of reified experience. Consequently, the repeated experience of systematization's failure is inverted to become further proof of the unity of the system, hence Debord's contention that 'separation is itself part of the unity of the world, of the global social praxis split up into reality and image' (1983, para. 7). The unrelenting picture of total domination and total passivity implied by Debord's account of the spectacle emerges most fully here. Because visual or 'spectacular' experience is irretrievably ensnared in the dominance of the system, the disparities and differences which emerge within experience are dismissed as so many 'pseudo-events', while any attempt to subject the claims of modern thought to immanent critique is rejected as complicity with the 'system's thought' (*ibid.*, para. 195).

Given the subsequent role of reification within recent accounts of the new condition of visual experience, Debord's shifting of the term's conceptual location and meaning becomes significant, and the consequences of this shift for vision need to be clearly identified. In Lukács, reification is understood as a means of moving between the transcendental and the empirical, or between apperception and perception. In Debord, however, the question of the *transcendental conditions* of perception are occluded and so reification is confined to empirical perception, a shift that effectively returns us to the pre-Kantian conception of vision which we encountered in Descartes. For Descartes, the question of vision is not conceived of in terms of the transcendental conditions which allow empirical intuitions to be presented to the understanding, but simply in terms of the understanding's reception or framing of sensory data that are already assumed to be conformable to it. Similarly, for Debord visual experience can be identified with the 'incessant spread of . . . technical rationality' because thought and visual experience are assumed to share the same organization of space and time, and thus to be in some sense *already* identical. In neither case are the conditions of possible experience – which would underlie both cognition and perception and provide the terms of their agreement – at issue. Descartes fixes them in God, as the guarantor of the formal correspondence of reason and extended substance, while Debord secularizes them as the 'social relations of production', which is perhaps why he does not feel the need to address the specific impact of technology. Consequently, Debord's conception of visual experience is bifurcated around an opposition between systematic coherence and the pure incoherence of 'what is really lived', which 'has no relation to the official irreversible time of society' and which 'remains without language, without concept, without critical access to its own past' (*ibid.*, para. 157). In contrast, for Lukács visual

75

experience offers one of a number of sites where the deformations of experience incumbent on the modern drive to systematization might themselves become 'visible', or available for cognition. Thus, while for Lukács the experience of modernity points to the need for a renegotiation of the relationship between the empirical and the transcendental, in Debord the opposition of 'real' experience to visual experience seals the fate of modernity as one of endless domination and the repetition of the same.

TECHNOLOGY AS *DÉJÀ VU*

This understanding of Debord's application of the commodity form to visual experience is valuable in assessing the kind of developments proposed by Baudrillard, although his approach also needs to be distinguished from Debord's conception of the spectacle in a number of ways. Like the Situationists, Baudrillard was initially influenced by the work of Henri Lefebvre, and he shares both their interest in post-war consumer society and their employment of the vocabulary of reification. However, Baudrillard's starting point was not the extension of reification to visual experience, but of Saussure's account of the sign to the objects and images of consumer society. The enthusiastic extension of Saussure's semiology was of course a widespread feature of French intellectual life through the 1960s, and its potential was explored perhaps most suggestively by Roland Barthes in his writing on photography and at a broader level of cultural analysis in *Mythologies* (1957). In *Mythologies*, Barthes was able to illuminate the dynamics underlying the meaning and affective power of advertising and media imagery by viewing them through the lens of semiotics, and reading them as a visual 'language'. However, like any such extension, the promise of new perspectives and understandings held out by such a theoretical translation also involves the danger of flattening out the specificity of the different 'languages', or configurations of meaningfulness. The issue of translation becomes particularly relevant to Baudrillard's writing through the late 1960s and early 1970s, from the structuralist approach of *The System of Objects* (1968) and *Consumer Society* (1970), through *For a Critique of the Political Economy of the Sign* (1972), *Symbolic Exchange and Death* (1976), and *Seduction* (1979).

Across this series of works Baudrillard attempted not only to combine the structuralist analysis of semiotics with the language of the commodity form, but also to rearticulate this fusion in the terms of the emergent discourses of post-structuralism.

In *The System of Objects*, Baudrillard observes that consumer imagery develops particular semantic charges through its interaction with a wider context of popular imagery and meaning. This leads him to ascribe a systematic structure to the appearance of consumer objects – the 'system of objects' – which is counterposed to 'the system of needs'. Here Baudrillard effectively transcribes Debord's opposition between 'reality' and 'image' into structuralist terminology: 'the system of needs' is seen to be grounded in experiential capacities and desires, and is thus understood as 'reality', while 'the system of objects' relates to the signifying 'system' of consumption, and thus stands as the opposite pole of 'the image'. However, where Debord projects 'real' experience back into the past, Baudrillard figures these two systems as a simultaneous hierarchy, within which the image predominates and organizes 'real' needs. In *For a Critique of the Political Economy of the Sign* this opposition is itself rewritten through a series of algebraic equations in terms of the parallel 'systems' of production and consumption, or economic and symbolic exchange. In turn these parallel systems are each internally organized around a second-order opposition between 'image' and 'reality': exchange value and use value, and sign value and symbolic exchange value respectively (1981, pp. 123–9). The effect of this double transcription is to set up a binary hierarchy of two orders of 'reality' and 'image' which sets in place the trajectory of Baudrillard's argument: on the one hand, Marx's relational concept of use value is presented as though it were the static 'real' underlying exchange value; on the other, the economic 'system' itself is presented as though it were the 'real' underlying the 'system' of symbolic exchange. The text thus identifies the 'reality' that it ascribes to use value as the real locus of fetishism, whose truth is exposed by the form in which it appears – namely exchange value. In turn, the 'reality' which has been ascribed to the economic is then identified as a second-order fetishism, whose truth is exposed by the form of appearance of the system of production – namely the signifying system of consumption.

It is at this point that the differences and continuities between Debord and Baudrillard can be seen to emerge. Baudrillard's simultaneous hierarchy of 'image' and 'reality', or consumption and production, is thus resolved into a 'general political economy . . . which is traversed throughout by the same form and administered by the same logic'; namely, that of the relationship between sign value and symbolic exchange value (*ibid.*, p. 144). For Baudrillard, this general logic identifies 'signification [as] in some ways kin to the notion of reification', and consequently 'all the repressive and reductive strategies of power systems' are understood to be 'already present in the internal logic of the sign'. In effect Baudrillard equates signification with reification, which again relocates it from the transcendental to the empirical by subordinating its operation to the 'general logic', or algebra, of signification. Like Debord, therefore, Baudrillard excludes the possibility of any point of critique or change from within the system's logic, because signification is understood as the 'functional and terroristic organization of the control of meaning'. The only alternative to this 'general logic' would be a pure non-signification or non-form, an absolute other to what Baudrillard terms 'the positivity of meaning'. Adapting contemporary vocabulary, Baudrillard calls this absolute non-signification the 'symbolic', which is defined as 'the beyond of the signification process through which sign exchange value organizes itself' (*ibid.*, p. 163). Thus the effect of Baudrillard's algebra is to retain Debord's opposition of 'image' and 'reality', yet at the same time to invert the valorization of its terms. For Debord, the domination of needs by the spectacle had implied the resurgence of 'real' needs or integrated experience, while for Baudrillard the promise of disruption or release is now located not in the 'real', but in the 'beyond' of the symbolic's non-signification. Where 'reification' designates the fragmentation of spectacular vision for Debord, for Baudrillard it designates meaningfulness or form *per se*, which he associates with claims to grasp or render 'reality'. Where Debord looks for a release from the fragmented visual experience of the spectacle in the upsurge of 'real' experience, Baudrillard celebrates the reversal of any moment of 'positivity' or meaningfulness – which he associates with 'the real' – because signification is itself equated with reification and is thus 'terroristic'.

Although primarily concerned with signification, the algebra of *For a Critique of the Political Economy of the Sign* can be seen to underwrite the subsequent development of Baudrillard's account of visual experience in his two subsequent books, *Symbolic Exchange and Death* and *Seduction*. Here Baudrillard transposes the opposition of signification and the symbolic into an account of the technological condition of appearances. Baudrillard does this by stressing technology's capacity for reproduction or simulation, so translating his analysis of political economy of the sign into the language of representation. This process is perhaps best illustrated by the comparison offered in *Seduction* between still-life painting and *trompe l'oeil*, where the opposition developed in *For a Critique of the Political Economy of the Sign* between signification and the symbolic is translated as the opposition between representation and anti-representation. In *Seduction*, Baudrillard argues that still life painting encapsulates 'the entire representative space of the Renaissance', which implies a 'hierarchical organization of space that privileges the eye and vision' and which renders appearances as the representation of 'reality' (1990, p. 61). The arrangement of the visible according to perspectival sight lines emanating from the eye is located as one pole of Baudrillard's guiding opposition, namely as the 'real'. The shadows which locate objects within the perspectival grid of the perceiving subject are seen to lend them not only visual, but also ontological substance, and thus they are read as evidence of a metaphysics of presence which is seen as irretrievably bound up with vision. In contrast, the exact duplication of *trompe l'oeil* anticipates the 'malevolent use of appearances' in technological simulation, where the claim to represent 'reality' is marred by 'the irony of too much reality', so that what is presented is 'pure appearances' (*ibid.*). For Baudrillard, therefore, *trompe l'oeil* encapsulates the new condition of the visual because it captures technology's capacity to exceed the representational techniques of painting through 'hypersimulation'. The exact visual reproduction of appearances creates a heightened sense of the 'tactile hyperpresence of things'; yet as Baudrillard explains 'this tactile fantasy has nothing to do with our sense of touch', but is rather 'a metaphor for the "seizure" resulting from the annihilation of the scene and space of representation'. The perfect clarity and visibility of appearances 'rebounds onto the so-called "real" world, to reveal that this reality is naught but a staged world, objectified in accord with the rules of perspective'. What the 'hypersimulation' of *trompe l'oeil* reveals, then, is that 'reality' is merely a 'principle' or a 'simulacrum' (*ibid.*, p. 63).

And yet in another sense *trompe l'oeil* reveals nothing, since within the terms of Baudrillard's opposition such an insight cannot be developed or have issue, because any such issue could only be identified as a resurgence of the 'real'. Or to put it in directly visual terms, in the absolute and perfect clarity of 'pure appearances' the spatio-temporal configuration of the visible cannot be registered, and so there is nothing to see. But having said this, although Baudrillard's discussion ultimately resolves itself into its governing opposition of 'image' and 'the real', the analysis which it offers is in fact more interesting. In terms of this governing opposition, the eye either sees things as they 'really are', or it sees only the pure and absolute emptiness of images; vision either describes a transaction in which the 'real' is returned in all its fullness and self-presence, or one in which there is nothing returned. But in analysing *trompe l'oeil*, Baudrillard identifies a transaction which exceeds these symmetrical alternatives. As he explains, in *trompe-l'oeil* objects 'do not flee before your gaze, but position themselves in front of you', so that 'perspective in the *trompe-l'oeil* is, in a sense, projected forward' and 'depth appears to be turned inside out' (*ibid.*, pp. 64, 63). What appears in these terms is not the 'real', but the co-ordinates of space and time which configure the image, or the mode of visibility within which appearances appear. It is possible to see a parallel here with Baudelaire's account of the photographic image in his review of the Salon of 1859. There, photography produced an awareness of technique's framing of appearances by interrupting the unity of the image; here, *trompe l'oeil* instances the ability of the technological image to throw back to the eye its own perspectival organization of space, producing the effect of *déjà vu* because it mirrors too closely the eye's organization of the visible. However, although his analysis of *trompe l'oeil* may raise this possibility, Baudrillard does not draw these conclusions, and here the parallel with Baudelaire reveals some of the consequences implicit in Baudrillard's opposition of the 'image' and the 'real'. Baudelaire can only understand the contingency thrown back by the photographic image as the interruption of aesthetic technique's aspiration to harmony, because he views technique and technology as opposed and mutually exclusive. Equally, Baudrillard's identification of aesthetic technique with representation means that he can only figure technology's role as the abolition of technique, as 'the annihilation of the scene and space of representation', and thus as an absolute and perfectly clear *non*-seeing. The difference between them of course lies in their respective valorization of these terms: while Baudelaire regrets photography's interruption of aesthetic harmony, Baudrillard celebrates what he sees as the collapse of representation's claim to reproduce the 'real'.

Curiously, then, although Baudrillard's analysis of *trompe l'oeil* identifies technology's potential to illuminate the spatio-temporal co-ordinates of vision, his eye is drawn only to the 'non-return' of anti-representation, and his discussion fails to register the significance of his own analysis. Thus he writes that in *trompe l'oeil*

> the eye, instead of generating a space that spreads out, is but the internal vanishing point for a convergence of objects. A different universe occupies the foreground, a universe without horizon or horizontality, like an opaque mirror placed before the eye with nothing behind it. This is properly the realm of appearances, *where there is nothing to see*, where things see you (*ibid.*, pp. 63–4; emphasis added).

Despite this passage's conclusion 'that there is nothing to see' in *trompe l'oeil*, its identification of a condition in which 'things see you' points to a kind of return that is absent in Baudrillard's subsequent writing. Instead of seeing vision as a transaction which either returns the illusory substantiality of a 'real' world or the blank image of simulation, the unsettling effect of *tromp l'oeil* points to another experience altogether: what is returned or made visible within the jarring experience of *trompe l'oeil* are the conditions of visibility themselves, at least within this particular instant of vision and within this particular configuration of experience. Or to adapt Baudrillard's own terms, what would be 'rebounded' in the unsettling experience of *trompe l'oeil* is not 'the annihilation of the scene and space of representation' which claims a substantial 'reality' that lies 'behind' the 'mirror' of appearance; rather, the *déjà vu* of simulation rebounds to the eye an image of its own spatio-temporal co-ordinates, which configure the *tain* or silvering that constitutes the image, but which do not of course lie 'behind' or 'beyond' the mirror itself.

In foreclosing the possibilities of vision by claiming that 'there is nothing to see' in *tromp l'oeil*, Baudrillard not only fails to see what might be thrown back or returned in technological appearances, but also locks himself into a conception of vision which organizes his subsequent accounts of the technological simulation of the simulacrum and the 'code'. And this is where the convoluted terminological translations that we have traced in Baudrillard's early writing become significant. In the algebraic equations of *For a Critique of the Political Economy of the Sign*, the spatio-temporal location of vision is bracketed out through the absolute convertibility of objects into the 'signs' of semiology, which are understood as being driven by an autonomous 'code' that is removed from spatio-temporal experience. By transmuting the appearance of objects directly into their signifying value, the processes of their visibility and recognizability in space and time are already assumed: Baudrillard's signs are always readable, and have always already been read in all their typographical clarity and distinctness. In effect, *For a Critique of the Political Economy of the Sign* takes for granted the perfect or absolute visibility of signs within a homogenous space and time, an assumption which contrasts markedly with significant strands of modernist poetry and visual art, which explored the spatial arrangement of letters on the page or canvas in terms of visual echoing and ambiguity, superimposition and illegibility. Baudrillard's algebra, we might say, reduces reading to the homogenous space and time claimed by the realist novel, which in *S/Z* Roland Barthes identified with 'transparency'. So it is that Baudrillard, rather than pursuing the unsettling experience produced by the re-folding of the gaze in *trompe l'oeil*, sees only 'the transparency of objects to a black sun'; and so he reduces the return of simulation to a 'fantastic vivacity' or an 'unmediated hallucination anterior to the perceptual order', which is understood as the 'hyperpresence of things' (*op. cit.*, pp. 62–3). And perhaps this is why the pleasure of *trompe l'oeil* is for Baudrillard only 'small', since it can only ever be 'the *ironic simulacrum* of that reality', the 'anti-representation' of representation, rather than an insight into the conditions of its possibility (*ibid.*, p. 64). A curious condition obtains in the absolute visibility and transparency of techno-logical appearances: for 'they are blank, empty signs' that 'describe a void, an absence . . . of the hierarchy that organizes the elements of a tableau, or for that matter, the political order'. And yet this 'void' can only ever be the glaring and absolute clarity of 'pure appearances' conceived of as 'hyperpresence', rather than a differential site where the play of presence and absence emerges in the folds and distortions of contingent vision.

It is therefore a mistake to accept at face value Baudrillard's subsequent claim to have left behind the subject's domination of the phenomenal world in vision, in favour of the 'pure appearances' of simulation or the autonomy of the visual. In fact, Baudrillard's account of simulation does imply a conception of vision, although it does not so much resemble Baudelaire's as Descartes'. The translation of the sensible world into signs effected by *For a Critique of the Political Economy of the Sign* had already been accomplished by Descartes in *The World*. In Descartes, resemblance is replaced by the arbitrary and conventional relationship between thinking substance's perception and the excitations of extended substance which underlie sensory data. Descartes' shift is of course underwritten by the analogy of speech rather than writing, but there is an important similarity nonetheless: rather than attending to mispronunciation, the overlay of sounds, or to the ambiguous semantic charge of homophones, Descartes' analogy assumes precisely the homogenous space and time of an absolute and pure apprehension which reoccurs in Baudrillard. The conception of vision which the analogy implies contains the problematic nature of visual experience within the dualism of the 'real' and the 'image' by privileging one pole over the other: the rational form of the *res cogitans* and the geometry of extended substance are privileged as the 'real' over and against the 'vacuous, false and worthless' images which confront the *cogito* in visual experience. Thus, Descartes' analogy confirms his rejection of any visual experience that is not consistent with the a priori co-ordinates of the *cogito*'s rational apprehension, hence his rigid opposition between certain and illusory appearance. This bifurcation reappears in Baudrillard's opposition between the illusory nature of the 'real' and the absolute certainty that 'there is nothing to see' in pure appearances; and although he inverts the valorization of Descartes' dualism, his conception of visual experience remains subject to the same homogenous time and space. And so, while Baudrillard may claim to have erased the subject in his notion of the code, along with its difficult, impure, and distorted vision, the Cartesian *cogito* continues to haunt the absolute visibility of Baudrillard's signs.

In Baudrillard's conception of the code, the fraught complicities and investments of vision that emerge in his own examination of *trompe l'oeil* are shrugged off, and his analyses become increasingly comfortable with the certainty of non-knowledge, or 'the loss of the real'. Thus in *America* (1986), Baudrillard's Cartesian heritage, although not recognized, is celebrated in the clarity of the 'European' eye which surveys the transparency of 'America'. 'It may be', suggests Baudrillard, 'that the truth of America can only be seen by a European', although the 'truth' revealed here is simply the certainty that 'this is the only country which gives you the opportunity to be so brutally naïve'; consequently, 'America' becomes 'the land of the "just as it is"', where 'things, faces, skies, and deserts are expected to be simply what they are' (1988A, p. 12. Although this 'truth' might be thought to 'rebound' back only the brutal naïveté of a gaze which is oblivious to the fixed parameters of its own vision, this is not what Baudrillard sees, but only an 'America' which has 'no past' and so 'lives a perpetual present' (*ibid.*, p. 76). Just as the complex histories of 'Europe' are collapsed in the brutal clarity of this naïve 'European' gaze, so the myriad histories of technique and technology that converge in 'America' are reduced to an absolute blankness. It turns out, however, that this blankness is not that of the urban space of Los Angeles or Las Vegas as we might be led to expect, but of the inert expanse of the desert. 'This is not narcissism', Baudrillard nonetheless claims, but 'a sublime form that banishes all sociality, all sentimentality, all sexuality', a gesture that recalls the Cartesian suppression of the contingency of the body and the corporeal world in its methodology of doubt (*ibid.*, pp. 37, 71). And so, in a sense, it is the return of the Cartesian subject, which cannot recognize a different kind of meaningfulness in the deformations of visual experience in modernity because its pure vision sees all appearances in terms of its own clarity and certainty. However, now that its faith in the certainties of God and geometry have been withdrawn, it is certain only that the absolute clarity and coherence which confronts it in vision is 'vacuous, false and worthless'.

This is not to say that Baudrillard ignores technology, but rather that his conception of technology is significantly restricted: technology is not conceived of in terms of the reformulation of the space and time of vision, but only as the capacity to reproduce or simulate appearances within homogenous and fixed spatio-temporal co-ordinates. This limitation can be clearly seen in Baudrillard's figuring of Disneyland, which plays an important role in his account of the 'precession of simulacra'. Disneyland is for Baudrillard 'a perfect model of all the entangled orders of simulation', and in it the 'objective profile of the United States . . . may be traced' (1988B, p. 171). The cartoon forms of Disneyland correspond to the 'pure appearances' of the *trompe l'oeil* in that they no longer claim to represent the 'real'; indeed, Disneyland is understood to provide an alibi for the 'real' by simulating a 'non-real' to set against it. But while this account rehearses once again the opposition between 'image' and 'real', what is perhaps more significant here is the way that its transposition of cartoon forms to the 'real' world of Southern California brackets the different configurations of space and time generated by the techniques and technologies of film animation. The 'cartoon forms' of Disneyland are of course already excised from the spatio-temporal conditions of film, and simply designate the iconography employed through the theme park. Just as the algebra of *For a Critique of the Political Economy of the Sign* erases the spatio-temporal contingency of writing, so this transposition erases the different configurations of visual experience generated by the techniques and technologies of film animation. Its histories are instead reduced to the cartoon forms of the Disney corporation, which are themselves reduced to the iconography of its theme parks, so that Disneyland becomes an algebraic sign for the platonic 'cartoon form'.

Notwithstanding the sense of contemporaneity and rupture which characterizes the writing of Debord and Baudrillard, the problems involved in their accounts of vision and technology point back to earlier moments within the tradition of modern thought. These problems centre on their shared failure to address the spatio-temporal conditions of visual unity or form, which are assumed to remain invariable even if, as is more evident in the case of Debord, the space and time of capital are recognized as changing. In turn this failure underlies their restricted conceptions of technology, which concentrate on technology's capacity to reproduce appearances at the expense of its reformulation of the space and time of visual experience. There is then a certain irony in the role which their work has played in locating Marx's conception of the commodity form as one of the central theoretical mechanisms for addressing the impact of technological reproduction on vision. For however Marx's account of capital is to be judged, both the *Grundrisse* and *Capital* are centrally concerned with the relationship between social experience and technology's reformulation of space and time.[2] Thus for Lukács, the critical potential of Marx's conception of the commodity form lay in its concern to identify the disparity between 'rational' social institutions and the spatiotemporal organization of the social world which they were intended to regulate, a disparity testified to by the disjunctive and violent experience of modernity. Lukács took this experience as an opportunity to question the claim of neo-Kantianism to enumerate the transcendental conditions of experience as the harmonious integration of the particular, by demonstrating that this claim depends on the suppression of the conflictual nature of experience and on the suspension of reason's legality. Because Lukács' critique reinhabits Kant's distinction between transcendental apperception and empirical perception, it does not counterpose experience to rationality, yet nor does it equate them. His critical conception of reification was therefore understood by a generation of intellectuals as calling for a reformulation of the conceptual machinery of neo-Kantianism, a call which centred on its restrictive conception of the spatio-temporal conditions of experience.[3] In contrast, the recent 'extension' of reification to visual experience tends to collapse the difference between apperception and perception, and so returns to a pre-Kantian conception of vision, with its opposition

[2] For a discussion of the philosophically innovative character of Marx's conception of the relationship between technology and politics, see Beardsworth, 1996, pp. 95–7.

[3] See Rose, 1978, ch. 3; Rose's discussion of the 'abuse of reification' remains relevant to the work of Debord and Baudrillard.

between the 'real' and the vacuous images of contingent visual experience. However this opposition is formulated, it remains bound within a fixed conception of space and time which restricts visual experience and the possibilities opened up by technology.

THE AESTHETICS OF LOSS

Debord and Baudrillard represent only one response to the technological condition of vision, and the work of Jameson and Virilio can be seen to offer a different kind of approach. Although Jameson locates his own conception of vision within an account of reification similar to that of Debord and Baudrillard, his approach ultimately turns on an analysis of the spatio-temporal co-ordinates of visual experience within the new conditions of appearance created by technology. Virilio, on the other hand, circumvents the problematic of commodification by concentrating on optical technologies, so that his conception of the 'vision machine' applies the development of technology directly to visual experience. Because their accounts seek to address technology's reconfiguration of space and time as well as its capacity to replicate appearance, they tend to emphasize the disparity between inherited configurations of vision and the new co-ordinates of technology. Consequently, they describe visual experience in terms of disorientation and dislocation, rather than seeing it, like Debord and Baudrillard, as a clear and monumental procession of images. And perhaps it is for this reason that their approaches take modern conceptions of vision more seriously, since they also address the conflictual character of visual experience; yet if this is true, these two approaches also register the inheritance of modern thought in another sense. For Jameson, the reformulation of space and time is conceived of aesthetically, as the suppression of time and the new predominance of space registered in the visual intensity of the image world of postmodernism; for Virilio it is conceived of primarily in terms of the disorientation and reformulation of cognition, where the temporal intensification of visual experience is registered as 'speed'. Significantly, and perhaps unexpectedly, this divergence repeats the central bifurcation between knowledge and the aesthetic which char-acterizes modern conceptions of vision, and as such it raises the question of inheritance in a new way.

Jameson's engagement with vision is bound up with the account of postmodernism presented most famously in his 1984 article 'Postmodernism, or the Cultural Logic of Late Capitalism', which was subsequently incorporated as the first chapter of his extended study *Postmodernism* (1991, pp. 1–54). The defining feature of this condition is the 'new spatial logic of the simulacrum', which is understood by Jameson to reflect not only the increasing predominance of new visual technologies over the printed word, but more broadly the reformulation of experience itself within specifically visual terms (*ibid.*, p. 18). This focus on the historical reformulation of experience underlines Jameson's concern to avoid technological determinism, and consequently he develops his account of this new condition in terms of an extension of the aesthetic. Where Baudelaire opposed aesthetic perception to the 'technological' vision of the camera, Jameson sees the proliferation of technologically mediated images in postmodernism as the generalization of aesthetic appearance, and it is therefore precisely here that the impact of technology is to be found. For Jameson, postmodernism is not simply the moment when the techniques of aesthetic modernism have been exhausted, but rather the condition within which that other kind of seeing signalled by aesthetic perception has itself become routine, and is now organized by technology.

The central statement of this new condition is provided by the essay's well-known account of the Bonaventure Hotel in Los Angeles, and its consequences are pursued through a reading of Lacan's linguistic description of schizophrenia. For Jameson, the experience of the Bonaventure Hotel is that of an 'alarming disjunction . . . between the body and its built environment', a disjunction which arises from a 'mutation in space' which has 'finally succeeded in transcending the capacities of the individual human body to locate itself, to organize its immediate surroundings perceptually, and cognitively to map its position in a mappable external world' (*ibid.*, p. 44). The reconfiguration of experience is thus primarily understood by Jameson in spatial terms: he terms this new condition 'postmodern hyperspace', and understands it to render 'our older systems of perception of the city somehow archaic and aimless, without offering anything in their place' (*ibid.*, p. 14). The 'everyday' experience of postmodernism is therefore one of the inability of the subject to 'map' the new configuration of the phenomenal world, an experience which itself stands as 'the symbol and analogon of that even sharper dilemma which is the incapacity of our minds . . . to map the great global multinational and decentred communicational network in which we find ourselves caught as individual subjects' (*ibid.*, p. 44). The root of this experiential failure lies in the predominance of visual intensity over and against temporal coherence, and it is in these terms that Jameson describes postmodern culture. Postmodern culture is seen to offer an 'indescribable vividness, a materiality of perception properly overwhelming, which effectively dramatizes the material [or] literal signifier in isolation'. But as such it presages a 'breakdown of temporality' wherein the present is 'released . . . from all the activities and intentionalities that might focus it and make it a space of praxis'; the 'present suddenly engulfs the subject' in its 'heightened intensity', and although it can be experienced as 'anxiety and loss of reality' or 'euphoria', it cannot become a moment of praxis (*ibid.*, p. 27).

However, as the essay argues at some length, the kind of intensification of visual experience described here is not unprecedented, but was in fact central to the aesthetic perception engendered by modernist art. Indeed, aesthetic modernism provides the essay not only with the model of vision which is to be generalized in postmodern culture, but also the conception of experience through which its broader implications are to be understood. Echoing Baudelaire, Jameson understands aesthetic perception in terms of its difference to utilitarian vision, and drawing on Marx's conception of the commodity form and Adorno's critique of modern rationality, this utilitarian vision is understood as the routinized perception incumbent on instrumental rationality – as the 'commodification' or 'reification' of vision. Against this condition, aesthetic modernism is understood as an intensification of visual experience which lifts aesthetic perception above or outside of utilitarian vision: thus Jameson describes Van Gogh's painting 'A Pair of Boots' in terms which anticipate the intensities of postmodernism, as 'the most glorious materialization of pure colour in oil paint'. And yet Jameson argues that this intensification should be differentiated from the inert intensities of postmodern culture, and understood instead 'as a Utopian gesture, an act of compensation which ends up producing a whole new Utopian realm of the senses, or at least the supreme sense

– sight, the visual, the eye – which it now reconstitutes for us as a semiautonomous space in its own right' (*ibid.*, p. 7). The importance of this distinction for Jameson lies in the fact that it is not a matter of the respective formal properties of modernist and postmodernist cultural artefacts, but is rather a measure of the reconfiguration of the conditions of experience in postmodernity, and this is why so much rides on the distinction. According to Jameson, aesthetic perception can now no longer offer an alternative to the routinized perception of utilitarian vision because it has itself become routine: in being general-ized in consumer society, the utopian potential of aesthetic perception is withdrawn and replaced by the 'reified eye' of the consumer (*ibid.*, p. 9).

While Jameson's invocation of reification recalls the work of Debord and Baudrillard, the concept is deployed here within a larger frame-work which revolves around the fate of aesthetic perception, which is understood to mark a fundamental reconfiguration of experience. Thus his account of the new conditions of experience, understood as 'the new spatial logic of the simulacrum' engendered by 'postmodern hyperspace', depends on an account of the disintegration of the autonomy of aesthetic perception (*ibid.*, p. 18). Therefore, to address Jameson's analysis in its own terms means focusing on the nature of this reconfiguration and the consequences it is seen to imply. From this perspective, what is most striking is that Jameson's conception of aesthetic perception takes the claims of aesthetic modernism entirely at face value. Baudelaire's art criticism, for example, claims to discover in beauty a spatio-temporal coherence and unity which stands outside of and in opposition to the contingency of utilitarian vision. As we have seen, within such a mode of vision the harmonious appearance of beauty anticipates its framing in perception, so returning to the gaze an image which confirms the proportionality of frame and appearance. The image is no longer haunted by the absence implied by contingency, but is experienced by the viewer in all its spatio-temporal fullness and self-presence. But as we have also seen, there are good reasons to be sceptical of such claims, not least because the practice of aesthetic modernism so often calls them into question. And yet Jameson characterizes the experience of aesthetic modernism in precisely these terms, as can be seen in his account of Rilke's 'Archaic Torso of

Apollo' from the *New Poems*. Rilke's short poem places an ancient statue of Apollo before a contemporary viewer, and for Jameson it serves to illustrate the affective power of modernist art. According to Jameson, the statue returns to the viewer's gaze a sense of another time and another place in all its experiential fullness and self-presence, and so embodies the spatio-temporal unification effected by modern art. He argues that 'the august premonitory eye flashes' of the Greek god revitalize the routinized vision of the bourgeois subject, imbuing its degraded perception with an experiential charge which famously warns it to change its life (*ibid.*, p. 10). In contrast, he argues, postmodernism withdraws the experiential 'depth' of cultural artefacts under 'the new spatial logic of the simulacrum', and so postmodern cultural artefacts are robbed of this affective charge and, bereft of the ability to return the experience of another time and place, they can no longer 'look back'. Consequently, Jameson declares that contemporary cultural production 'can no longer gaze directly at some putative real world, at some reconstruction of past history which was once itself a present'; and as a result he claims that 'we are condemned to seek History by way of our pop images and simulacra of that history, which itself remains forever out of reach' (*ibid.*, p. 25).

The point of Jameson's account of modernist visual art is that it puts in place the trajectory which governs his understanding of the conditions of experience in postmodernity: the postmodern is defined precisely by the loss of the spatio-temporal unity and self-presence ascribed to aesthetic modernism, a loss which leaves the subject bound within the purely spatial intensities of the perpetual present. In these terms the spatio-temporal unity which Jameson sees returned in the aesthetic is understood as the basis for the subject's capacity to 'actively . . . extend its protentions and retentions across the temporal manifold and to organize its past and future into coherent experience' (*ibid.*, p. 25). That is, Jameson identifies the temporal continuity of experience with aesthetic autonomy, which he also describes as 'critical distance'. According to Jameson, then, both historical orientation and critique require a 'certain minimal aesthetic distance', which is to be conceived of as 'the possibility of the positioning of the cultural act outside the massive Being of capital' (*ibid.*, p. 48). What characterizes the new condition of postmodernism, then, is the loss of aesthetic autonomy, a loss that underlies the inability of contemporary cultural production to return the past fully and authentically. However, such a trajectory misreads both the visual experience of aesthetic modernism and the conception of aesthetic autonomy described by modern thought. For although modern artists like Baudelaire may have claimed that the aesthetic image returns the harmonious unity of appearances to the gaze, modernist practice belies such claims, and indeed it is possible to see a quite different notion of return in Rilke's 'Archaic Torso of Apollo'. Jameson understands the poem to convict modernism of being an aesthetics of full presence because he sees in 'the august premonitory eye flashes' of the statue the return of the past in all its fullness and self-presence. But what Jameson appears to forget is that the torso in Rilke's poem is headless and *has no eyes*. The statue does not stare back at the contemporary viewer, offering an image of the past in its own gaze: what is returned to the gaze of the present as the admonition to 'change your life' is not the past as it once 'really was', fully present and integral in the moment of its apprehension, but the moments of loss or absence which are paradoxically 'embodied' or 'made present' in the ruin of the statue's integrity, and in the scarring and dismemberment which it has suffered in time. What underlies the affective power of the statue, therefore, is not the transmission of a past configuration of appearance in its self-identity, but the appearance of different possible configurations of the statue's form which emerge in the interplay of presence and absence. The statue invokes the integral unity of form as memory, or rather as different possible memories, and so it involves the gaze in an activity which simultaneously sees the statue's ruin and the possible shapes of its unity. What the gaze of the present 'sees' or experiences, then, is the interplay between its own framing of the dismembered torso and a configuration which remains unexhausted by the forms within which it is framed. The play of presence and absence therefore points to the disparity between the object's appearance – which bears the marks of its persistence in time – and the gaze of the present – which disavows its inhabitation by time and claims to occur just now, in an absolute and pure instant. What art makes visible in Rilke's poem are the moments of loss or absence which configure the gaze of the present, but which of course are invisible to it. If the poem sees the 'return' of

the past, it also points to the prospect of different possible configurations of form, and therefore of different possible configurations of
vision and appearing.

By suggesting a different conception of aesthetic experience to that
provided by Jameson, Rilke's poem not only questions Jameson's
account of what has been lost, but also raises important questions
about his understanding of aesthetic autonomy as 'critical distance'.
For if the ruined torso can be said to offer an intensification of vision,
this intensification does not occur 'outside' of the gaze of the present,
as an experience unrelated to or incommensurate with the subject's
routine gaze; rather, it occurs in the folding back of the subject's gaze
and the consequent experience of superimposition and multiple resolution. Its critical potential lies in the awareness it provides of different
possible configurations of appearance, but this awareness only emerges
and has definition within the determinate experience of this moment
of vision and within these particular co-ordinates of space and time. In
contrast, Jameson sees aesthetic experience in terms of a 'fundamentally spatial' notion of 'critical distance': accordingly, aesthetic autonomy lifts perception 'outside' of the routinized vision of instrumental
reason, which can only ever see the empty repetition of second-hand
images (ibid., p. 48). Jameson identifies this conception of critical
distance with Peter Bürger's influential Theory of the Avant-garde, which
locates the historical specificity of the avant-garde in terms of the
negation of aesthetic autonomy or 'the institution art'. But in drawing
on Bürger, Jameson misreads his notion of aesthetic autonomy by
seeing it in quasi-spatial terms, as though it were a quite literal
'distance' which might be widened or closed. Such a notion is in fact
quite alien to Bürger, whose conception of autonomy does not involve
any such spatial 'distance' but develops out of Kant's characterization
of aesthetic experience as disinterested (1984, pp. 41–6). For Kant,
the ascription of autonomy to the aesthetic relates to the status of
aesthetic perception as 'disinterested', a term which refers to the
temporal organization of ends and not to the 'position' of the cultural
act. In the apprehension of beauty, intuitions themselves give rise to
the principle of their own unification, and the apprehension of form is
thus 'disinterested', or free from the external imperatives of cognition;
and yet the reflective judgement of aesthetic taste points to the

compatibility of intuition and unification which also underlies cognition. The significance of beauty for Kant therefore lies precisely in the fact that its perception is not external to experience. The feeling of pleasure evoked by the unforced agreement of beauty points from within experience to the transcendental unity of apperception which underlies cognition, but which cannot itself be grasped in concepts.

The significance of Rilke's poem is then twofold. First, it suggests that Jameson's concept of postmodernism implies and depends on a restricted conception of visual experience; and second, it points to the problematic nature of the relationship between the experience of postmodernism and knowledge. Jameson conceives of vision as purely spatial, and so the visual intensification characteristic of postmodern culture is understood by him as 'the breakdown of temporality' (*op. cit.*, p. 27). But Rilke's poem reminds us that vision must be understood in terms of the configuration of space *and time*, and that it is a mistake to think of it only in spatial terms: to conceive of vision as somehow 'purely spatial' means that its intensification can only be understood as the 'loss of historicity' and of what Jameson calls 'the retrospective dimension indispensable to any reorientation of our collective future' (*ibid.*, p. 18). However, once the involvement of space and time in vision is remembered, the technological intensification of visual experience need not be thought of as necessarily blank and disabling, nor disorientation assumed to be a permanent or fixed condition. Rather, this intensification might be taken as opening up possibilities for different configurations of experience. But this understanding of vision also suggests something else, namely how visual experience might be thought of in relation to knowledge without being made identical to it, and in doing so it reveals a much broader and more wide-ranging problem in Jameson's account of postmodernism. For Kant, the feeling of pleasure in the apprehension of beauty points to the unity of the transcendental conditions underlying perception and cognition, although perception and cognition are not the same. For Jameson, however, the purely spatial, 'aesthetic' experience of postmodernism is opposed to knowledge, which is somehow free from the loss of critical distance and the anxieties over 'absorption' which so limit 'everyday' experience. Indeed, Jameson is quite unequivocal on this point: 'it has never been said here', he writes, that the new 'global world system . . . was unknowable but merely that it was unrepresentable'; the world can be known, he explains, by way of 'Mandel's great book', *Late Capitalism* (*ibid.*, p. 53). Jameson thus exempts knowledge from the reconfiguration of experience in postmodernity, invoking an Althusserian conception of 'science' which separates his own approach from Lukács, despite his frequent citation. As we have seen, *History and Class Consciousness* insists that the possibility of knowledge is itself implicated in the reformulation of experience in modernity, and therefore knowledge cannot be presented as external to or unaffected by experience. In separating his *concept* of postmodernism, as 'the cultural logic of late capitalism', from the experience of postmodernity, Jameson's approach necessarily begs the question of the relationship between them.

LOGICS OF REINTEGRATION

Like Jameson, Virilio addresses vision in terms of its spatio-temporal conditions, and therefore he also sees the fate of visual experience in terms of a growing disparity between an inherited configuration of vision and the technological reformulation of the phenomenal world. However, Virilio does not structure his analysis around an account of the historical transformation of the aesthetic nor a conception of reification, but maps technological developments directly onto the organization of the gaze. Consequently, while the disparity between a routinized aesthetic perception and the 'global space of late capitalism' coalesces as a fixed opposition in Jameson, Virilio is able to introduce a dynamic element into his account, in that technology is understood to produce not only a new condition within which vision takes place, but also a new configuration of vision itself. And so where Jameson's account of the history of vision comes to an end in the spatial intensities of postmodernism, Virilio offers an account of visual experience whose trajectory seeks to anticipate the direction of ongoing technological developments. For Virilio, vision is not inherently abstract, as it is for Debord, nor is it inherently spatial, as it is for Jameson, but rather it is understood as a historically variable configuration of space and time.

In *The Vision Machine* (1988), Virilio draws on Merleau-Ponty's notion of embodied perception in order to develop a conception of vision that is ordered according to the human body's spatial reach and time of response. He sees this initial configuration of vision as an 'original, ideally human happiness', because it orders appearances within 'the "I can" of sight', and so renders the visible world in terms of the capacities of the embodied subject (1994, p. 7). Modern vision thus emerged out of the inhabitation of a world that could be assimilated by the human organism, and which therefore allowed it to develop a correspondingly secure sense of itself. The visual apprehension of a 'world-within-reach' gives rise to what Virilio calls 'topographical memory', the subject's memory of itself within an enduring three-dimensional space, which allows it to imagine itself and the universe which it inhabits as substantial entities persisting through time. Against this backdrop Virilio charts the impact of technology, which he introduces in the form of the telescope. The historical emergence of the telescope in early modern Europe is understood to have destabilized this sense of secure inhabitation because it 'projected an image of the world beyond our reach and thus another way of moving about the world', so 'telescoping near and far' and 'obliterating our experience of distances and dimensions'. The subsequent development of optical instruments and mechanisms of visual reproduction is seen to bring about a profound reformulation of visual experience by 'delocalizing' vision, or withdrawing vision's imbrication within a configuration of space and time that could be assimilated to the human body. The telescoping of space by the lens disrupts the secure image world of properly human vision, producing 'a phenomenon of acceleration' in which the stable arrangement of space gives way under the accelerated time of technology (*ibid.*, p. 4). What is lost here is the sense of the determinate spatial relations which would cohere as a substantial world, but which are now shown to have depended on topographical memory and the subject's ability to imagine or represent itself within secure spatio-temporal co-ordinates.

The initial impact of technology is thus understood as the creation of a disparity or conflict between the phenomenal world and an inherited configuration of vision, and Virilio emphasizes the violent nature of this conflict by siting his history of vision on the modern battlefield. The battlefield replaces the city as the exemplary locus of vision in modernity, and the conflictual nature of vision is developed in military terms, so that the rapidly shifting world of technological appearance is imaged in the constantly mutating landscape of the front, where time and space are given by the range and speed of artillery, ground attack aircraft, surveillance instruments, and command and control systems. However, the crucial point for Virilio is not simply that the technological landscape of war is visually disorientating, but that it presages a reformulation of the stable co-ordinates of vision which the modern subject had inherited. The response which such a predicament produces is understood as a new 'faith in the technical sightline' within which 'the visual field' is 'reduced to the line of the sighting device' (ibid., p. 13): in the face of the terrifying acceleration of appearances, the isolated subject feverishly presses its eye to the instrument's eyepiece, hoping that its 'delocalizing geometrical optics' will bring the visual flux to order (ibid., p. 12). Ironically then, the disorientation generated by technology is met by a desperate and unreserved faith in that very same technology, which Virilio identifies in terms of an unprecedented 'dependence on the lens'. Technology is seen as replacing the 'natural speed and sensitivity' of vision by a 'logistics of perception', a usage designed to stress the violent dynamic underlying technology's role in reorganizing the subject's gaze. This dependence on technology imposes a 'rigid and practically invariable structure of immobility' on the eye: 'One can only see instantaneous sections seized by the Cyclops of the lens', observes Virilio, and so 'vision, once substantial, becomes accidental' (ibid., p. 13). For Virilio, contemporary culture mirrors the experience of the front, and the soldiers' terror in the face of a landscape that exceeds their conceptions of proximity and causality exemplifies the broader reformulation of vision in modernity. The condition of modernity is thus described as a 'moment of panic when the mass of Americans and Europeans could no longer believe their eyes' (ibid., p. 13). The new technological condition of appearance is exemplified by cinema, since the technology of film organizes visual coherence primarily in temporal rather than spatial terms. Just as much as the computer maps of the military commander, the diegetic image space of Hollywood film offers a compensatory synthesis of appearances which provides the spectator with a coherent image of the world. But crucially for Virilio this 'coherence' does not arise from the substantial space of 'human' sensory perception, but from the speed at which truncated image fragments are spliced together.

The trajectory which Virilio maps out here moves from an initial disparity between an inherited configuration of vision and the techno-logically ordered co-ordinates of appearance, to the penetration and colonization of vision by technology. The condition of appearances is now ordered according to the temporal succession of cinema, rather than the stable spatial arrangement of embodied vision and its topo-graphical memory. But if the technologically organized world of modernity mutates according to logics which exceed the capacities of the subject, then once the co-ordinates of vision are themselves supplied by technology, this trajectory implies the inescapable liquidation of 'human' sight. Thus Virilio argues that 'the absolute culmination of the inexorable march of progress of representational technologies, of their military, scientific and investigative instrumentalization over the cen-turies', means the 'solemn farewell to the man behind the camera' and 'the complete evaporation of visual subjectivity into an ambient technical effect' (*ibid*., p. 47). Virilio refers to this condition as the 'industriali-zation of vision', yet this is only an intermediary step: 'after synthetic images [and] after the digital image processing of computer-aided design', he writes, 'we are on the verge of *synthetic vision*, the automation of perception'. Virilio's trajectory thus leads to a technological condition which he calls the 'vision machine', within which properly visual images are transcoded into the digital information of computer systems, whose 'sightless vision' is in fact a matter of the sequential flow of information (*ibid*., pp. 61–2). The 'sightless vision' of the 'vision machine' marks the end of the modern paradigm of vision, which Virilio understands to have depended on the confrontation of the subject and a substantial world set over and against it. Technology both colonizes the subject's framing of appearance and reorganizes the phenomenal world in terms of its own autonomous logics, and so there can no longer be a conflict between the configuration of vision and that of the phenomenal world. Visual experience no longer offers the subject a sense of its inhabitation and imbrication within space and time, Virilio argues, because 'the categories of space and time have become relative' (*ibid*., p. 71). Technology withdraws what Virilio calls the 'extensive' time which was understood to have been made possible by a substantial and independent world. This is what he means when he refers to the 'cinematic derealization' or 'dematerialization' of the world, a new condition in which 'the image prevails over the object present' so that 'the virtual prevails over the real' (*ibid.*, p. 73).

If this new condition of vision is ordered according to the temporal acceleration of cinema, the corresponding organization of vision is identified by Virilio in the phenomenon of retinal retention or persistence. Retinal retention occurs as the prolongation of activity in the retinal receptor cells for a short period after stimulation has ended; the receptors continue to signal an image, although without an accompanying stimulus. Virilio sees retinal persistence as underlying the perception of movement in film, and thus as the perceptual corollary of film's temporal organization of appearance: in retinal persistence, each projected image is understood to persist for a short time after the photogram has moved on so that, if the film speed is sufficient, the black spaces between the projected images are not registered, and continuous movement is perceived. Crucially for Virilio, this virtual image is a 'time take', a discrete fragment within a temporally ordered succession that is determined by the filmic apparatus, and which depends on its protocols of editing and on the speed of projection. Thus, where the spatial image-world of embodied vision corresponded to the secure co-ordinates of a world within reach, the disconnected 'virtual images' of retinal retention are understood to correspond to this new technological condition by releasing the image from its reliance on an 'external' stimulus (*ibid.*, p. 61). Retinal retention thus offers a kind of finality which confirms the trajectory of Virilio's analysis, since now that the virtual images of retinal retention correspond to the accelerated time of technology, the human organism is finally attuned, or 'plugged in', to the technological apparatus: 'It is the discovery of a *freeze-frame effect* which speaks to us of some kind of unscrolling', Virilio argues, which points to 'the intensive time of human perceptiveness' (*ibid.*, p. 75).

The significance of retinal retention, then, is that it reveals the predominance of time over space, so that time becomes a principle of flux that sweeps away the conceptual frameworks of modern thought and culture, and its comfortable illusions of subjective autonomy and agency. And Virilio's sober new view is indeed uncomfortable. In *War and Cinema* (1984) he identifies the emergence of this new condition as the historical development of the total and inescapable power of technology after the Second World War:

> Cinematic derealization now affected the very nature of power, which established itself in a technological Beyond with the space-time not of ordinary mortals but of a single war machine. In this realm sequential perception, like optical phenomena resulting from retinal persistence, is both origin and end of the apprehension of reality, since the seeing of movement is but a statistical process connected with the nature of the segmentation of images and the speed of observation characteristic of humans (1989, p. 79).

The 'derealization' or 'dematerialization' of the world effected by the new optical technologies generates a culture which liquidates the modern paradigm of vision, and so locks the subject into the 'vision machine' which is in truth identical to the 'war machine'. The urge towards the mastery of the phenomenal world which Virilio sees as being inherent within modern vision is now radicalized under the increasing dependence on technology, and so modern societies are characterized by a propensity to war. If visual coherence once entailed the violent ordering of the phenomenal world by the subject, this 'sightless vision' marks a massive intensification of violence: ordered only by purely technological logics, the 'vision machine' is unencumbered by the social, political, economic, or moral goals pursued by the modern subject, and so is freed from any restraint or mitigation such goals may once have imposed. Virilio thus draws a straight line between the cultural forms of technology, the structure of human consciousness, and the violent nature of modern societies: 'the macro-cinematography of aerial reconnaissance, the cable television of panoramic radar, the use of slow or accelerated motion in analysing the phases of an operation', Virilio contends in *War and Cinema*, 'all this converts the commander's plan into an animated cartoon or flow chart' (*ibid.*). In the retinal persistence generated by the technologically mediated form of film animation, the violence of the military–industrial complex finds its truth.

Virilio's approach is significant because it rejects the kinds of fixed conception of vision offered by Debord, Baudrillard, and Jameson, which cast vision as, alternatively, abstract, homogenous, and purely spatial. Instead, Virilio sees vision as a historically determinate configuration of space and time, and as such, his analyses are often suggestive: his siting of visual experience in the landscape of modern warfare, for example, restores its conflictual and fraught nature by reminding us of vision's location in a world that increasingly comes into conflict with its inherited co-ordinates. And yet the very forcefulness and single-mindedness of the trajectory we have traced here raises significant questions about Virilio's approach. Centrally, this trajectory depends on a fixed moment of origin which reduces the histories which precede it, and which circumscribes the conceptual understanding of vision that lies at its heart. Virilio's conception of an 'original' configuration of visual experience, measured against a conception of the 'technologically naked' human body, underestimates the role of technology in the historical constitution of what he conceives of as a purely 'human' perception. Equally, it implies a restricted conception of experience which limits his subsequent analysis. Virilio's account of embodied vision at the beginning of *The Vision Machine* is intended as a critical description of the experiential limits inherited by the modern subject, but in fact it does not only function in these terms. Crucially, this conception of visual experience organizes the relationship between subjectivity and the phenomenal world around an a posteriori conception of form, and it is this conception of form which drives Virilio's teleology. The coherence of perception is not discovered or produced through the activity of the subject, but occurs as the correspondence of the spatio-temporal co-ordinates of the phenomenal world and the configuration of subjectivity: thus, Virilio identifies the initially stable 'personality' of the modern subject as a function of 'the permanence of the natural environment' in pre-industrial Europe (1994, p. 13). Such an a posteriori conception of form ties subjectivity to the configuration of the phenomenal world, so that its historical development is directly read off from technology's recasting of the world. The central problem here is that such a conception of visual experience assumes the terms of its formal coherence: vision may be active for Virilio in the sense that it *forms* appearances, but its activity does not extend to any role in *configuring* form, which instead occurs as a correspondence whose terms are simply given. Consequently, while the spatio-temporal co-ordinates of vision may be variable, the goal of visual experience is fixed as the achievement of a coherence which is defined at the outset, in terms of the 'world-within-reach'. Thus, in the face of technology's reformulation of the phenomenal world, the subject mechanically responds by attempting to restore this original coherence of the world over and over again.

This restricted conception of visual experience is best illuminated by the pivotal role played by retinal retention in Virilio's conception of the vision machine. Retinal retention provides the bridge that links the new technological condition of appearance to the consequent reformulation of consciousness by providing a physiological mechanism for moving between the visible world and the activity of consciousness, much like the pineal gland in Descartes. It identifies a temporal organization within the physiological processes underlying perception which matches that of the cinematically organized world of appearance: 'How can we have failed to grasp', asks Virilio, 'that the discovery of retinal retention [has] propelled us into the totally different province of the mental retention of images?' (*ibid.*, pp. 60–1). The significance of retinal retention, then, is that it provides a new physiological basis for perception, which functions in terms of the same kind of mechanical correspondence which Virilio sees in the stable spatial perception of the 'technologically naked' human body: its direct correspondence with the new condition of technological appearance effectively 'updates' the correspondence between topographical memory and the stable environment of pre-industrial humanity. However, Virilio's reliance on retinal retention is curious: although it was initially proposed as an explanation for the perception of motion in film, it was soon realized that the phenomenon does not give rise to the perception of continuous movement, but to a blurred vision composed of superimposed images. While the phenomenon certainly exists, it has long been discounted as a plausible explanation for the experience of cinematic movement, and the current scientific consensus identifies Wertheimer's 'phi effect', first proposed in 1912, as the most plausible explanation (Aumont, 1994, pp. 30–2). Significantly, the phi effect primarily involves post-retinal processes, and therefore applies just as much to the movement of objects in space as it does to the apparent movement of film. The point here is not simply that Virilio fails to keep up with the scientific literature, but that his enthusiasm for retinal retention points to broader problems in his conception of visual experience. The pivotal role played by retinal retention arises because it appears to offer a direct homology between the technological condition of appearance and the physiological processes underlying perception, within which the spatio-temporal co-ordinates of perception can simply be read off from the configuration of appearances. Such a homology therefore reduces visual experience to an automatic mechanism of correspondence, casting it as a mechanical reflex rather than an inventive or active production. The irony here is that Virilio deploys retinal persistence in order to present visual experience as ineluctably caught within a technologically organized coherence, yet the visual experience produced by retinal persistence is in fact one of blurring and superimposition, varieties of visual experience which are ignored by Virilio's approach.

Despite Virilio's invocation of the battlefield, within his account visual experience is not the site of a conflict between configurations of vision and the changing co-ordinates of the visible world, but simply the site for an automatic transcription. This is why the historical trajectory of vision is so undifferentiated and unidirectional, since each reformulation of the phenomenal world leads to a single response which points in only one possible direction. At each step along the way, the impact of technology produces an automatic reconfiguration of vision, which doggedly plays out technology's internal logics. In turn, consciousness is conceived of as an extension of vision, and so rationality is understood as the reflection of technology in consciousness. The delocalized geometrical optics of the vision machine thus translate technology's invisible logics into the principle of modern rationality, which is defined in visual terms as 'the will to see all, to know all, at every moment, everywhere' (Virilio, 1994, p. 70). According to Virilio this 'omnivoyance' produces coherence 'by repressing the invisible', and so is identified with 'Western Europe's totalitarian ambition' (ibid., p. 33). Yet it might just as easily be objected that it is Virilio's assumption of a fixed configuration of form which orders visual experience according to the unchanging goal of coherence, and so suppresses the activity of vision. Visual experience becomes the perennial search for an integrated image-world that harks back to the integrated appearance of an originary, embodied vision, and in this sense, technology changes nothing, but simply offers new mechanisms for achieving the unchanging goal of visual coherence. Virilio fails to consider the experiences of incoherence, blurring, superimposition, or dissonance implied by his own account, preferring instead to focus only on visual coherence. This means that the emergence of other possibilities within the history of vision go unnoticed and remain invisible, and so he is unable to envisage any way in which vision might negotiate or reconfigure technologically organized appearance.

THE EYES OF THE POOR

As Baudelaire had realized, albeit uneasily, technology has a profound impact on vision. Whether thought of in terms of new optical instruments, new capacities for image reproduction and circulation, or more broadly in its recasting of the sensible world, technology reformulates the spatio-temporal conditions of appearance, and so provides new contexts for visual experience. Contemporary cultural theory has sought to radicalize this awareness, and sees the emergence of a technological condition that overturns the existing parameters of vision, whether as a direct function of the technological organization of sight, or through the mechanism of reification. Although the four accounts considered here describe this condition differently, they all see it as redrawing the terms of cultural meaning and social action, and therefore as marking a radical break with modernity. Yet significantly, all of these accounts associate technology with a single condition of visibility which imposes a monolithic and inescapable mode of visual experience. In the case of Debord and Baudrillard, the visible world becomes a series of autonomous images which dominate the gaze, and which reduce visual experience to the uniform perception of 'pure appearances'. In the case of Jameson, the intensification of the visible robs perception of temporal orientation, withdrawing its critical potential and casting it adrift among purely spatial patterns of intensity. And in the case of Virilio, the acceleration of appearances evacuates perception of any sense of spatial location, reordering visual experience around a temporally derived coherence inimical to the body's inhabitation of space. In each case, the world becomes purely and completely visible, never blurred, ambiguous or unresolved, but always appearing in high resolution and high definition. And yet, if the image-world is inevitably and absolutely visible, it is also irretrievably empty and worthless, since vision can no longer offer either knowledge of the world that stretches beyond the subject, or a sense of its own capacities or disposition. For all their claims to shift the focus of attention from the subject to the scene it confronts, these positions in fact imply the disappearance of the world.

The central claim shared by these accounts is that technology breaks the paradigm of representation underlying modern conceptions of vision by freeing the image-world from its connection to a 'reality' that exists behind or beyond appearances. As we have seen in the case of Cartesian vision, the paradigm of representation not only subordinates vision to knowledge, but reduces the visible to an inert collection of objects which serve only to reflect back the abstract rationality of the sovereign subject. For these recent critics, the new technological condition of appearance frees the image-world from any such connection, and so transfers the activity of vision from the subject to the image. And while the image's new found autonomy may imply the loss of depth and of 'the real', it nonetheless brings to an end the dangerous illusion of the sovereign subject's agency, which is understood to have permeated modern thought and culture. But, in examining these positions more closely, it becomes apparent that they remain within the limits of the paradigm of representation to an extent that they fail to acknowledge: for while the primary focus of these critics has been the rejection of the epistemological claims of representation, they prove much less aware of its figuring of form. As we have seen, despite their claims to effect a radical break, each of these approaches assumes the terms of visual coherence and so fixes the configuration of form. In the case of Debord and Baudrillard, the coherence of visual experience is assumed in the homogenous space and time of the image's absolute visibility, and by the pure and total apprehension that it implies. In the case of Jameson and Virilio, while the co-ordinates of space and time are reformulated by technology, it is only to lock visual experience within an integrated image-world, conceived of as purely spatial or purely temporal. None of these approaches can envisage the emergence of different configurations of experience in response to technology's reformulation of space and time, because each implicitly assumes that the configuration of form is given and so already fixed. But in that case, the claim made by these critics to have fundamentally broken with modern thought and the paradigm of representation must be re-evaluated. Although the announcement of the loss of 'the real' is taken to mark such a break, from this perspective it appears in a different light, as marking instead the continued inhabitation of a conceptual terrain organized by the opposition of illusion and the 'real'. As we have seen in examining Cartesian vision, the paradigm of representation implies a fixed configuration of form to guarantee the correspondence of thinking and extended substance, so making it possible to see 'through' illusion and grasp the substantial 'reality' that lies 'behind'. While these accounts may have withdrawn the subject's capacity to effect such a violent and all powerful vision, they retain its fixed conception of form in the autonomous but illusory image.

Yet if claims for the autonomy of the image involve an unacknowledged inheritance from Cartesian thought, when set alongside Baudelaire's conception of aesthetic perception it becomes a little easier to see why this might be the case. Technology leads to a single and ineluctable fate in these accounts because in order to envisage different configurations of visual experience, it is necessary to acknowledge the role of subjectivity in producing the configuration of form. Such an acknowledgement is understood to involve a wholesale return to the spontaneity of the modern subject and its aesthetic vision, which opposes the pure interiority of its eternal Imagination to the degraded and broken contingency of the world. If technology casts appearances as irretrievably illusory within these accounts, their proponents can at least argue that their positions disallow the return of the self-sufficient and self-deluding modern subject: for after all, had not the artist's marvelling at the visual dynamism of the city in 'The Painter of Modern Life' ended up celebrating the dashing appearance of Napoleon III and his imperial soldiers, so proving blind to the colonial violence inflicted beyond the borders of the metropolis? From the vantage point of the end of the twentieth century, Baudelaire's artistic eye thus appears in another light, making it much harder to think of its harmonizing of the disparate scene of modernity as heroic. Rather, its integration of appearances smacks of a violent and authoritarian will to power, while the beauty towards which it directs technique seems only fitted to the concealment of systems of entrapment and domination. And yet if this is the case, it is also possible to identify different ways of thinking vision in Baudelaire. As we have seen, while his art criticism locates the activity of aesthetic perception in the pure interiority of the Imagination, his poetic practice suggests a different relationship between subjectivity and the contexts which it inhabits, which draws attention to its contingency, rather than claiming to soar above the specificity of time and place. The alternative avenues for thinking vision opened up by Baudelaire's poetic technique are made more explicit in 'The Eyes of the Poor', one of a series of short prose poems published as feuilleton pieces in the Paris press (1989, pp. 111–14).

'The Eyes of the Poor' takes the form of a lover's complaint in which the narrator remembers an evening spent with his beloved at a café on one of Haussmann's new boulevards. The lovers are seated outside, while across the rubble-strewn boulevard they are observed by a father and his two sons, a boy and a young infant; inhabitants of the poor quarter through which the boulevard has just been driven, the watching group are dressed in rags. The narrator's complaint revolves around his failure to achieve a rapturous communion with his beloved, a failure that arises obliquely from the presence of the poor. For although he takes his own view of the poor family to be sympathetic and sensitive, his lover brusquely complains of their presence and demands their removal. The narrator is thus thrown back into his own isolation, and the prose poem ends with a statement of the failure of communion in love: 'So you see, how hard it is to understand one another, my angel, how incommunicable our thoughts are, even between those who love each other' (*ibid.*, p. 113). Yet while this complaint may seem to affirm all the more emphatically the pure interiority of the subject in the failure of even love to transcend the isolated ego, in fact the poem works in quite a different direction. For the failure which it describes is in fact the simultaneous failure of aesthetic and utilitarian perception, a failure which reformulates the terms of Baudelaire's art criticism and which suggests a different way of conceiving vision.

The narrator's search for the rapturous communion of love is articulated in terms of aèsthetic perception, as the search for an image which anticipates the terms of his own gaze: as the narrator explains to his beloved, what he desires is to look into her eyes and 'read my thoughts in them' (*ibid.*, p. 111). However, the visual condition of the city interrupts the easy achievement of this harmony, and the poem's central axis of vision is complicated, first, by the ersatz beauty of the café and, second, by the eyes of the wretched figures who gaze from across the boulevard. If the dominant visual trajectory of the poem is provided by aesthetic perception, the technologically organized appearance of the café introduces a disturbing parallel. Through the eyes of the narrator we see in the café the dazzling intensity of appearances which is emerging in the technological reconstruction of Paris: the café 'glittered all over with lights', its 'new gas-jets cast their incandescent novelty all round, brightening the whiteness of the walls, the dazzling planes of a multitude of mirrors [and] the gilt of the mouldings and cornices'. But the visual power of the café is not only constituted by the intensity of its gas lighting, but also by its organization and integration of appearances around a unifying telos. As the narrator notes, the gas light also casts its 'incandescent novelty' on 'the rosy-cheeked pageboys . . . the nymphs and goddesses . . . the Hebes and Ganymedes' painted on its walls, and its enchanted appearance is constituted as much by its unification of the image world of tradition as by its visual intensity: indeed, as the narrator remarks sardonically, 'all history and mythology' are 'exploited in the service of gluttony' (*ibid.*). Just as in the aesthetic image, so in the integrated appearance of the café 'all shapes speak to us, and nothing is indifferent or unnecessary' − at least to the hungry eyes of the paying customer. Yet if this is the case, the organized appearance of the café is confidently dismissed by the narrator as a degraded and ersatz beauty because the telos which orders it is indifferent to the images it deploys. Just as much as the gastronomic delights on the café's menu, these images have become objects of consumption, image-commodities plucked from their original location in tradition and now set 'free' to work in the market. Thus separated from the traditional conditions of their meaningfulness, they are evacuated of their particular character and specificity, becoming empty ciphers interchangeable with any number of other such cherubs or deities, or indeed with bottles of wine and bunches of fruit.

The destruction and recombination involved in the café's mobiliza-
tion of traditional images might seem to mirror the creative activity of
art, yet for the narrator appearances are not organized here according
to the telos of the Ideal, but simply in order to stimulate appetite. In
the narrator's gaze the traditional images of beauty, fecundity and
harmonious nature jar with the café's ultimate commercial imperative,
for if their original significance is sacrificed, it is not in order to achieve
the transcendent meaningfulness and harmony of the Ideal, but for the
altogether more prosaic and contingent goal of profit. Against this
ersatz organization of appearance the narrator offers his own gaze,
which is able to draw both the watching poor and the opulence of the
café into its regime of meaning: in the father's gaze he sees wonder at
the visual riches of the café; in the gaze of the boy he also sees an
awareness of their own inevitable exclusion; and in the eyes of the
infant he sees 'a mindless, deeply felt joy' (*ibid.*). This 'family of eyes'
thus bears out his own disdain for the café, while his 'understanding'
of their apprehension of the scene stands as proof of the sensitivity of
his soul and the depth of his sympathy: 'Not only was I moved by the
family of eyes', he confides, 'but I felt a little ashamed of our array of
glasses and decanters, all so much bigger than our thirst' (*ibid.*,
p. 113). In taking in the scene before him and integrating it within his
own framework of experience and memory, the narrator finds a unity
and harmony which counters the degraded 'beauty' of the café; and it
is precisely this harmonizing of appearances that he looks for in the
eyes of his beloved. In the narrator's eyes at least, her failure to
reciprocate his own harmonious vision testifies to the singularity of the
Imagination, and to its location deep within the inner recesses of the
soul.

But in fact the poem deliberately undercuts this interpretation. In
truth it is not the case that appearances fail to cohere as beauty for the
narrator, nor that his beloved fails to reciprocate his gaze, for in
looking into her eyes he does see an image of beauty. Indeed, it is at
this very moment, in the instant of the experience of beauty, that a
paradoxical failure occurs, as the narrator makes clear:

I was turning my eyes towards yours, my dear, to read *my* thoughts
in them; I was plunging into your beautiful, strange eyes, your

emerald eyes full of caprice and the inspirations of the Moon, when you remarked, 'I just can't stand those people, with their eyes wide as open gates' (*ibid.*).

With these words, the narrator complains, his lover reveals her lack of the sensitivity and generosity that animates his own gaze, and so in failing to reciprocate his gaze she shatters the promise of the harmonious unification in beauty. But despite the narrator's claims to the contrary, in fact the eyes of his lover do return to him an image of his own gaze – though not of course the one which he intended. For the harmony he desires depends on the integration of the scene, and thus it requires the eyes of the poor to be rendered according to the coordinates of *his* experience, so as to reflect his own sensitivity and generosity of heart rather than the experience that animates their apprehension of the scene. Thus, although they are captured in the image and given an integral place there, the eyes of the poor – unlike those of his beloved – cannot look back: they cannot reciprocate the narrator's gaze within the terms of their own configuration of experience, but can only appear as an expression of his. Therefore, while to his eyes they provide a moment within the larger unity of appearances, when his vision is reflected back in his lover's gaze the eyes of the poor appear as the looming and empty remainders of a configuration of experience which *cannot itself appear*, except negatively or as loss. The eyes of the poor gape back blankly 'as wide open as gates' from within the beautiful image constituted by his beloved's gaze, because their appearance is premised on their failure to appear *differently*, on the denial of their capacity to look back in other terms. Blank and impassive in their rendering, the eyes of the poor mark out the limits of the narrator's aesthetic perception in that they imply a different configuration of vision upon whose suppression the unity of his own gaze depends. As the residue or reminder of other gazes, and thus of other possible configurations of visual experience, they interrupt the enclosed circularity of aesthetic perception by pointing from within it to what it excludes, and therefore to what underlies and makes possible its organization of appearance.

What is most disturbing here for Baudelaire's art criticism is that the eyes of the poor reveal the affinity between the aesthetic image and the ersatz beauty of the café. Just as the visual unity of the café proves indifferent to the appearances it subordinates to its own imperatives, so the ragged family across the boulevard are drained of their significance in order to assume their allotted place in the scene, becoming an image of the narrator's good conscience, sensitivity, and generosity of heart. But a further irony also arises here, for, if the narrator's confident perusal of the scene from within the brightly lit halo of the café contrasts with the blank gaze of the 'family of eyes', this comparison suggests that its vision depends on the particular circumstances of time and place: upon the leisure that the bourgeois lovers enjoy; upon the narrator's wealth which allows them to stop without a second thought at the glittering new café; upon the willingness of his female lover to provide the mirror for his own reflection; and perhaps above all, upon his ability to take in the scene freely and to view it as an occasion for the exercise of his own visual prowess, rather than having to direct his vision towards more prosaic goals. And in these terms, both ersatz and 'real' beauty find themselves immersed in the contingency of the historical world. For just as the images of tradition are 'freed' in the marketplace of consumption, so the gaze of the bourgeois narrator also depends for its 'freedom' on the society of commodity production, not only in terms of his wealth, his leisure time, and his sphere of action as a male citizen, but also in his consciousness of himself as the autonomous source, or 'free producer', of the formal unity of the scene.

'The Eyes of the Poor' thus refuses the opposition proposed by Baudelaire's art criticism between aesthetic and utilitarian vision by placing aesthetic vision within the technologically organized space of the city. Like the photographic image, the city produces configurations of appearance which cannot be harmonized without some residue or remainder. But while his art criticism disregards the experience of the photograph as incoherent and without return, here the looming holes figured by the eyes of the poor present an experience that is not without value or affect. In ruining the harmony desired by the gaze, they do not communicate the substantial reality lying behind appearances – or in contemporary terms, they do not represent the return of the 'real': the narrator does not come to know these other contexts of experience which they evoke, nor does he understand the family as they 'really are'. But equally, the juxtapositions and associations produced by the new space and time of the city do not simply coalesce as a monolithic image landscape, nor do they lock visual experience within inescapable patterns of spatial intensity or rhythms of acceleration. Rather, the charge that is communicated occurs within the narrator's activity of framing appearances as an experience of dislocation or '*dis*-appearance', which reinscribes the residual inherence of other configurations of experience within the apparently inert images that confront the gaze – albeit negatively, as distortion or loss. And if technology denies visual experience the sovereign independence promised by beauty over and against the riotous contingency of the visible world, visual experience is not thereby necessarily rendered inert or without significance. In a very important sense this return is not narcissistic, for in registering the disparity between the configuration of appearance and their framing, it points beyond the sovereign limits of the subject's gaze.

CHAPTER 3

Technics of Vision

. . . vision happens among, or is caught in, things . . .
Maurice Merleau-Ponty, 'Eye and Mind'

VISION AMONG THINGS

The challenge technology poses for thinking vision requires more than
a recognition of its animation of the visible or its capacity to reproduce
appearances. It also demands that the visible world's contribution to
vision be recognized not simply as passive matter to be formed, but
rather in its constitutive role in giving the conditions of visual
experience. Such a recognition raises significant questions about the
spatial and temporal co-ordinates of vision, about the relationship
between sensory perception and discursive conceptuality, and about
the limits of experience. Technology therefore requires a broader
rethinking of the nature of the subject and its relation to the world.
Debord, Baudrillard, Jameson, and Virilio all seek in different ways to
register the new contexts for vision generated by technology, but their
various accounts of the autonomy of the image fail to consider how
technology might reformulate the terms of visual experience. In
particular, the spatio-temporal parameters of experience remain fixed
around the telos of a formal unity whose terms are already given. For
Debord and Baudrillard, technology produces an image-world that
anticipates the formal unity of the subject's vision, a situation that
ironically resembles the Cartesian correspondence between consciousness and the world, although now the unity of appearances is given by
technology rather than by God. Jameson and Virilio, on the other
hand, depart from Descartes in recognizing technology's reorganization
of space and time. However, because the terms of formal coherence

THE ARCHITECTURE OF THE VISIBLE

are fixed, this reformulation can only ever be understood in terms of an absolute loss or the absence of a unity that was once fully present. Notwithstanding the claims made by these critics for a radical break with modern thought, the Cartesian subject persists as a kind of implicit structuring principle, although now it functions negatively to describe the inability of appearances to provide either certainty or knowledge.

One important consequence of this inheritance has been the overriding concern with the collapse of the Cartesian paradigm of representation, a concern reflected in the centrality of claims for 'the loss of the real' and 'the dematerialization of the world'. Within the paradigm of representation appearances are in the strict sense illusory, but because they are understood to correspond to an underlying world of substances, cognition is able to see through the scene of illusion and grasp the substantial reality lying behind it. The persistence of a fixed conception of formal unity has meant that the impact of technology has tended to be conceived in terms of this model, or rather in terms of its breakdown. Because appearances are now understood to be organized according to autonomous technological logics, they are seen as no longer reflecting or corresponding to a substantial reality that might lie behind or beyond them. Technology therefore gives rise to the autonomy of the image, although this autonomy is understood in a number of different ways. In the case of Debord and Baudrillard, because their conceptions of experience admit no externality, technology's organization of appearance is transposed directly to consciousness itself. Consequently, there is always a correspondence between appearances and their framing in perception, although as such it is absolutely blank and worthless. Jameson and Virilio on the other hand both acknowledge an element of non-identity in visual experience, and so they conceive of vision as a confrontation between an inherited model of subjectivity and an autonomous world of images. However, because the site or ground of this conflict cannot itself be reformulated then the subject's disorientation becomes an inescapable fate: overwhelmed and disorientated, it vainly seeks to impose a model of visual coherence upon a world whose spatial intensity or acceleration exceeds its terms. Thus, despite very real differences, the impact of technology is understood by all of these critics primarily in epistemological terms, as the perceiving subject's incapacity to know the world; or in Jameson's case, its inability to produce representations adequate to Marxism's 'scientific' cognition.

Given this focus on technology's disruption of the Cartesian paradigm of representation, Baudelaire's prose poem 'The Eyes of the Poor' is illuminating. As we saw in chapter two, its examination of vision is not orientated towards the question of knowledge conceived in terms of the adequacy of appearance in relation to an underlying substance; rather, it explores the relationship between the parameters of formal unity and the spatio-temporal co-ordinates of the visible. In line with his art criticism's assessment of photography, Baudelaire's poem criticizes the technologically organized appearance of the café, not because it fails to represent 'the real', but because the spatio-temporal harmony which it achieves is ordered according to contingent goals rather than the telos of the ideal. More disturbingly – at least for Baudelaire – the poem also describes the narrator's gaze in similar terms: not only is the unity it seeks animated by the narrator's own anxieties and desires, it is shown to depend on the contingent circumstances of a particular time and place. The central irony of the poem is that the very autonomy claimed by aesthetic vision – its liberation from the worldly imperatives of utilitarian perception – is made possible and is conditioned by the world of commodity production, within which the subject ironically comes to regard itself as the 'free producer' of the scene it confronts. Just like the technologically organized appearance of the café, aesthetic appearance is revealed to be implicated in the society of commodity production at the very moment when the claims for its autonomy are loudest.

What begins to emerge here, at least implicitly, is a quite different conception of experience from that informing recent cultural theory. Unlike Debord and Baudrillard, Baudelaire's poem acknowledges the non-identity of the spatio-temporal co-ordinates of the visible and its framing by the subject, as is evident in the disparity between the telos of the narrator's gaze and the scene it apprehends. Visual experience is therefore understood as a conflictual or discontinuous site, rather than occurring as the homogenous scene for an automatic process of correspondence. But equally, in contrast to Jameson and Virilio, the terms of this framing are themselves shown to be bound up or implicated within the changing spatio-temporal co-ordinates of the world, rather than being locked in a static transcendental structure or a fixed a posteriori form. Consequently, the narrator's gaze is located within the particular histories which converge at this site, and so rather than being thought of as unique and universal, it can be recognized as constituting one configuration of visual experience among many. The figuring of vision within Baudelaire's prose poem thus moves beyond the opposition of consciousness and the world implied by the paradigm of representation, and as such it suggests a different approach to vision's fate in technology. For the world that is to be known cannot simply be separated from appearances, as the substance or 'reality' lying behind them. It is not simply opposed to and separate from the terms of vision which organize and frame appearances, but in some sense inheres within them. What is to be seen then is not just what appears *in* vision, but also its mode of appearing or its failure to appear; for the conditions which frame appearances are themselves in the world, and the world therefore lies embedded in their configuration. From this perspective the incoherence which for Jameson and Virilio signifies the failure of vision can be understood instead as marking the limits of visibility within a particular regime of vision. Such moments of incoherence need not then be thought of as necessarily blank, as a pure absence in opposition to the full presence of representation's clarity and coherence, but can be understood to offer a certain kind of 'knowledge'. And, conversely, in moving beyond the paradigm of representation it also becomes possible to reconsider the broader theoretical assumptions involved in statements concerning 'the loss of the real'. As we have seen, such statements essentially conceive of technology's impact in terms of the autonomy of the image and the consequent disruption of the paradigm of representation: because appearances are now seen to be driven by purely technological imperatives, the image is freed from any relationship with social existence and so no longer represents an underlying 'social reality'. But this conception of technology's impact throws up a particular paradox. Contemporary cultural theory has emphasized the technological organization of the visible in order to undermine the idealized notion of vision implied by representation; yet because this mediation is understood in terms of the autonomy of the image, appearances are no longer located within the contingency of worldly existence. Above and beyond the epistemological claim for 'the loss of the real', then, we might identify the disappearance of the world here in another sense: for in being granted their autonomy by technology, appearances are no longer imbricated in the space and time of *Dasein*, or being-in-the-world. Thus, although the claim for 'the loss of the real' is designed to locate vision within the material processes of technological mediation – to place it, as it were, among things – it is predicated on a conception of technology which withdraws visual experience from the contingency of worldly history.

Although it is possible to identify a different conception of visual experience in Baudelaire's poetic practice, such an identification of course involves reading Baudelaire against the grain. Not only does his art criticism fail to acknowledge such a conception of experience, its understanding of the purely subjective origin of the Imagination is opposed to it. Baudelaire's poetic practice is open to different configurations of visual experience because his conception of the fallen state of creation demands a productive conception of form. But in his art criticism he limits the nature of this productivity by locating it within the pure interiority of the soul, so fixing the terms of formal coherence as the Ideal. It is worth recalling Baudelaire's restriction of experience within the pure interiority of the subject at this stage because it points to broader problems in the history of thinking vision. Looking back at the different accounts we have considered, vision seems inevitably to imply a basic polarity between the eye and the world which structures it according to the opposition of subject and object. This polarity underlies both those positions that celebrate the epistemological or aesthetic possibilities of visual perception, and those that criticize its complicity with subjective domination and mastery. Indeed, the hostility to vision evident in twentieth-century thought can be understood as a reflection of changing attitudes to the modern subject, whose perspective is increasingly understood as inherently instrumental, parochial, and violent. But equally, this hostility also provides a context for understanding why recent accounts of vision have been reluctant to acknowledge the productivity of visual experience in response to technology, and instead prefer to see either the colonization of vision by technology or its disintegration into incoherence. This reluctance is understandable, since within modern thought the productivity of visual experience has tended to be identified with the agency of the self-sufficient and absolutely spontaneous subject, so that ultimately visual experience becomes a reflection of the subject's interiority however understood. As a result, within recent cultural theory the dynamism of the visible is recognized but at the cost of the productivity of visual experience, which is reduced to the automatic reproduction of a prior configuration of form.

In reviewing these different approaches to vision, a certain symmetry therefore emerges, a symmetry which can perhaps best be described in the Kantian terms introduced in chapter one. In Baudelaire, subjectivity is understood as active in that it organizes the matter of sensation within the forms of human intuition, namely space and time. In cognition, this productivity is subordinated to the categorical framework of the understanding, but, in aesthetic perception intuition legislates itself and organizes appearances according to its own law. Consequently, for Baudelaire it is only in aesthetic perception that subjectivity experiences its own productivity and autonomy. However, while this conception of perception recognizes the productivity of visual experience, its terms are fixed within a model of subjectivity that is absolutely separate from and uncontaminated by the world. Baudelaire is hostile to photography because its reorganization of visual experience disrupts the terms of intuition's self-legislation by reformulating the very conditions of law and legislation. This hostility leads Baudelaire to ascribe an absolute sovereignty to the isolated and self-possessed subject, an ascription which reduces the harmony of beautiful appearances to an inert reflection of the subject's gaze. Contemporary cultural theory has therefore been wary of acknowledging the productivity of visual experience, and has tended to look to technology as a means of countering claims for subjective mastery. Yet in doing so the positions we have examined either suppress the activity of perception outright, or fix it within invariable limits. In the case of Debord and Baudrillard, the malevolent demon of technology legislates the terms of formal coherence as imperiously as Descartes' benevolent deity, so that visual experience is reduced to a procession of spectacles or simulacra which are always clear and have always already been read. For Jameson and Virilio, the subject's activity in attempting to legislate the unity of appearances is recognized, but it finds itself disorientated and overwhelmed by technology's intensification of, alternately, space and time. However, because the subject's legislation of form is locked within invariable parameters it cannot respond or reformulate its own terms, and it remains implacably fixed in the face of technology's reorganization of the world. In the case of Jameson this impasse gives rise to a permanent condition of temporal disorientation, while in the case of Virilio it results in the increasingly violent imposition of a rigid and disproportionate law. Thus in Baudelaire's art criticism the agency of visual experience is limited to the autonomous subject, subordinating it to a mysterious and invariable law of form; while in contemporary cultural theory this agency is transferred by technology to the autonomous image, leaving subjectivity transfixed and unable to reformulate the terms of its legislation.

What this symmetry suggests is that positions which locate the activity of perception either exclusively in the subject or in the world of objects remain restricted. Yet if it is necessary to develop an approach to visual experience that is no longer organized around this opposition, such a project raises its own difficulties, as is evident in the critical response to phenomenology since the 1960s. Phenomenology, whose emergence is primarily associated with the German philosopher Edmund Husserl and which became particularly influential in French intellectual life in the period immediately before and after the Second World War, offers the most sustained and systematic attempt to overcome these symmetrical alternatives.[1] Instead of taking as its starting point either the capacities of the subject or the properties of the object, phenomenology sought to circumvent these alternatives by concentrating on the activity of perception itself. In contrast to the paradigm of representation which separates frame and sensation, so conceiving of perception as the process of bridging the gap between distinct entities, phenomenology sees perception as an activity within which the terms of subjectivity and objectivity are themselves

---

[1] For an account of French philosophy in this period, see Descombes, 1980, chs. 1 and 2. For a sense of the perceived promise which phenomenology held out within a French intellectual context, see the early essays collected in Levinas, 1998, especially 'The Work of Edmund Husserl'.

produced. In perception, subjectivity 'intends' or organizes sensation as objectivity, so that it is understood to involve the mutual interaction of the perceiving and the perceived. Perception, then, is not a matter of apprehending isolated and independent objects, but designates the integral structuring of intentionality which gives the conditions of appearance within which 'objects' are constituted. This approach can be understood as an attempt to radicalize Kant's concern for experience by stressing the derivation of the transcendental conditions of experience – the forms of intuition and the categories of the understanding – from the activity of perception, rather than adopting Kant's table of categories or his conception of space and time. However, if phenomenology holds out the promise of moving beyond the opposition of subject and object, it also points to the difficulties involved in doing so, as became apparent in the reaction against phenomenology which was such a feature of French intellectual life in the 1960s. The powerful critiques levelled against phenomenology have left their mark on contemporary cultural theory, and can be seen as an important factor underlying its reluctance to acknowledge the productivity of visual experience.

Within the present context both the promise and the problems associated with phenomenology can perhaps best be summarized by returning to Maurice Merleau-Ponty's essay 'Eye and Mind' introduced in chapter one (1964A, pp. 159–92). Although there are important differences between Merleau-Ponty and Husserl, Merleau-Ponty's essay deals explicitly with vision and technology in ways which illustrate both phenomenology's wider appeal and its limitations. As we have seen, the essay challenges the Cartesian separation of the *cogito* and the corporeal world by conceiving of vision as being embodied, and therefore as involving the interpenetration of consciousness and the world. In the words of the essay, 'vision takes place among, or is caught in, things', and so it testifies to 'the undividedness of the sensing and the sensed' (*ibid.*, p. 163). For Merleau-Ponty it is this 'undividedness' which underlies the philosophical value of visual experience and grants it a revelatory power that exceeds the limits of Kantian knowledge, with its restriction to the space and time of human intuition. From this perspective the essay launches a critique of modern science which is structured by the diremption of subject and object, and instead argues for the philosophical value of visual art. Science's reliance on a disembodied rationality is seen as self-defeating, since in imposing a fixed conceptual structure on the sensory world it disfigures precisely what it aims to grasp. In contrast, the essay argues that visual experience should not be conceived of as the seeing of discrete and external objects, but as an activity which discloses 'a texture of Being of which the discrete sensorial images are only the punctuations or caesurae'. Visual experience is thus to be understood as an inhabitation of being which performatively maps or traces its texture: in Merleau-Ponty's words 'the eye lives in this texture as a man lives in his house' (ibid., p. 166). It is in these terms that the essay identifies visual art, exemplified by painting and sculpture, as 'a figured philosophy', since it is seen to involve a sensitivity or reflexivity that escapes the utilitarian vision ordered according to the opposition of subject and object (ibid., p. 168). The painter's gaze does not simply function within the terms of a given intentional structuring but interrogates them, asking 'what they do to suddenly cause something to be and to be this thing, what they do to compose this worldly talisman and to make us see the visible' (ibid., p. 166). In capturing the responsiveness of the artist's eye to the shifting contours of the visible, painting traces the conditions of visibility that constitute a particular structuring of intentionality. What the painting images, then, is not so much the subjective expression of the artist nor the contingent appearance of objects, but the 'undividedness' of sensing and the sensed that 'hides itself in making the object visible' (ibid., p. 167). Painting thus moves beyond the limits of Kantian knowledge in being able to disclose a texture of being which precedes the separation of subject and object, and so in a sense 'sees beyond' the limits of experience.

Merleau-Ponty's phenomenological approach is clearly suggestive in its conception of visual experience as performatively embodying or tracing the conditions which configure its intentional structuring. In focusing not on the objects seen in vision, but the intentional activity performed or described in visual experience, his approach seeks to map the configuration of being that underlies and makes possible the opposition of subject and object. Such a change of focus therefore aims to 'see beyond' the limits of the subject by tracing the texture of being which configures the parameters of its vision. But it would be premature to conclude that it escapes the problems that we have seen in Descartes and Baudelaire, and which continue to haunt contemporary cultural theory. Although Merleau-Ponty claims to be able to recognize the active nature of visual experience without falling back into their conceptions of subjective sovereignty and mastery, it is significant that his approach evinces an assessment of photography which in at least in some ways recalls that of Baudelaire.[2] According to the essay the revelatory power of painting depends on its fundamental difference to photography, and it cites Rodin's comparison of sculpture and photography, which judges the artist to be truthful and the photograph to lie, since 'in reality, time never stops cold' (ibid., p. 186). In the living moment of perception, the artist's eye adjusts its own parameters of vision to the spatio-temporal co-ordinates of the world which it inhabits, and so its structuring of intentionality embodies this configuration as a unity. And in the resulting painting, the different temporal moments involved in motion can be rendered together. But the optical parameters of the camera are indifferent to the world's appearing and proceed according to a different law, and consequently the photograph proves unable to capture the spatio-temporal unity of appearances. Instead the camera reproduces discontinuous fragments of the visible, presenting 'a rigid body as if it were a piece of armour going through its motions' (ibid., p. 185). The reason why photography is inferior to painting therefore is that the frozen photographic image 'keeps open the instants which the onrush of time closes up forthwith' and so 'destroys the overtaking, the overlapping, the "metamorphosis" of time' (ibid., p. 186). Where painting blurs or smudges the temporal heterogeneity involved in the perception of motion in order to sustain the coherence of appearances, photography captures frozen glimpses which are held in suspension outside of the flow of time. In the photograph of the galloping horse invoked by the essay, what is jarring is the lack of relation between horse and ground, which appear to inhabit different configurations of apprehension, yet are made simultaneous in the photographic image.

[2] This is not to say that Merleau-Ponty ignores the impact of technology on vision or is unremittingly hostile to it; see for example his essay 'The Film and the New Psychology' (1945) in Merleau-Ponty, 1964B.

In effect, the photograph superimposes temporally heterogeneous moments of perception, and so remains irreducible to a single, unified structure of intentionality.

What is troubling about the essay's opposition between fine art and photography is that it presupposes a conception of the human experience of time as a unified and successive flow of discrete, punctual moments. Consequently, although human vision is seen to respond to the changing spatio-temporal co-ordinates of the visible, the parameters of this responsiveness are fixed according to an understanding of the body's occupation of space and time as fully present. This assumption is betrayed in the way that Merleau-Ponty conceives the task of painting. Because 'the visible in the profane sense forgets its premises', and so fails to see 'the play of shadows and light' as well as the object, it is painting's task to 're-create' the object in its 'total visibility'. That is, painting reproduces the intentional structuring of perception in all its fullness, so 'liberat[ing] the phantoms captured in it' (*ibid.*, p. 167). In these terms, vision occurs as a discrete moment of intending which grasps the scene as a unity, as fully present right there and just now in the instant of perception. By contrast, the photographic image remains haunted by multiple and shifting structures of intentionality, 'phantoms' which are not fully present or unambiguously visible, but which appear in the failure of the image to cohere absolutely, or finally resolve 'the play of shadows and light'. As such, Merleau-Ponty can be seen to circumscribe the nature of visual experience, which is assumed to function in terms of a cohesive temporal flow. And this is why he fails to appreciate the significance of the photographic image, whose organization of space and time exceeds the integrated unity of such a visual experience. But in that case, Merleau-Ponty's attempt to *discover* the texture of being underlying the diremption of subject and object must be scrutinized, since the uniform and homogenous character of this conception of visual experience presupposes a prior configuration of being and time.

The ambition of Merleau-Ponty's essay 'Eye and Mind' is nothing less than to escape the parochial perspective of the subject and so locate vision among things. But its rejection of photography betrays the promise of this different kind of seeing, since it reveals that Merleau-Ponty's vision cannot countenance a concept of visibility that

exceeds the limits of the subject. And in these terms the broader
significance of phenomenology becomes discernible. The collapse of
the phenomenological project looms large in the development of
French thought since the 1960s: for if phenomenology had held a
particular promise in the preceding period, then the measure of this
promise is also a measure of its failure (see Descombes, 1980, ch. 5).
Its impact on the subsequent development of cultural theory can be
seen in terms of the reluctance to acknowledge the productive
character of visual experience we have identified in recent approaches
to visual culture. This role emerges most clearly in the work of Virilio
in France and Jameson in the United States. As we have seen in the
case of Virilio, Merleau-Ponty's conception of the embodied eye and
of 'the world within reach' provides the model of vision and subjectivity which technology exceeds and constantly threatens to obliterate.
And it is the repeated imposition of this model of vision upon a world
it can no longer assimilate that generates the escalating violence which
Virilio sees exemplified in modern, technological war. Equally, for
Jameson, phenomenology furnishes the model of subjectivity which
technology's visual intensification overwhelms and disperses. For what
technology brings is the withdrawal of the subject's capacity to 'actively
. . . extend its protentions and retentions across the temporal manifold
and to organize its past and future into coherent experience' (1991,
p. 25). Phenomenological vision does not simply disappear with its
critique in the 1960s, but continues to set the limits of much of the
subsequent discussion of vision and visual culture on both sides of the
Atlantic. If phenomenology represents the high-water mark of confi-
dence in the productivity of visual experience, the limit it marks out
remains as the measure against which to gauge our subsequent retreat.

The question pursued in this chapter is whether such a retreat is the
necessary response to the powerful critiques levelled against phenomenology in the 1960s. It takes as its focus a pivotal moment in the
critique of phenomenology, namely the publication in 1967 of Jacques
Derrida's *Speech and Phenomena*. Derrida's text offers a penetrating
deconstruction of the central terms of Husserl's theory of meaning,
and has therefore come to symbolize the subsequent shift of interest
away from perception and towards the critique of language and
discursive conceptuality. Yet, as a number of critics have pointed out,

what is striking about Derrida's deconstructive reading of Husserl is that it does not articulate a hostility to visual experience *per se*; nor does it seek to counterpose textuality to a conception of the visual as irretrievably bound up with the metaphysics of presence (Jay, 1993, p. 496). As we shall see, Derrida's critique of Husserl is misunderstood if it is read in terms of subsequent statements of the loss of 'the real', and consequently it cannot be taken to underwrite accounts of the inescapably blank and inert nature of visual experience, nor the relativism which is seen as its philosophical analogue.[3] Rather, Derrida's reading of Husserl calls for a rethinking of the relationship between the 'interiority' of consciousness and the 'exteriority' of the world which subtends the different formulations of vision we have considered here, and it is in these terms that Derrida's reading suggests opportunities for thinking vision and for addressing the impact of technology.

VISION AND THE VOICE

Derrida's engagement with Husserl forms an important early part of his writing, providing the context for the development of his hugely influential neologism 'differance'(*différance*). In a series of essays culminating in *Speech and Phenomena* (1967), Derrida questions Husserl's central claim to escape the tradition of Western thought, with its perennial opposition of subject and object, and, as it were, to 'begin again' by building a philosophical foundation for knowledge directly out of the activity of perception. While by no means ignorant of philosophical tradition, phenomenology aims to avoid its prejudices and arbitrary assumptions by returning to first principles and isolating the fundamental co-ordinates of thought from perceptual experience. It seeks to do this through a double process of 'bracketing' or 'reduction', wherein the contingent elements of perceptual and cognitive experience are stripped away in order to reveal the underlying forms of consciousness which make experience possible, or what Husserl calls the 'eidetic forms'. Derrida's deconstruction of Husserl's project involves demonstrating that the very point on which it erects

---

[3] See Beardsworth, 1996 for a reading that stresses Derrida's distance from such a relativism.

its claim to escape the dogmatism of tradition – its isolation of form from the activity of perception – is in fact profoundly traditional; therefore, notwithstanding its impulse to break free, phenomenology remains bound within the terms of tradition. Thus in 'Form and Meaning', also published in 1967, Derrida identifies Husserl's attempt to isolate the eidetic forms underlying experience as the repetition of a kind of thinking that reaches back to Plato and Aristotle (1973, pp. 107–28). 'Formality', Derrida writes, 'is what is presented, visible, and conceivable of a thing in general', so that the tradition of Western thought is itself identified as 'the thought of being as form', as a mode of 'putting-on-view' which marks the 'subjection of sense to seeing' and 'of sense to the sense of sight'. Thus, although Derrida recognizes significant conceptual resources in Husserl's thought – indeed, his deconstructive 'method' depends on this recognition – phenomenology is nonetheless understood to rehearse 'the metaphysical domination of the concept of form' which 'cannot fail to effectuate a certain subjection to the look' (ibid., pp. 108–9).

Taken in isolation, this assessment seems to identify vision wholly with the ambitions of a metaphysics which privileges being over becoming, a thinking whose insistence on self-identity and sameness mirrors the apparently stable and substantial object world of the visible. This impression would appear to be corroborated by Derrida's focus here and elsewhere on Husserl's theory of signs, which might suggest a deep-seated suspicion of perceptual experience; while his announcement in the closing pages of *Speech and Phenomena* that 'there never was any "perception"' seems to present nothing less than a categorical rejection of perception (ibid., p. 103). This kind of interpretation sees a specifically linguistic differance opposed to a vision that is ineluctably ensnared in the claim to full presence, and so would find in Derrida a philosophical complement to the accounts of visual culture examined in chapter two. But in fact vision plays a quite different role in Derrida's reading of Husserl. Derrida neither accepts this equation as inevitable and invariable, nor does he counterpose linguistic differance to an inherently 'metaphysical' vision; after all, as many critics have pointed out, the difference involved in Derrida's term 'differance' is not registered phonetically, in the modulation of the voice, but visually, in striking the eye. The fact that Derrida's deconstruction of Husserlian phenomenology should centre on its theory of meaning and signs is, however, significant, and to fully grasp the potential Derrida sees in vision it is necessary to locate its role within Husserl's broader account of signification.

While Husserl's authorship involves major shifts and developments, stated baldly its aim can be understood as the attempt to establish universal and objective grounds for knowledge from within the flux of experience. Crucially, in *Ideas I* Husserl refuses to import an external categorical frame to order experience, but seeks instead to isolate the underlying forms of consciousness and meaning from experience itself, which is why perception provides the starting point for his analysis. However, if his project involves a commitment to perception and its imbrication in the externality of the world, it also involves a movement away from it. If the eidetic forms that are isolated from experience are nonetheless to be objective and therefore universally valid, they must be infinitely repeatable without variance; that is, they must be conceivable as pertaining to a realm of ideality which is unaffected by the world and the contingency of experience. Derrida identifies the distinction between ideality and the worldly as fundamental to phenomenology, since it is necessarily implicit in its method of reduction; and his reading of Husserl traces how this duality organizes both his conception of perception and the theory of meaning which it is seen to entail. In terms of perception, it is necessary for Husserl to be able to distinguish between an invariable and purely interior element, and the contingent and variable elements which properly originate in the exteriority of the world. That is, Husserl's method of reduction implies an invariable 'core' of pure intuition within perceptual experience which is not itself affected or conditioned by its engagement with the world, but which, as purely interior, is infinitely repeatable without variance. However, if the centrality of this pure intuition appears to corroborate the phenomenological claim to 'begin again' on the basis of perceptual experience, Derrida emphasizes the fact that within Husserl's own terms it remains insufficient. If phenomenology is to be anything more than a radical intuitionism, it is not enough to isolate a pure moment of intuition within consciousness, since as such it cannot be transmissible or communicable within other contexts or for other subjects. To attain the status of objectivity this pure intuition must give rise to a conceptuality or meaningfulness which is not tied to the particularity of intuition, but which is universally valid.

The central problem pursued by *Speech and Phenomena* therefore revolves around the question of how the non-discursive moment of pure intuition which Husserl identifies in perception is to give rise to the universal validity of conceptual meaning. This problem is made all the more acute by Husserl's recognition that this pure moment of intuition cannot be reliant on or contaminated by the particular systems of discursive meaningfulness constituted by empirical languages. As Derrida details in his introduction to Husserl's *Origin of Geometry*, Husserl was well aware that in language meaning is tied to 'the de facto and actual intentionality of a speaking subject or community of speaking subjects', and thus to the particular circumstances of time and place. If this pure intuition were simply to be converted into linguistic meaning then its interiority would be contaminated and 'marked by the empirical subjectivity of an individual or society'; and so rather than being universally valid, it would remain immersed in the contingent circumstances of worldly history (Derrida, 1978, pp. 88, 82). In *Speech and Phenomena* Derrida identifies Husserl's solution to this problem in terms of the silent inner voice of the *Logical Investigations*, and the two central distinctions which he understands it to sustain and imply: that between 'expression' (*Ausdruck*) and 'indication' (*Anzeichen*) in the *Logical Investigations*, and a 'pre-expressive strata of sense' (*Sinn*) and 'meaning' (*Bedeutung*) in *Ideas I*. The pivotal significance of the inner voice lies in its capacity to guarantee the self-identity of form in its passage from intuition's sense to expressive meaning: in the silent inner monologue of the inner voice, the pre-expressive sense becomes instantly present to consciousness without the involvement of the externality of indication or signs. And by radically excluding the indicative dimension from expression, Husserl's meaning is orientated towards 'the telos of perfect expression' which is the 'total restitution, in the form of presence of a sense actually given to intuition' (Derrida, 1973, pp. 74–5). However, Derrida argues that in the process, the contingency involved in intuition is retrospectively erased in the claim that 'pure . . . logical expression must be an "unproductive" medium which "reflects" the pre-expressive stratum of sense' (*ibid.*, p. 74). Expression is to repeat exactly the pre-expressive sense of intuition, but this 'exact' and 'unproductive' repetition purges sense of its involvement in the world and externality, and converts it without residue into an ideal and purely logical expression.

By posing the 'problem' of phenomenology in this way, Derrida effectively undermines its central methodological claims by reversing the trajectory it ostensibly pursues. The centrality of the silent monologue of the inner voice to Derrida's account of Husserl in *Speech and Phenomena* calls into question phenomenology's claim to begin with perception and work back to the transcendental conditions of consciousness which make experience possible. For Derrida, Husserlian phenomenology begins not with perceptual experience but with the objectivity and ideality of meaning, its infinite repeatability as the same. The self-identity of meaning is then projected backwards through the mechanism of the silent inner voice, which casts perception as absolute and fully present. In these terms, the act of reduction does not lead back from perception to the ideality of eidetic form, but occurs at the level of language in the inner voice, which 'phenomenologically reduces itself, transforming the worldly opacity of its body into pure diaphaneity' (*ibid*., p. 77). That is, phenomenological reduction is not a method which teases out the pure forms of consciousness and meaning underlying experience, but a mechanism for excluding the externality necessarily involved in perception and in language. As a purely interior 'auto-affection', and indeed one 'of a unique kind', the inner voice is understood by Husserl to allow mental acts to enter expression and become meaningful 'without passing through an external detour, the world'. Meaning thus remains within the sphere of lived, interior experience, and 'does not risk death in the body of the signifier that is given over to the world and the visibility of space' (*ibid*., pp. 77–8). According to Derrida, then, what is primary here is the self-identity of meaning in expression, which retrospectively discovers its origin in the pre-expressive sense of a pure moment of intuition, and not the other way around.

Derrida thus argues that the inner voice in fact takes conceptual precedence in phenomenology over other forms of experience, such as vision or touch: for as Derrida points out, 'when I see myself, either because I gaze upon a limited region of my body or because it is reflected in a mirror, what is outside "my own" has already entered the field of this auto-affection'; while in the case of touch, 'the surface of my body , as something external, must begin by being exposed in the world' (*ibid*., pp. 78–9). In contrast, the soliloquy of the inner voice appears to be uncontaminated by exteriority, since

> the operation of hearing oneself speak seems to reduce even the inward surface of one's own body; in its phenomenological being it seems capable of dispensing with this exteriority within interiority, this interior space in which our experience or image of our own body is spread forth. This is why hearing oneself speak is experienced as an absolutely pure auto-affection, occurring in a self-proximity that would in fact be the absolute reduction of space in general . . . Requiring the intervention of no determinate surface in the world, *being produced in the world as pure auto-affection*, it is a signifying substance absolutely at our disposition (*ibid*., p. 79).

The unique auto-affection of the inner voice thus comes retroactively to subtend a notion of lived experience (*Erlebnis*) as fully present, as a 'self-proximity' founded on the 'non-alterity' and 'nondifference' of 'the identity of presence as self-presence'. But as Derrida argues, 'this concept of experience not only involves the enigma of a being appearing in absolute proximity to one-self', but 'also designates the temporal essence of this proximity', wherein 'the self-presence of experience must be produced in the present taken as a now' (*ibid*., pp. 58–9). Thus, employing Husserl's own phrase, Derrida writes that 'if mental acts . . . do not have to be informed about themselves through the intermediary of indications, it is because they are "lived by us in the same instant" [*im selben Augenblick*]'; or translated more literally, they are lived by us 'in the blink of an eye'. The absolute reduction of space in the self-proximity of presence therefore implies a purely temporal self-presence or pure temporality, which would be 'as indivisible as the *blink of an eye*' (*ibid*., p. 59).

What is particularly significant about Derrida's approach to Husserl in the present context is that its focus on the unique auto-affection of the inner voice works to question phenomenology's commitment to perception; and in turn, this questioning qualifies Derrida's apparent equation of seeing and presence in 'Form and Meaning'. If, to use

Merleau-Ponty's formulation, phenomenology claims to escape philo-sophical tradition by according 'primacy' to perception, then Derrida's emphasis on the role of *phone*, or the voice, implicitly questions the centrality of perception, and specifically vision, to Husserl's project.[4] And indeed, this questioning is made explicit by Derrida both in *Speech and Phenomena* and in 'Form and Meaning'. In the case of the latter, the initial subordination of meaning to the pre-expressive unity of pure intuition is reversed in Derrida's question as to whether 'the expressive stratum' of meaning had not 'secretly guided the analyses of the pre-expressive stratum', so allowing 'us to discover in its core a logical sense under the universal and allegedly silent-form of being present' (1973, p. 126). In the case of the former, the role of vision in providing the telos for meaning as 'presence to intuition' is shown to depend on its articulation within a broader conceptual nexus, which Derrida characterizes as 'the unity of *technē* and *phōnē*'. In securing a realm of pure interiority, the inner voice implies a pure exteriority awaiting manipulation and organization, an objectivity at the disposal of the technical operations of rational consciousness; that is, the inner voice requires a vision that sees a world of objects spread before it, discrete and fully present in the blink of an eye. For Derrida, then, it is the rigid opposition between the interiority of the voice and the externality of the worldly that casts vision as a function or instrument of 'the epoch of speech as *technical* mastery of objective being'. And so rather than according 'primacy' to perception, phenomenology is seen within these terms as constituting a certain *technic* of vision, one that subordinates the visual to the form of technical objectivity, as 'being-before the gaze' (1978, p. 75).

Rather than rejecting phenomenology's engagement with perceptual experience, *Speech and Phenomena* in fact points to its failure to carry through with this engagement, and so make good on its own promise. Despite his best intentions, Husserl is shown to subordinate perception to the pure interiority and self-presence of the inner voice, rather than according it 'primacy'. The impossibility of this absolute self-presence provides the focus for the final section of *Speech and Phenomena*, which

---

[4] The formulation is taken from the title of Merleau-Ponty's well-known essay 'The Primacy of Perception and its Philosophical Consequences' (1964A).

in examining the articulation of the 'I' in speech demonstrates that it 'has its norm', not in the fullness and self-presence of the inner voice, but 'in writing and its relationship with death' (*ibid.*, p. 97). It is here that the broader significance of Derrida's reading of Husserl emerges most clearly since, as Derrida observes, it is through the inner voice 'that the *ergo sum* is introduced into the philosophical tradition and that a discourse about the transcendental is possible' (*ibid.*, p. 95). But while the final discussion of writing provides a powerful lens for reviewing Husserl's location within modern thought and his relation-ship to tradition, it should not obscure the range of possibilities opened up by the text. If one important element within *Speech and Phenomena* is its discovery of similarities which link Husserl's transcendental consciousness to the transcendent co-ordinates of the Cartesian *cogito* through their shared reliance on the self-presence of the inner voice, the text's deconstruction of Husserl's central claims takes place not only at the level of language, but also at the level of perception. And just as Derrida's questioning of phenomenology's claims for the ideality of meaning employs Husserl's own account of signification, so his deconstruction of the pure moment of intuition draws on Husserl's own figuring of perception in a short but pivotal text, *The Phenomenology of Internal Time-Consciousness* (1928). In revealing phenomenological perception to be just one possible organization or *technic* of vision, *Speech and Phenomena* thereby raises the prospect of thinking vision differently. A crucial part of Derrida's reading therefore involves identifying a different conception of perception already at work within Husserl's own text.

IN THE BLINK OF AN EYE

The Phenomenology of Internal Time-Consciousness comprises two extended series of lectures given by Husserl between 1904 and 1910, which were brought together and published in 1928 by Husserl's erstwhile student Martin Heidegger. The lectures engage with two distinct but related questions. Their initial concern is to account for the immanent activity of consciousness through which temporally discrete acts of perception are able to give rise to the interrelatedness of lived experience. But their broader aim is to identify the necessary and universal character of internal time-consciousness, and so accord objectivity to the human experience of time. In order to achieve the latter, the lectures seek to establish 'consciousness of a unitary, homogenous, Objective time' through an account of the interiority and self-presence of intuition; but in pursuing the former, they offer an engagement with the specificity of experience which implies a quite different conception of perception and time (1964, p. 94). Consequently, Derrida's assessment of the lectures in *Speech and Phenomena* is nuanced. Not only does he acknowledge the text's 'admirable analysis' of the temporality of perception, but he cites approvingly Heidegger's assessment of it as 'the first in the history of philosophy to break with the concept of time inherited from Aristotle's *Physics*' (Derrida, 1973, p. 61). Yet at the same time Derrida also draws attention to the ways in which this analysis is subordinated to the project of securing an invariable and ideal transcendental consciousness. His discussion of the text therefore centres on the conceptual contradictions and inconsistencies that are thrown up in the process.

The immediate problem addressed by *The Phenomenology of Internal Time-Consciousness* involves the intuition of temporal objects. Such objects would include visual phenomena whether moving or at rest, although Husserl chooses to focus on the tonal sequence of a melody, a choice which as we shall see is not insignificant. While perception might be conceived of as an act that takes place 'just now' in relation to an object present to consciousness, this scenario becomes more difficult when a temporally extended phenomena like a melody is considered. The question is necessarily begged as to how the perception of the individual notes in each now could be experienced not as unrelated and discrete tones, but as a melody that depends on the variation, patterning, and interrelation of tonal values over time. As Husserl observes, if perception is conceived of as discretely locked within each successive now, then 'we should have a note at every instant, and possibly [an empty phase] in the interval between the sounding of the next, but never the idea [*Vorstellung*] of a melody'. The solutions that had been proposed to this problem involved either positing a time-lag within consciousness – whereby sensations persist for a short while after the stimulus has ceased – or appealing to the activity of memory. Such solutions see each perceived now as being accompanied by the preceding moments of perception, which either persist unchanged within consciousness, or are reproduced by memory and so are re-experienced as they once were. But for Husserl such accounts prove insufficient, since they cannot provide a sense of temporal duration or succession. If the preceding notes simply remain or are reproduced within consciousness without being modified, then as Husserl points out, 'instead of a melody, we should have a chord of simultaneous notes or rather a disharmonious jumble of sounds such as would obtain if we struck all the notes simultaneously' (1964, p. 30). Or in the case of visual phenomena, he notes that if a moving body 'were to be held fast unaltered in its momentary position in conscious-ness, then the space traversed would appear to us to be continuously occupied [and] we should have no idea of motion' (*ibid.*, p. 32). Whether conceived of in terms of memory or sensory persistence, such approaches fail to account for the continuity of experience or register the pastness of the past in relation to an ever-renewed present. And as such, they cannot account for the experience of duration nor the successive nature of perception.

Husserl's keen grasp of the problems of duration and succession leads him to qualify the commitment to the pure *now* of intuition that is so central to his larger project. The solution which *The Phenomenology of Internal Time-Consciousness* proposes seeks to maintain the pivotal position of the perceptual now, but crucially conceives of it as a complex formation rather than a simple unity. While the originary and self-giving centre of intuition comprises an ever-new moment of perception – what Husserl calls the 'primal impression' – this now is extended temporally to include immediate remembrance and antici-pation through the introduction of two new conceptual terms, 'reten-tion' and 'protention'.[5] Following his former teacher Brentano, Husserl sees each now of perception as being continually 'shoved back' by the succession of new impressions. But, unlike Brentano, he conceives of this process of 'shoving back' as a formal modification in which the impressional now 'just past' is *retained* within the emergence of the

---

[5] Husserl's term is to be distinguised from the physiological phenomenon of retinal retention, which is akin to the first position above which Husserl rejects as unable to account for duration and succession.

new now, but is marked or formally modified as 'just having been'. The dynamic role of retention can be illustrated by following Husserl's account of the perception of a melody, which begins with a fresh primal impression, the apprehension of the first note. As a new impressional now emerges with the sounding of the next note, this 'just past' now is retained and modified. The emergent now is therefore a 'nexus' or complex which comprises both the fresh primal impression of the second note *and* the retentionally modified impressional now 'just past' of the first. With the sounding of the third note, this now is in its turn 'shoved back', but this time what is retained is the whole complex that is just past. That is, what is retained *and modified* in its entirety is the complex comprising the perception of the second note and the retained (and previously modified) impression of the first. The impressional now of the third note therefore comprises a complex that carries an immediate memory of the complex of the second note, which in turn carries within itself an immediate memory of the first note – and so on, up to a given limit. In being retained, impressions are successively marked as further and further away from the actual now until they are no longer retained and fall away, so that their accumulation occurs as a 'diminution' or 'shading off' from the 'source point' of the impressional now.

Husserl's attentiveness to the temporal character of perception significantly reformulates the nature of what is perceived. Each impressional complex is now understood as 'bear[ing] in itself the heritage of the past', although modified and marked as past in relation to the experiential priority of the present (*ibid.*, p. 51). And further, since the perception of a melody involves not only the immediate memory of notes already struck but also an immediate expectation of the notes that are to come, Husserl also extends perception to include anticipation through the concept of protention. Consequently, a train of anticipated impressions is projected forwards from the primal impression on the model of retention. Each primal impression is therefore supplemented or extended by what the lectures describe as an intentional 'double halo', the complex or 'nexus' of retentions and protentions receding back into the past and forwards into the future (*ibid.*, pp. 139–40). By extending the perceptual now in this way, Husserl argues that he can overcome the problems associated with the perception of temporal objects. But he also argues something more than this: namely that such an account of perception can provide the basis for establishing the objectivity of the subjective experience of time. This larger claim depends on his ability to demonstrate that, although he has extended the perceptual now, it remains anchored by and centred on the fixed point of the primal impression. By maintaining the centrality of the primal impression, Husserl can conceive of the retentional train as being organized as a consistent and invariable linear succession, and it is this aspect which is developed by the lectures in order to secure a consistent and linear temporality underlying internal time-consciousness. Because retained or anticipated impressions are marked as progressively removed from the actual now through their differing levels of formal modification and re-modification, their 'shading off' is seen to follow a regular and uniform pattern. Husserl illustrates this effect by way of an analogy, arguing that the temporal diminution generated in retention can be understood as 'a kind of temporal perspective . . . analogous to spatial perspective'. Just as visual objects appear to recede towards a single point on the horizon, so Husserl argues that 'as the temporal Object moves into the past, it is drawn together on itself and thereby also becomes obscure' (*ibid.*, p. 47). What is central to this analogy is the stable relationship between a proportional recession and the co-ordinates of, alternatively, space and time: just as perspectival recession supplies the co-ordinates of three-dimensional space, so the retentional 'shading off' supplies a temporal gradient falling away from the ever emergent now. This temporal gradient establishes the successive nature of the temporal flux in relation to the experiential priority of the impressional now, arranging the multiplicity of impressions as a continuous, linear duration. As such, Husserl understands perception to occur as a series of discrete moments which nonetheless carry an immediate memory of their past within their temporal form.

For Husserl, then, it is vital that perception remains centred in the living and punctual now, even though it is extended via retention and protention in order to account for the continuous and successive nature of experience. And in turn, this requirement has important consequences for perception, for memory, and for the relationship between them. Although extended through retention and protention, the perceptual complex must remain centred on the primal impression, which anchors perception in a discrete and punctual instant. In order to establish this priority, the now of primal impression is identified as singularly generative and originary, as opposed to retention and protention which are secondary and dependent on it. Thus Husserl insists that the primal impression alone is the living 'act which primordially constitutes the Object *(Objekt)*' *(ibid.,* p. 63). What this means is that the perceptual 'object' – the complex of retentions and protentions centred on the primal impression – is perceived 'as complete givenness', or is given absolutely and in its integral entirety in the instant of apprehension *(ibid.,* p. 94). Notwithstanding the temporal dispersal involved in retention and protention, then, Husserl maintains that in the pure instant of primal impression, perception occurs once and for all and is fully present. But for Husserl, it is not only the primal impression that is fully present to consciousness, but also retention and protention since, as he argues, 'consciousness is necessarily *consciousness* in each of its phases' *(ibid.,* p. 162). That is, perception in the widest sense is to be understood as fully conscious, as Husserl makes clear by insisting that 'retention of a content of which we are not conscious is impossible' *(ibid.,* p. 163).

Such a conception of the absolute productivity of perception has important consequences for memory since, as Husserl continues, 'it is certainly an absurdity to speak of a content of which we are 'unconscious', of which we are only conscious later' *(ibid.,* p. 162). Thus the corollary of the originary and absolutely spontaneous nature of perception is that memory is reproductive and derivative, and adds nothing to perception; and on this basis the two terms must be rigorously separated and distinguished. However, the distinction between the productive character of perception and the *re*productive character of memory also ranks these acts within an inviolable hierarchy, a hierarchy given an emphatic formulation in Husserl's lapidary dictum that 'I can re-live [*nachleben*] the present' in memory, 'but it can never be given again' *(ibid.,* p. 66). Within these terms, Husserl can argue that the perceptual complex is ideally reproducible in memory, and so the original perception can be reproduced – or 'presentified' – in recollection exactly as it once was. As Husserl explains, to every formative act of consciousness 'there corresponds the ideal possibility of an exactly matching presentification of this consciousness', while every perceptual content can be reproduced in all its manifold sensory richness (*ibid.*, p. 115). As we shall see, this ideal reproducibility is understood by Husserl to establish the objective and linear character of subjective time.

But as Derrida observes in *Speech and Phenomena*, the concepts of retention and protention in fact radically undermine the self-presence of intuition 'in the blink of an eye', and so the larger claims pursued by the lectures are already undone by their opening analysis. Indeed, although Husserl claims that he can establish the continuity of perceptual experience while still maintaining the priority of the pure now of primal impression, his own discussion consistently indicates the reverse. His strictures regarding the perception of a melody require that for consciousness to be able to grasp the interrelation of a series of notes extended over time, it cannot simply be locked within a series of discrete and unrelated moments. The apprehension of a melody must therefore involve both the perception of the note heard now and the perception of those that are just past and yet to come; that is, it necessarily involves the interplay of presence *and* absence in the ostensibly indivisible now. Thus, within Husserl's own terms, his apparently innocuous claim that 'the *whole melody* . . . is *perceived*' presents an extraordinary extension or dispersal of perception. His subsequent qualification – that this temporally dispersed perception is always centred on an instant so that 'only the now-point actually is [perceived]' – does not in fact establish the integrity of the perceptual now, but only underlines the inherence of absent moments in what had claimed to be indivisible and fully present (*ibid.*, p. 60). Indeed, Husserl states quite emphatically that 'the just-having-been, the before in contrast to the now, can be *seen directly*' in retention, while in protention the 'about-to-be-perceived is now; it endures and fills the *same time*' (*ibid.*, pp. 64, 169; emphasis added). 'We have then characterized the past itself as perceived', he observes, since in retention we are 'directly conscious of the *just-having-been* of the "just past"'; and he goes on to conclude that 'obviously the meaning of "perception" here does not coincide' with the claim for the pure self-presence of the primal impression (*ibid.*, p. 61). In fact the very possibility of a discrete point or moment of perception is effectively undermined when Husserl acknowledges that 'we . . . can only have continuities of apprehension', and that any attempt to identify a discrete, punctual instant 'immediately breaks down again into a finer now and past, etc.' (*ibid.*, p. 62). The purely punctual now, it transpires, is only the 'ideal limit' of what is really 'a *continuum of gradations*', and is therefore 'something abstract which can be nothing for itself' (*ibid.*, pp. 62–3).

In *Speech and Phenomena* Derrida inserts this dispersal of the now into Husserl's broader account of meaning and signification. For Husserl, the self-presence of mental acts effected by the inner voice 'in the blink of an eye' maintains the interiority and self-identity of pre-expressive sense in its passage to expression, and so grounds the possibility of a pure, logical meaning obtaining within a realm of ideality. The universality of conceptual meaning therefore depends on the spontaneous generation of a succession of discrete nows by consciousness, through which the 'movement' of temporalization is produced. As Derrida observes, this implies, first, that the auto-affection of the inner voice is purely temporal, and second, that transcendental consciousness is self-identical and uncontaminated by the contingency of the world. However, the dispersal of the perceptual now implicit within *The Phenomenology of Internal Time-Consciousness* undermines the self-identity of transcendental consciousness, since the 'movement' of temporalization produced by consciousness in fact depends on its difference with itself. As Derrida points out, for the living now 'to be a now and to be retained in another now' it must 'affect itself . . . with a new primordial actuality in which it would become a non-now, a past now'. Auto-affection therefore becomes a process 'in which the same is the same only in being affected by the other, only by becoming the other of the same'. By recognizing the inherence of absence and externality within perception, Derrida argues, Husserl in fact describes the perceptual now not as a punctual and indivisible point, but as a 'trace'. Consequently, Husserl's claim for the priority of the primal impression as the living source point and centre of the intentional halo is unsustainable. The primal impression cannot be conceived as an integral present prior to the absence of retention, but 'springs forth out of its nonidentity with itself and from the possibility of a retentional trace'. As Derrida observes, the pre-expressive sense of intuition 'is never simply present; it is always already engaged in the "movement" of the trace', and therefore it is already inhabited by the absence and dispersal that characterize signification and writing (1973, p. 85).

Derrida develops this insight by pursuing its implications for the transcendental conditions of what had claimed to be pure logical expression. He argues that the formative activity of intuition cannot be isolated as the purely temporal organization of an inert and static spatial content, because the dispersal of the perceptual now reveals the inherence of space in time. '*The temporalization of sense is, from the outset, a "spacing"*', writes Derrida, and therefore 'Space is "in" time; it is time's pure leaving-itself; it is the "outside-itself" as the self-relation of time'. Time cannot be opposed to space, nor space to time, but these terms must be thought together. Consequently, the formative activity of consciousness cannot be isolated as purely temporal from the externality of space, but is contaminated by the world. Indeed, as Derrida explains, 'there can no longer be any absolute inside, for the "outside" has insinuated itself into the movement by which the inside of the nonspatial, which is called "time", appears, is constituted, is "presented"'. Husserl's attempt to examine the uncontaminated operation of consciousness by bracketing the externality of the world thus finds both its 'power and limit' in its analysis of time, for the world that is to be excluded in the transcendental reduction is itself 'primordially implied in the movement of temporalization' (*ibid.*, p. 86). Husserl's own account of perception is therefore shown to strike at the heart of the phenomenological method and to undermine its claims for the ideality of a pure logical expression. With the dispersal of the perceptual now, the essential distinctions required by Husserl's theory of meaning – between 'sense' and 'meaning', 'indication' and 'expression', 'speech' and 'writing' – begin to unravel. Intuition's pre-expressive sense cannot give rise to the universality of conceptual meaning because its 'purely' temporal form is already immersed in the 'externality' of space; equally, the inner voice cannot guarantee the self-presence of meaning to consciousness, since its silent monologue is already inhabited by the absence and deferral that characterize signs and writing. Consequently, a purely logical expression cannot be separated from indication, because the contingency of indication is shown to be inherent within signification from the outset. Crucially, for Derrida, this means that rather than guaranteeing the ideality of pure logical expression, the inner voice betrays the dependence of meaning on the supplement of writing. Meaning finds its condition not in the self-presence of auto-affection, but in the contingency and deferral – or differance – at work in signs and indication. Differance undermines the pure interiority of transcendental consciousness by revealing its contamination by worldly history.

SPACE AND TIME

Derrida's reading of Husserl in *Speech and Phenomena* therefore moves from perception to the transcendental conditions of logical expression in order to discover the exteriority and absence inherent within meaning. The linguistic character of logical expression belies the self-presence of intuition that is supposed to supply its foundation, and discursive conceptuality finds its condition in the absence and deferral of writing rather than in the self-presence of the inner voice. Thus, although perception plays a pivotal role in his argument, Derrida does not pursue the specifically visual implications of Husserl's extension of the now, which remain largely implicit. Instead, his discussion concentrates on identifying the implications of this extension for discursive conceptuality, and for the notion of a transcendental subject structured around the consistency and invariability of pure logical expression. Or, in Kant's terms, Derrida's critique is primarily concerned with the discursive or acroamatic categories of the understanding rather than with the 'visual' axioms of intuition, although its force emerges precisely in its movement between the two. Crucially, then, Derrida does not simply counterpose the absence and externality inherent within language to the self-presence and interiority of a pure core of intuition, for any such notion is undermined by the dispersal of the perceptual now in the retentional trace, which is itself described as a 'protowriting' (*ibid.*, p. 85). If vision supplies Husserl with the metaphor for the self-presence of meaning 'in the blink of an eye', it is central to Derrida's argument that perception in fact works quite differently. Consciousness is not to be conceived on the model of an intuition fully present to itself, because in vision the very terms of seeing are in fact already implicated in the contingency of the world. As Derrida observes, 'Hearing oneself speak is not the inwardness of an inside that is closed in upon itself; it is the irreducible openness in the inside; it is *the eye and the world within speech*' (*ibid.*, p. 86; emphasis added).

But if *Speech and Phenomena* points to the emergence of a different conception of vision within Husserl's thought, the nature of this other conception needs to be drawn out. The central importance of *The Phenomenology of Internal Time-Consciousness* is seen to lie in its potential for articulating the space and time of experience in terms which would reformulate the opposition between inside and outside that has governed the thinking of vision. Derrida sketches out the central issues involved for vision in an extremely compressed formulation, observing that 'There is a duration to the blink, and it closes the eye' (*ibid.*, p. 65). Despite its economy, the central thrust of this statement is recognizable within the broader context of Derrida's reading of Husserl. It neither offers a confirmation of the necessarily 'metaphysical' nature of visual experience nor an announcement of its redundancy, but alludes to a vision that no longer occurs in the pure and fully present instant. The first part of this statement inserts the spreading of the now into the idiomatic eye-blink, revealing its apparently pure punctuality to be inhabited and extended by other moments of perception; and the second part reinscribes the element of repetition inherent in the eye's incessant blinking, a repetition that had been obscured by the claim for the self-presence of the undivided now. Yet while this statement points to some of the visual implications raised by the dispersal of the now, albeit in a condensed form, *Speech and Phenomena* does not develop them; nor does it elaborate how the space and time of vision might be thought once the opposed poles of inside and outside become untenable. The question thus remains as to how this repetition might reformulate the string of oppositions which flow from this polarity and which have recurred in our examination of vision: between clarity and distortion, activity and passivity, form and content, and between what appears and what is invisible. In order to understand the alternative possibilities which Derrida sees in Husserl's analysis of perception it is necessary to return to *The Phenomenology of Internal Time-Consciousness*: for although the text seeks to suppress the broader implications of its dispersal of the now, this dispersal continually re-emerges. Read against the grain, then, the text offers an important insight into how the space and time of vision might be thought differently.

The central importance of the punctual nature of the now for Husserl lies in the fact that it fixes the perceptual nexus once and for all. Because perception occurs instantaneously and in the blink of an eye, the halo of retentions and protentions leading forwards and backwards from the primal impression is frozen in the instant, caught, as it were, in the snapshot of the eye-blink. The completeness and finality incumbent on the instantaneous nature of perception allows Husserl to posit the ideal reproducibility of the original perception in memory: 'I always presentify the same', he maintains, and consequently the same temporal form and the same sensory content are always reproduced in memory (1964, p. 71). And it is through this ideal reproducibility that Husserl claims to establish the consistent and linear nature of subjective temporality, and hence its 'objective' character. To illustrate this argument, the lectures return to the analogy between spatial and temporal perspective that was originally employed to illustrate the idea of retentional diminution or 'shading off'. Initially it was introduced in order to lend the notion of retentional diminution a certain uniformity and consistency, and the lectures increasingly emphasize this aspect in pursuing their larger goal. Thus, in discussing the perception of motion, Husserl maintains that:

> The originary temporal field is obviously circumscribed exactly like a perceptual one. Indeed, generally speaking, one might well venture the assertion that *the temporal field always has the same extension*. It is displaced, as it were, with regard to the perceived and freshly remembered motion and its Objective time in a manner similar to the way in which the visual field is displaced with regard to Objective space (*ibid.*, p. 52; emphasis added).

What is central to the analogy, then, is its assumption of the fixed parameters of Euclidean space which categorically '*always has the same extension*', and it is this static geometrical perspective which it transposes to time. Visual experience is located within a three-dimensional spatial framework that is rigid and invariable. Within these terms the diminution of objects conforms to a regular and predictable geometry, which is arranged around a central axis running from a single vanishing point on the horizon to the perceiver's eye. Consequently, if the surrounding field were blocked off so that only a segment were visible, the viewer would nonetheless be able to extrapolate the lines of recession within the segment, and so fill in the distance intervening between the segment and its own position, and between the segment and the horizon. As long as their position is constant and the scale and proportions of recession are unaltered, the viewer can therefore fix the segment's relative distance and location, since the uniform recession of objects within the segment conforms to the regular geometrical co-ordinates of Euclidean space. Thus, for Husserl the temporality of perception is to be understood as analogous to the fixed spatial co-ordinates of Euclidean geometry, and he transposes this logic of geometrical location to his account of memory in order to see it as a kind of internal measure for calibrating time-consciousness.

The extension of this spatial model to internal time-consciousness depends on the fixed and invariable nature of the remembered perception, which allows Husserl to see the temporal gradient implied by the train of retentions as analogous to the uniform geometry of perspectival recession. Observing that spatial perspective involves a uniform diminution from foreground to background, Husserl argues that 'it is the same with regard to the unity of time-consciousness', where 'the duration reproduced is the foreground', while 'the classifying intentions make us aware of . . . a temporal background' (*ibid.*, p. 78). The remembered contents therefore become the 'bearers of rays of apprehension' within their temporal form, which in turn imply 'lines of memories which discharge in the actual now', 'lines' that are understood as analogous to those organizing perspectival space (*ibid.*, p. 139). Because each remembered duration 'encloses in itself, in a chain of mediate intentions, the entire series of intentions which have expired' from the remembered past to the present of recollection, Husserl argues that it is possible to extrapolate 'a longitudinal intentionality' which 'goes through the flux' and remains 'in continuous unity of coincidence with itself' (*ibid.*, pp. 162, 107). This continuous chain constitutes 'an order' comparable to the fixed dimensions of

Euclidean space, so that just as any segment of the perspectival field occupies a determinate position within fixed spatial co-ordinates, so 'every temporal interval . . . [is] part of a unique chain, continuing to the point of the actual now' (*ibid.*, p. 96). When reproduced, each moment of perception 'still has its connections' encoded within its intentional nexus, and so although shorn of its surrounding context, it 'nevertheless lies "potentially" in the [longitudinal] intention' (*ibid.*, p. 139). It is not necessary, then, to reproduce the actual series of memories that leads from the past perception to the present of remembrance in order to locate the remembered perception in time, for the self-identity of the remembered perception enables consciousness to 'go back at a bound to the past and then again intuitively presentify the past progressively to the now' (*ibid.*, p. 140). That is, the exact reproduction of an earlier moment of perception allows the duration intervening between the past remembered and the now of recollection to be extrapolated according to a uniform and consistent longitudinal intention. Individual durations of perception can therefore be plotted within an invariable and regular linear sequence which, because based on the necessary temporal form of perception, is universally valid for consciousness and hence objective.

It is worth dwelling on Husserl's re-employment of his analogy between space and time, because the second time around it functions not only to illustrate the mechanism of recollection, but also to describe the relationship between perception and memory. Just as in its initial deployment – where it serves to illustrate the temporal structure of perception by way of a parallel between retentional diminution and perspectival recession – the analogy aligns temporal organization with the static co-ordinates of three-dimensional space. However, in this second instance the analogy establishes a parallel between the spatial location of a segment within a three-dimensional field and the temporal location of the remembered perception; that is, the analogy functions by moving from perception to memory. As such, the analogy bears a considerable weight, since by illustrating the operation of memory through perception, it also articulates their relationship. As we have seen, for Husserl, perception and memory are not only distinct, but are ranked according to a strict hierarchy that is integral to the whole project pursued by the lectures; for while the act of perception is originary and productive – and so absolutely spontaneous and 'self-giving' – the act of memory is *reproductive*, since the terms of its activity are already given. Husserl's use of the analogy to move from perception to memory appears to respect this hierarchical separation, in that the secondary and unproductive nature of memory is reflected precisely in the exemplary status of perception: just as the remembered perceptions are reproductive and derivative, so the operation of memory simply reproduces the terms of perception. But although the analogy may appear to function in these terms, there is in fact an important aspect of recollection which it cannot assimilate, and given its dual role this failure not only questions Husserl's account of memory, but also his account of perception. Significantly this failure emerges at the very point when the lectures offer their most forthright and affirmative statement of the analogy between perception and memory. 'We have', Husserl explains, 'the following analogies':

> for the spatial thing, the ordering into the surrounding space and the spatial world on the one side, and on the other, the spatial thing itself with its foreground and background. For the temporal thing, we have the ordering into the temporal form and the temporal world on the one side, and on the other the temporal thing itself and *its changing orientation with regard to the living now* (ibid., pp. 78–9; emphasis added).

But despite Husserl's claim for a rigorous correspondence, there is of course no analogue within this account of visual perspective for the ever-emerging now of recollection and its continual reorientation of the lines of memory. Were the vantage point of vision to change, or were there to be a multiplicity of vantage points, then the strict and invariable correlation between geometrical recession and spatial extension upon which the analogy depends would no longer hold.

The inconsistency that emerges here is not incidental but reveals the assumptions on which Husserl's analogy is built, and by extension points to possibilities that are excluded. The analogy is able to secure the uniform and invariable co-ordinates of its respective spatial and temporal poles precisely because it isolates them, strictly counterposing the spatial plane of simultaneity and the temporal flow of succession.

In the case of visual perspective the analogy assumes an absolute simultaneity in order to describe a purely spatial form: there is a uniform correlation between the geometry of recession and the fixed dimensions of spatial extension only because the possibility of different or multiple vantage points is excluded, and so the vista appears all at once within a single set of spatial co-ordinates. Equally, the analogy's account of 'temporal perspective' posits an absolute succession in order to isolate a purely temporal form: the co-ordinates of recession are unidirectional and fixed only because the different impressional complexes are homogenous units deployed within a discrete succession, so that there is no possibility of the simultaneity or co-extensivity of heterogeneous temporal moments. This emphasis on pure succession is reinforced by the lectures' central example of the perception of a melody, which lacks a visual component and so gives the impression of a discrete sequence more easily than say the example of a moving object, where the coincidence of alteration and stasis is more readily observable. In this way the succession observed in temporal perspective is accorded a uniformity and consistency modelled on that of spatial perspective. But were the changing location of perspective that is figured in the analogy's temporal pole registered within its spatial pole, then the strict separation of simultaneity and succession would break down. The visual pole of the analogy would not occur as an absolute simultaneity, so giving an image organized by a uniform geometry of recession arranged around a single axis; instead it would involve a multiplicity of perceptual moments superimposed on top of one another, so giving an image comprising heterogeneous perspectival axes. In terms of visual representation, then, what would be described here is not the single-point perspective of Renaissance painting, but the multi-perspectival image space which Cubism was just then in the process of exploring.

The analogy between space and time proves revealing in ways that Husserl had not intended, and points to fundamental tensions in his claims for the ideal reproducibility of recollection and the absolute givenness of perception. Most immediately, the disparity that becomes evident in the analogy's extension from perception to memory challenges the very conception of time it is designed to establish since, in introducing the changing location of recollection it raises the prospect of multiple temporal perspectives. This issue is confronted by Husserl in his discussion of the retroactive nature of memory, memory's ability to 'see' the past perception differently from later vantage points. Husserl has to concede an element of retroaction within memory, but recognizes that it potentially threatens the self-identity of the remembered perception. He therefore seeks to contain this threat by restricting this retroactive dimension to protentions, assuming retentions to be determinate and fixed. If each perception involves anticipations of what is to come, then in being recalled these anticipations will be confronted by a future in which they are either fulfilled or not fulfilled; consequently, the remembered perception is necessarily adjusted or modified by the circumstances of its recollection. However, Husserl maintains that what looks like a significant problem for his account of memory simply resolves itself: for 'if the primordial protention of the perception of the event was undetermined and the question of being-other or not-being was left open', he argues, 'then in recollection we have a predetermined expectation which does not leave all that open' (*ibid.*, p. 76). That is, the initially indeterminate – or as it were 'blurred' – protention is focused through the actuality of succeeding events, so that the 'rays of memory' are concentrated and the resultant reproduction achieves a higher resolution and a surer outline.

However, this account of retroaction remains partial within Husserl's own terms, and neither its restriction to protention nor its characterization as final and progressive can be sustained within the arguments developed through the lectures. The problem of retroaction is limited to protention because the retentional train is assumed to be determinate and already informed by the perceptual complex within which it is retained. But what this assumption ignores is that the retained impression is itself a complex comprising three elements: an earlier primal impression, its receding train of retentions, *and* its projected train of protentions. According to his own analysis of perception, then, Husserl is wrong to restrict the question of retroaction to protentions, since each retention includes earlier protentions and so is also inhabited by an element of indeterminacy. Equally, according to Husserl's account of the absolute reproducibility of the original perception, memory's retroactive determination cannot be figured as final and progressive. For if memory's reproduction is exact in each instance, then the original indeterminacy cannot be factored out; and indeed Husserl admits as much, conceding that the undetermined element 'is also included in recollection' and so is reproduced again and again (*ibid.*, p. 76).[6] Therefore, if the remembered perception is determined by subsequent experience, as Husserl argues, the original indeterminacy – its openness to 'the question of being-other or not-being' – must nonetheless also recur in each subsequent moment of recollection. Recollection does not therefore constitute a process whereby the remembered perception is focused more and more narrowly through a determinate actuality proceeding to the present, since the interplay between the determinate and the undetermined is continually renewed. Paradoxically, then, the ideal reproducibility of the original perception does not guarantee its self-identity, but provides the condition for its continual modification in memory. Even though reproduced exactly, the past does not return 'as it once was'; for in its return, the reproduced perception inserts the memory of different pasts and different possible futures into the changing actuality of remembrance. Such a conception of memory destabilizes the unity of the remembered perception, and identifies any moment of unity as provisional and incomplete. Any such moment of unity is bought at the cost of the suppression of the play of memory, which must necessarily emerge again and again.

The problems posed for Husserl by memory's retroactive power also extend to perception, and it is here that we can begin to identify that other conception of vision which Derrida indicates is implicit within Husserl's extension of the perceptual now. First and foremost, memory retrospectively reinstates the multiple and heterogeneous nature of the perceptual complex which had been obscured by the priority granted to the primal impression. For the element of indeterminacy that emerges within the remembered perception is itself originary, and is rooted in the retentions and protentions that comprise the impressional complex of the original perception. Rather than constituting a unified and unidirectional halo receding back into the past and forwards into the future, the perceptual complex points back

---

[6] Indeed, Husserl accepts that the necessary reproduction of this original indeterminacy presents certain 'difficulties', although he does not pursue them (*ibid.*).

to a number of different pasts and forwards to a number of possible futures. And as such, it cannot give rise to a conception of time constituted by the linear succession of discrete perceptual nows, like beads on a string or links in a chain. But once the purely successive nature of subjective time becomes untenable, then like memory, perception must be also recognized as being inhabited and conditioned by other moments of perceptual experience. Perception cannot be absolutely opposed to memory, as originary and self-giving, but must be understood as being inhabited by memory in the broadest sense of the term: that is, the spontaneity of perception must be conceived of as inhabited by the absent histories of other moments of experience and of remembrance and anticipation. Husserl's example of the perception of melody obscures this more complex temporality by always beginning with 'the first note'; but from this perspective, *there is no 'first' note.* Just as our memory of the unfolding of a melody is overshadowed by the experience of its actual tonal progression, so our 'original' perception is guided by the experience of similar melodies or patterns of tonal progression. And once the perceptual act is recognized as being informed and inflected by prior transactions with the externality of the world, then it can no longer be seen as wholly originary and 'interior'; and in turn this world can no longer be conceived as wholly unproductive and 'exterior'.

The Phenomenology of Internal Time-Consciousness therefore returns us to Derrida's reading of Husserl in *Speech and Phenomena*; for just as the exteriority of indication and signs is shown to inhere within the pure interiority of the inner voice, so the contingency of worldly experience is shown to inhere within the spontaneity of perception. But this detour allows us to draw out the specifically visual implications of Derrida's argument in *Speech and Phenomena* and elsewhere. Centrally, the dispersal of the now reveals the apparently fully present moment of perception to be inhabited by other moments of experience, and therefore undermines the opposition between inside and outside which governs Husserl's conception of perception. This insight allows us both to identify the historically determinate character of phenomenological perception, and to develop the terms of visual experience beyond the limits which it implies. The three-dimensional space and linear time presupposed by phenomenology are not, then, the necessary perceptual co-ordinates of a fixed transcendental consciousness, but themselves emerge from the contingency of experience and worldly history; therefore, they must be recognized as one possible configuration of perception. And indeed, in *Speech and Phenomena* Derrida identifies this particular transcendental organization of experience as 'one with the historical advent of the *phōnē*' and its conjunction with *technē*; that is, he identifies it with the historical culture of Europe, which is characterized by a conception of consciousness as fully present to itself, and a conception of the world as inert matter available for human manipulation and use (1973, p. 75). The separation of space and time which Husserl marks out in his analogy can itself be seen as a particular spatio-temporal configuration, and by recognizing it as such we can both identify how it structures vision according to the series of oppositions we have identified, and examine how vision might be thought beyond them.

THE EYE AND THE WORLD WITHIN SPEECH

Given Derrida's insistence on the inherence of contingency within the phenomenal eye, it is necessary to address a specific occasion of visual experience in order to illustrate the visual implications of his reading of Husserl. And in the light of the complex interplay of language, vision and 'lived experience' within this reading, a valuable site for drawing out these consequences is provided by a poem written by Frank O'Hara in 1959, 'The Day Lady Died' (1995, p. 235). O'Hara, an American poet closely associated with the New York 'schools' of painting and poetry, is perhaps now best remembered for infusing the often earnest poetry of post-war America with a quick-fire wit and camp sensibility, inspired in part by the linguistic experimentalism of Apollinaire and Reverdy's 'Cubist' poetics. Like Baudelaire, his poetry is intricately involved with the question of seeing in the city, although O'Hara's Manhattan of the late 1950s is of course much closer to the technologically organized visual culture of our present than is Baudelaire's Paris. But, perhaps most significantly, the reception of O'Hara's most well-known and frequently anthologized poem traverses the intellectual trajectory traced at the beginning of this chapter, from phenomenology to postmodernism. Initially the poem was seen to embody the central tenets of a phenomenologically inspired literary criticism, while more recently it has been read in terms of postmodern conceptions of the commodification and reification of vision. By examining these two different readings of the poem, it is possible to identify how Derrida's reading of Husserl points to different ways of approaching urban visual experience.

Written soon after Billie Holiday's death, 'The Day Lady Died' is one of O'Hara's characteristic 'I do this, I do that' poems, and revolves around a moment of interruption and recognition in which the voice of the poem is confronted by an image of the dead singer. But the poem does not take the form of a lament or a meditation on memory or death; instead, it traces the associative itinerary of the poem's perceiving consciousness during a lunchtime stroll. However, the patterning of lyric associations is complicated by their idiosyncratic location within the fragmentary perception of time and place established in the opening stanza:

> It is 12:20 in New York a Friday
> three days before Bastille day, yes
> it is 1959 and I go get a shoeshine
> because I will get off the 4:19 in Easthampton
> at 7:15 and then go straight to dinner
> and I don't know the people who will feed me

For early, phenomenologically inspired accounts, this temporal disconnection sets the scene for the essential drama of the poem, which occurs in the final moment of interruption. The poem is therefore seen to fall into two parts: the first part, comprising the bulk of the poem, is read as registering the contingency and arbitrariness of successive temporal moments through its informal register and wayward point of view:

> I walk up the muggy street beginning to sun
> and have a hamburger and a malted and buy
> an ugly NEW WORLD WRITING to see what the poets
> in Ghana are doing these days
> . . .
> and in the GOLDEN GRIFFIN I get a little Verlaine
> for Patsy with drawings by Bonnard although I do

> think of Hesiod, trans. Richard Lattimore or
> Brendan Behan's new play or *Le Balcon* or *Les Nègres*
> of Genet, but I don't, I stick with Verlaine
> after practically going to sleep with quandariness

Plans for dinner jostle with an incongruously significant date – it is 'three days before Bastille day' – and the stroll through the sunlit city bustle takes in 'a hamburger and a malted' just as easily as Ghanaian poets, Classical mythology, or Irish playwrights. According to this reading, the first part of the poem embodies linguistically the disconnection and meaninglessness of urban appearance by recording the arbitrary and fleeting impressions of the perceiving consciousness. Set against the numerical notation of exact chronological time, the profusion of proper names evokes disparate times and places, so serving to emphasize the spatial and temporal disconnection of meaning. Equally, parataxis, the persistent use of enjambment and minimal punctuation all work, in the words of one critic, to 'cal[l] attention to the rush of time piling up details united only by sequential time alien to specifically human patterns of relationships' (Altieri, 1979, p. 122). The scene of urban modernity is thus seen to comprise a series of unrelated appearances that lack any intrinsic temporal organization, and so constitutes an external world that is indifferent to the terms of human meaning.

The pivotal moment of the poem, according to this reading, occurs in the closing stanzas. Suddenly, the contingency and disconnection of urban appearance is interrupted by the jolting and instantaneous recognition of Billie Holiday's face on the front page of the newspaper, and of the headline that announces her death:

> then I go back where I came from to 6th Avenue
> and the tobacconist in the Ziegfeld Theatre and
> casually ask for a carton of Gauloises and a carton
> of Picayunes, and a NEW YORK POST with her face on it
>
> and I am sweating a lot by now and thinking of
> leaning on the john door in the 5 SPOT
> while she whispered a song along the keyboard
> to Mal Waldron and everyone and I stopped breathing

The radical disjunction between the penultimate and the last stanza is understood as marking an instant of recognition that freezes the arbitrary flow of impressions; in the words of another critic, 'finally the sequence of meaningless moments is replaced by the *one* moment of memory when Lady Day enchanted her audience', and 'time suddenly stops' (Perloff, 1977, p. 182. Within the terms of this reading, the poem itself performs the phenomenological reduction, or bracketing of the world, and so dramatizes the dynamics of perception and memory central to its account of internal time-consciousness. The instantaneous character of the final moment of recognition, its occurrence 'in the blink of an eye', is figured by the sudden temporal break that occurs in the gap between the last two stanzas. This instant marks a singular act of perception capable of gathering up and ordering the temporal disconnection of the perceptual flux. But, crucially, this temporal organization is not borrowed from the disconsolate objects of the external world, but is internal to the poem's perceiving consciousness. By recalling the dead singer in memory, the poem's perceiving consciousness orientates itself in time, setting the perceptual now alongside the reproduction of a past moment of perception. In this way, the instant of recognition provides the perceiving consciousness with the means to recollect, order, and give meaning to its own experience of time. The remembered scene of the final stanza, which reproduces a past moment of perception in all its vitality and self-identity, therefore reflects the fullness and self-presence of *this* moment of recognition, here and now, and so testifies to the unity and spontaneity of the perceiving consciousness over and against the arbitrariness of appearances.

But as recent commentators have pointed out, stated in these terms the moment of recognition offers only the circularity of *self*-recognition, for what the poem's persona sees is ultimately a function of its own intending vision (see Ross, 1990, pp. 380–91). From this perspective, the memory of the final stanza is simply a moment of the voice's self-projection, which imposes its own image of the singer rather than seeing her as she once 'really' was. The intentional nature of perception therefore becomes a kind of blindness, for such a seeing cannot see beyond the terms that structure its gaze. Thus, phenomenology's attempt to isolate a pure interiority within the productivity of perception finds itself snagged on the sharp edges of post-war American racial politics; for in such terms, the voice's identification with an image of abused African-American femininity appears as an arrogant gesture of appropriation by a white, gay, middle-class poet. Recent accounts of the poem are not surprisingly wary of making claims about this final moment of identification, and yet for John Lowney the poem nonetheless retains a certain interest (1991, pp. 244–64). Lowney seeks to identify a different kind of visual transaction at work in the poem by approaching it through Frederic Jameson's account of post-modernism. Consequently, his reading concentrates on the world of appearances detailed in the first part of the poem, so avoiding the pitfalls of intention and identification that lie in the final moment of recognition. Where phenomenological readings had dismissed this first part as mere temporal discontinuity, Lowney regards it as an assemblage of commodified meanings whose semantic intensity awaits interpretation. The apparently incongruous and superfluous reference to Bastille Day in fact fans out into a complex web of historical and geographical references. Ghana, formerly the Gold Coast, had gained independence only two years before the poem was written, offering an instance of political change that recalls the French Revolution; but it also serves as a reminder of the role of slavery in the historical foundation of the Enlightenment republic, since the Gold Coast had been an important centre for the transatlantic slave trade. As Lowney notes, this reference therefore locates Billie Holiday's African-American identity, and the police harassment she suffered towards the end of her life, within a wider set of political histories. Equally, the books that the poem's persona considers buying for Patsy open up another dimension: Behan was twice imprisoned as a member of the IRA, Genet spent much of his life in jails, and Paul Verlaine was sentenced to two years in a Belgium prison for shooting his lover Arthur Rimbaud. Set against the moral didacticism of Hesiod, these references present a potted history of modern poets and writers at odds with social authority and the *mores* of bourgeois society. Thus, the city's semantically rich but arbitrary display of cultural goods presents a composite image, which juxtaposes these moments of aesthetic transgression to the past of slavery and to Ghana's postcolonial present. The image of Billie Holiday therefore finds inadvertent resonances in the profusion of cultural commodities that saturate postmodern social space.

Lowney is able to restore a semantic richness to what had once been dismissed by earlier readings, recasting the perceptual flux as the spectacular image landscape of postmodernity. Yet he proves unable to address the questions of intentionality and recognition raised by the poem, instead offering only the conclusion that the poem 'constantly remind[s] us that the subject both constructs and is constructed by "the stream of events"' (*ibid.*, p. 263). However, this circularity is troubling, since Lowney has already defined this cultural condition through its imposition of 'the reified subjectivity of consumer capitalism' (*ibid.*, p. 259). If the parameters of the subject's seeing are ineluctably given by the scene it confronts, then visual experience is locked in a closed and unbreakable circle. The problem that emerges here is not unfamiliar, and has already been encountered in the various accounts of vision considered in chapter two. As we have seen, because these accounts simply transfer the agency of vision from the subject to the world of appearances, they render visual experience as inert and empty. Once the parameters of the subject's reified gaze are given absolutely by the commodified appearance which it confronts, then all sights have already been seen. And indeed, the limits of Lowney's reading reflect the limits of Jameson's conception of postmodern visual experience. Just as the postmodern can only be grasped by way of concepts – because the experience of postmodernity is blank and without charge – so the semantic resonances which Lowney discovers emerge only cognitively and for the critic, and are not available *within* the visual experience described by the poem. It is the critic who cognitively grasps the semantic intensity of these commodified objects, while the poem's perceiving conscious sees only the blank reproduction of the same. But in failing to address the final moment of recognition and memory, Lowney ignores the patterning of visual experience figured or performed by the poem, restricting his observations to the viewpoint of the critic. Packaged and commodified as cultural goods, the reified objects of consumer society have, in Jameson's words, 'become a vast collection of images, a multitudinous photographic simulacrum' which, unlike Rilke's statue of Apollo, can no longer 'look back' (1991, p. 18).

While phenomenological and postmodern approaches produce different readings, they are nonetheless both informed by a concept of visual experience which remains recognizably within Husserl's terms. Centrally for Husserl, perception is fully present to consciousness 'in the blink of an eye'; what is perceived is conscious, and there is nothing in perception which is not immediately available to consciousness. It is therefore 'an absurdity', as Husserl insists in *The Phenomenology of Internal Time-Consciousness*, 'to speak of a content of which we are "unconscious" [and] of which we are conscious only later' (1964, p. 162). In its initial reception, the poem is understood to exemplify the instantaneous and fully present character of the moment of perception, which locates its productivity in the interiority of consciousness and not in its transactions with the contingency of the world. Thus, while the instantaneous character of perception is figured by the radical break between the last two stanzas, its productivity is figured not by an image of what is exterior – the front page of the newspaper – but by the reproduction of a prior perception in all its vitality and self-identity. By recalling the dead singer to life, as it were, memory's exact reproduction of the intentional nexus points back to the full presence of an original moment of intending, and so confirms the interiority and unity of consciousness in the now. In Lowney's reading, this conception of intentional perception persists, although its claims for the spontaneous and originary character of consciousness have been rejected. Just as in the earlier reading, the vision of the lyric 'I' is circular – it sees just what it sees; but now consciousness is no longer the productive and originary source of coherence and meaning, but simply *reproduces* the spatio-temporal ordering of the image world which it confronts. While Jameson emphasizes the inability of the subject to unify its retentions and protentions, Lowney concentrates on pursuing the role that this inability ascribes to the critic, which is to unearth the meanings that are sedimented in commodified objects, and relate them to the new, global space of capitalism. Yet although the critic's interpretative work comes after the fact of the poem, the structure of meaning it uncovers is already in place, immured within the semantically intense but static co-ordinates of the reified appearance of the city.

Derrida's reading of Husserl allows a different understanding of the visual experience described or performed by the poem. His location of the world within the phenomenological eye allows the final moment of recognition to be conceived in terms other than phenomenology's claim for the pure interiority of perception; while his identification of the duration of the eye-blink places the temporality of seeing within the worldy history which Lowney's reading implicitly opposes to such claims. Lowney's reading is certainly valuable in tracing the patterns of significance which inhabit the cityscape as linguistic resonance, and he is right to insist that they remain irreducible to subjective intention. But what he forgets is that the objects he interprets are not offered immediately, but as *perceived*: therefore they bear not only the pasts which he finds there, but also the imprint of the pasts that have shaped their perception, a kind of recollection that cannot be reduced to conscious memory. Memory is not therefore to be separated from and opposed to perception – as either the spontaneous act of a unified consciousness or as the exclusive province of the critic – since it inheres within perception in ways that exceed the conscious recollection of the subject. From this perspective it is possible to approach the final moment of recognition without understanding it either as confirming the self-identity of the lyric 'I', or as recalling the image of Billie Holiday as she once 'really' was. The first part of the poem, which describes the routine events of a middle-class, cosmopolitan, intellectual lifestyle, can be understood as tracing a particular structuring of perception which is established linguistically through the construction of the voice of the poem. This regime of vision is characterized by a playful and apparently unrestrained engagement with the world of appearances, and by the enjoyment of the 'freedom' of commodity consumption in the metropolitan centre of Manhattan. Yet if this regime of intending is shaped by the histories which coalesce in the present, it is not identical with the social world it confronts. Indeed, as Lowney himself observes, the camp tone of 'practically going to sleep with quandariness' suggests a sensibility and a sexuality that finds itself distanced from what, in 1959, were the legally enforced norms of 'decency' and 'propriety'.

However, the point of contact between aesthetic history and the social regulation of sexuality on the one hand, and the history of imperialism and the legacy of racism on the other, only emerges

retrospectively, in the interruption and distortion of the structuring of
vision mapped in the first part of the poem. The final instant of the
poem can be understood in these terms as a moment of recognition
and recollection which makes a past nexus of intentions visible within
the perceptual present; as such, it distorts and deforms both this prior
nexus and the context of vision into which it is returned. The instant
of recognition is not a moment of fully present perception; rather,
what the lyric 'I' sees is a flickering image, inhabited or haunted by
earlier moments of desiring and intending. The memory of the final
stanza cannot therefore be isolated from the perceptual present, as the
reproduction of an earlier moment of consciousness in all its integrity
and self-identity. For its reproduction within this new context rear-
ranges the intentional nexus and so discovers a perceptual past that
was not previously available to consciousness. The heterogeneity of the
remembered perception is figured linguistically by the lineation and
lack of punctuation of the final stanza, which allows the two 'ands' of
the last line both to connect the 'I' to the remembered scene, and
simultaneously to register its distance from it, while the abrupt ending
of the poem keeps this oscillation open. In one sense the 'I' joins all
of those in the audience ('and everyone and I') in a moment of stopped
breath; but equally it remains apart, out of breath and isolated ('and I
stopped breathing') from the scene in which Lady Day sings to 'Mal
Waldron and everyone'. The memory of the 5 Spot is thus one of
both proximity and separation, identity and difference, and in its
recollection the 'I' both remembers itself and its difference to itself.
The point of contact that the poem discovers in the figure of Billie
Holiday between marginalized racial and sexual identities can therefore
be located in the play of presence and absence that occurs in the final
instant of perception. In discovering an echo of Holiday's death in its
own suspension of breath, the voice discovers unexpected and unlooked-
for histories, which become available only now, in the distorted and
inauthentic return of the past into the present. The remembered
moment in the 5 Spot interrupts and disfigures the regime of vision
established by the voice's playful and apparently unrestrained enjoyment of the cultural commodities of mid-century Manhattan, and so
forces a reconceptualization of this seeing and the pleasures which it
affords. What becomes visible through the distortion of this regime of

vision is what is of course invisible within the terms of its unity and coherence: namely the suppressions and restrictions which constitute its conditions of possibility. After all, the unseen person who gives the shoeshine in line three is more likely than not an African-American. It is significant that the image of Billie Holiday which provokes this final moment of recollection is neither named nor described in the poem; for what the image makes possible is not the certainty of an identification fully present to itself, but a glimpse or intimation from *within* this structuring of vision of the histories which configure it. What the lyric 'I' sees, then, is not an image of the dead singer as she once 'really' was, but a glimpse from within its own structuring of vision of the histories which configure the terms of its unity and coherence.

Perhaps what is most valuable about O'Hara's poem within the present context is that it dramatizes the temporal implications of what might be thought of as the purely spatial question of form. The yield which the poem identifies in visual experience is located *within* the parameters of visual coherence; but it occurs retrospectively, in the distortion of its formal unity, a distortion which opens up the after-event of the 'becoming conscious' of the different possible futures latent in the past. As Derrida observes in *Speech and Phenomena*, 'it is no accident that *The Phenomenology of Internal Time-Consciousness* both confirms the dominance of the present and rejects the "after-event" of the becoming consciousness of an "unconscious content"' (1973, p. 63). And in 'Form and Meaning', he identifies the discrete and punctual now as the principle underlying 'the metaphysical domination of the concept of form' and 'the thought of being as form' (*ibid.*, p. 108). But equally, if Derrida questions the stable distinction underlying the unity of transcendental consciousness – between 'sense' (*Sinn*) and logical 'meaning' (*Bedeutung*), or between intuition and discursive conceptuality – in this latter essay he also insists that this 'is not to contest, against Husserl, the duality of the strata and the unity of a certain passage that relates them'. Rather, he explains, it is to ask whether 'the relationships between the two strata [can] be conceived within the category of expression', and therefore 'to ask a question about *another relationship* between what is problematically called *sense* and *meaning*' (*ibid.*, p. 127).

While this proposal may seem modest, it involves a theoretical reorientation which cuts across the central approaches to vision and technology which we have examined. As the subsequent discussion of 'Form and Meaning' makes clear, Derrida explicitly distinguishes his own approach from two symmetrical responses which remain within phenomenology's terms. First, he argues that to question the relationship between sense and meaning is not 'to wish to reduce one stratum to the other, or to judge the complete recapture of sense into meaning to be impossible'; and specifically it does not seek 'to reconstruct experience (of sense) as a *language*' (*ibid.*). That is, Derrida urges against identifying intuition and concept, or perception and meaning, so reducing visual experience to the co-ordinates of discursive conceptuality. And second, the essay argues against producing 'a critique of language based on the ineffable richness of sense'. That is, Derrida rejects the alternative of simply counterposing the protean nature of intuition to the rigidity of the concept, so opposing the dynamism of visual experience to a fixed and invariable structure of rational consciousness.

Derrida's rejection of these two responses to the deconstruction of phenomenology allows us to reconsider the problems identified in chapter two in the work of Debord, Baudrillard, Virilio, and Jameson. The positions developed by Debord and Baudrillard can both be recognized in terms of the first of these responses. As we have seen, in Debord's spectacle, visual experience is equated with modern rationality and abstract meaning, leaving open only a desperate appeal to the richness of 'real' experience. In Baudrillard's notion of 'the code' the visible is identified absolutely with its framing in perception, so that visual experience is subsumed under the fixed form of logical conceptuality which he understands as the terroristic simulation of 'the real'. Consequently, the visual is reduced to the supposed clarity and absolute visibility of signs, which are to be read in terms of post-Saussurean semiotics. The positions developed by Virilio and Jameson, on the other hand, can both be recognized in terms of the second response. In each case their accounts are split between a dynamic and excessive visual realm and the perceptual unity incumbent on the rational framework of the subject, whose discursive logic demands a space and time which can be assimilated within its terms. For Jameson, technology's spatial intensification of the visual generates a 'hyperspace' that can no longer be mapped within this perceptual grid, resulting in an irreparable disjunction between experience and cognition. On the other hand, for Virilio the perceptual unity required by the rational subject migrates to the vision machine, even though the spatio-temporal conditions underlying it have been superseded by technology itself. Consequently, the repeated imposition of this perceptual frame-work takes place within an image-world whose accelerated time exceeds its spatial terms, so giving rise to a spiral of violence. In each case, the 'ineffable richness' or speed of appearances is counterposed to the conceptual co-ordinates inherited from the rational subject, which is either left disorientated before the intensity of the visible, or subsumed within inescapable technological logics. But as such, none of these four positions reaches the level of analysis demanded by Derrida's reading of Husserl. By choosing either to intensify or merge – rather than reformulate – Husserl's opposition between 'sense' and 'mean-ing', or intuition and concept, they remain within its terms. Conse-quently, none of these positions is capable of envisaging visual experience other than in terms of the perennial imprisonment within, or absolute loss of, the clarity, unity, and distinctness which have been such a feature of modern accounts of vision.

The importance of Derrida's identification of phenomenology as a particular *technic* of vision is that it articulates a different kind of questioning, one which asks how the terms of coherence and incoher-ence are themselves framed. It therefore expands the scope of analysis, from the transcendental conditions which govern the unity of percep-tual form, to the 'condition' of transcendental unity or form itself. Or to put it in visual terms, it raises the prospect of other modes of visual experience outside of the clarity, unity, and coherence that remain central for Debord, Baudrillard, Virilio, and Jameson; since from this perspective, the superimposition, blurring, or irresolution that may occur within one *technic* of vision points to other configurations of visual experience that cannot appear within its terms. If we are to pursue Derrida's insights for thinking the specifically technological condition of visual culture, it is therefore necessary to step outside the intellectual ambit of French cultural theory post-1968. Instead, the next chapter looks to the writing of the Weimar philosopher and critic Walter Benjamin in the light of his recent reinterpretation by Howard

Caygill as primarily a thinker of the visual. Read in terms of the philosophical and cultural history which we have traced, Benjamin's analysis of the technical reproducibility of the image can be recognized as an important attempt to rethink the conditions of appearance within the technologically organized experience of urban modernity.

CHAPTER 4

Urban Optics

... where nearness looks with its own eyes ...
Walter Benjamin, 'Surrealism'

TECHNOLOGY AND FORM

If the philosophical critique of phenomenology in the 1960s involved a fundamental questioning of the concept of form, the adequacy of form as a category for addressing visual experience had in fact already been put in question by technological developments dating back to the nineteenth century. As we saw in chapter one, Baudelaire's hostility to photography stemmed from his appreciation of the threat to the unity of aesthetic form posed by the photograph's inclusion of contingency. Baudelaire's insight soon found an echo in subsequent reactions to the high-speed photography famously exploited by Muybridge, Marey, and Janssen from the 1860s. While exposure time for the daguerreotype and the calotype was several minutes, the development of the collodion and then the gelatin-brominde dry-plate processes achieved exposure times of 1/1000th of a second by the 1870s and 1/6000th of a second by the 1880s; at the same time, devices like the photographic revolver allowed the rapid replacement of the photographic plate. Such exponential improvements made possible a high-speed photography that revealed a visual world not available to the naked eye, as most famously exemplified by Muybridge's photographs of a galloping race-horse. As Aaron Scharf notes, contemporary reactions to high-speed photography perceived this revelation as a challenge to the authority of the human eye and the representational conventions considered proper to it (1974, pp. 14–15). For what high-speed photography captured was a visible world that escaped the unaided vision of the human eye.

However, Steven Neale has argued that a counter-tendency also emerged through the nineteenth century with the development of devices like Plateau's Phénakistiscope, which was able to produce the illusion of movement by running a series of images before the eye in quick succession. While high-speed photography produced an image-world which disconcertingly exceeds the space and time of human vision, such devices appeared to reintegrate the visible within specifically human terms, so restoring the eye's authority and the representational unity on which it rested. Thus Janssen, the inventor of the photographic revolver, counterposed his own invention to the Phénakistiscope, observing that each addressed a complementary problem: while the photographic revolver 'provides analysis of a phenomenon' by breaking it down into 'the series of its basic component elements', the 'Phénakistiscope is designed to reproduce the illusion of movement' by running together or reunifying 'the series of elements that comprise the movement'. For Neale, the subsequent development of Edison's Kinetograph and Kinetoscope in 1890, and of projected film by the Lumière brothers in 1895, strengthened this sense of reunification and reintegration, and so worked to contain the unsettling effects of high-speed photography by reinstating the formal unity of vision (1985, pp. 37–40).

Whether or not this account of film's role in re-establishing the unity of form and the authority of the eye is accepted, its conjunction of filmic technology and optical authority is representative of broader tendencies within contemporary understandings of film and its exemplary status for contemporary visual culture. Of particular relevance here is the work of critics associated with 'apparatus theory', a term identified most prominently with the writing of Christian Metz and Jean-Louis Baudry. While Baudelaire saw in technology an implacable challenge to the formal unity desired by aesthetic perception, apparatus theory stresses the ideological function of film technology, and more broadly the institutional apparatus of cinema. For apparatus theory, the spectator identifies not so much with the characters on the screen as with the camera's privileged viewpoint, which produces the effect of a unified 'reality' through its organization and arrangement of temporally and spatially discontinuous visual fragments. The spatial and temporal disjunction that appears to be inherent within film technology is therefore understood as the necessary prerequisite for the construction of a unified diegetic world – the fictional space and time within which the profilmic 'story' unfolds. In a certain sense the screen becomes analogous to the mirror in Lacan's account of the 'mirror stage', in that it provides an image-world whose intensified 'reality' or coherence subordinates the spectator and binds it within a unified and necessarily ideological identity. In these terms, technology determines and is identical with the formal parameters of perception, which reduces the experience of viewing to an inert reproduction of a technologically ordered form.[1] For Martin Jay, apparatus theory marks the culmination of the 'anti-ocularcentrism' of twentieth-century French thought, and as such it provides an important context for the work of post-1968 cultural critics (1993, p. 484). This affinity has been elaborated by Josh Cohen, who, while identifying significant differences, nonetheless argues that Paul Virilio's analysis of the 'cinematic derealization' of social space effectively extrapolates apparatus theory's understanding of technology, form, and spectatorship into an account of contemporary culture (1998, pp. 75–7). Cohen's insight might also be extended to Baudrillard, since Metz's account of film's construction of a fetishistic, 'hyper-real' image-world as a compensation for the inaccessibility of the 'real' finds a significant echo in Baudrillard's conception of the simulacrum and the 'loss of the real'. In these terms, the affinity between apparatus theory and the concerns of a broader cultural criticism locates film as a key location for thinking the relationship between technology and form.

Given the broader conceptual role of film, it is significant that both Virilio and Baudrillard ascribe a paradigmatic role to film animation in particular. The attraction of animation for these critics lies in its ability to exemplify a particular paradox central to their respective accounts of contemporary culture; namely that the loss of the 'real' is accompanied by its widespread simulation. The dominant style of Hollywood animation is seen to capture this paradox perfectly, for while it employs the representational conventions of live-action film – so signifying the 'real' – the world it represents is itself 'unreal', or a world of images. Thus, for Baudrillard, the cartoon form seems to

---

[1] For major statements of these positions, see Metz, 1986 and Baudry, 1974–5.

perfectly embody his most economical formulation of the simulacrum, which he describes in 'Simulacra and Simulations' (1981) as an image that 'bears no relation to any reality whatever' (1988B, p. 170). In contrast to, say, the photographic image, which might claim to stand for or reproduce an original 'reality', the cartoon form is a reproduction that lacks any such moment of origin. Baudrillard's claim that 'Disneyland is a perfect model of all the entangled orders of simulation' effectively inverts the fetishistic status ascribed by Metz to the cinema screen: where film provides a simulation of a 'real' that is unattainable, Disneyland provides the simulation of the 'unreal' which would provide an alibi for 'Los Angeles and the America surrounding it', which are in fact 'no longer real' (*ibid*., p. 171–2). Virilio's understanding of animation echoes this approach, although, as we might expect, his analysis is less static and more nuanced due to its awareness of the temporal implications of reproduction. While his account of the 'vision machine' is centred on the wider historical impact of film, his most sustained statement of the violent implications of visual technologies in *War and Cinema* allots a paradigmatic role to film animation. Here, the conjunction between the optical regime of the vision machine and the violent prospects of contemporary society are located within an extended genealogy which stretches back to the Bayeaux tapestry and culminates in animated film. Animation exemplifies the impact of a wide range of optical technologies because its articulation of vision perfectly describes their direct temporal organization of consciousness: 'the macro-cinematography of aerial reconnaissance, the cable-television of panoramic radar, the use of slow or accelerated motion in analysing the phases of an operation', Virilio writes, 'all this converts the commander's plan into an animated cartoon or flow chart' (1989, p. 79).

While the jump from cartoons to military technology may appear exorbitant, the central issue for Virilio is animation's illumination of 'the segmentation of images'. This segmentation reduces visual experience to an 'unscrolling', ordered according to an abstract temporal logic rather than the particularities of spatial location, a reduction which Virilio sees as underlying modernity's increasing propensity for violence. 'In this realm', he argues, 'sequential perception, like optical phenomena resulting from retinal persistence, is both origin and end of the apprehension of reality'; for once technology obliterates any stable sense of spatial dimension, then the perception of movement 'is but a statistical process connected with the nature of the segmentation of images and the speed of observation characteristic of humans' (*ibid.*). For Virilio, then, animated film describes the fundamental rearticulation of visual experience through which technology meshes with the physiological mechanism of retinal retention. Animation's exemplary status derives from its basic technical principle, which is simply the capacity to take frame-by-frame exposures. Unlike live-action film – where at least within individual shots the 'natural' flow of events might be understood to be recorded – in animation the tempo of succession is ordered exclusively by the technical apparatus and its relation to retinal retention. Because the shot is reduced to a single frame, and every shot is therefore followed by an edit, then the achievement of coherence has no relation to the spatial relations in which events occur – as in live-action film – but is purely temporal. The effect of continuity in animation is therefore more completely artificial, since it borrows nothing from 'nature', but is wholly derived from the technological arrangement and sequencing of disconnected images. In animation, according to Virilio, the technological ordering of images is 'plugged' directly into consciousness, circumventing the attentiveness to the texture of environmental space once exhibited by phenomenology's embodied eye.

For Baudrillard and Virilio, cartoon animation dramatizes both the spectator's subordination to the technological image and the inert character of visual experience, in which all sights have already been seen. Yet animation sits uncomfortably within critical frameworks organized around the oppositional categories of the 'real' and the 'non-real', categories which appear to have little purchase on its characteristics as a visual medium. In order to construe animation in these terms, it must be thought of primarily in terms of the Disney style that came to dominate American animation in the 1930s, a style which can be associated with the classic Hollywood narrative system and its protocols of shot construction and invisible editing. But while the frame of 'realism' remains ill-fitting even in this case, it is much less appropriate when applied to early animation. As a number of critics have demonstrated, notions of 'realistic' representation are not particularly helpful in examining the development of animation in the United States in the first decades of the twentieth century. But, if early animation challenges the basic assumptions involved in claims for the 'loss of the real', it also provides a valuable way of approaching the work of the German philosopher and critic Walter Benjamin. Benjamin's cultural criticism is often assimilated to contemporary understandings of the spectacle or the simulacrum because of its engagement with the technical reproducibility of images, most famously staged around his discussion of the technology of film. However, this chapter argues that Benjamin's understanding of technical reproducibility needs to be placed within a quite different conceptual trajectory, central to which is his consideration of visual experience in terms of colour. In revealing a different conception of the relationship between technology and form, early animation dramatizes some of the central issues involved in Benjamin's approach.

CAT AND MOUSE

The commercial dominance achieved by the Disney studios in the late 1930s makes it tempting to see the development of animation as leading ineluctably towards an increasingly 'realistic' animation. In these terms, the history of animation traces a halting progression towards the simulation of live-action shot construction and match cutting, and the adoption of a 'personality animation' which focuses narrative action on individualized and consistent characters (see, for example, Maltin, 1987). However, in *Before Mickey*, Donald Crafton argues that such an understanding of the emergence of animation in the United States remains unsatisfactory, first because it underestimates the extent to which animation was influenced by a range of visual registers and narrative forms above and beyond the important influence of live-action film, and second because it misunderstands the pleasures offered by film animation. Early animation was strictly limited by what were relatively high production costs in comparison with live-action film, and within these economic and technical constraints, the spare visual style and episodic nature of the newspaper cartoon strip provided a more serviceable model than live-action cinema. Therefore, by the 1920s, American animated cartoons tended to concentrate on a central protagonist defined by a number of repeated actions or characteristic gestures, and to follow a short, episodic narrative based around a series of loosely related visual jokes or transformations. Within these conditions, differentiation and innovation were achieved through the development of a range of distinctive visual regimes, which defined the parameters of humour and mood associated with the different 'trade-mark' protagonists. 'Thus', Crafton writes, 'when we think of Koko or Felix, we invariably associate them with the idiosyncratic visual environments we have come to recognize by viewing more and more of their films' (1993, p. 272). These visual environments each present different 'imaginative attempt[s] to assimi-late the staggering developments of . . . science and technology' by harnessing the technical possibilities of animation within a range of existing narrative and visual forms (*ibid.*, p. 32). For Crafton, the two most prominent visual environments were associated with the cartoons directed for Disney by Ubbe Iwerks – especially the Oswald series and the early Mickey Mouse films – and the series which dominated animation in the mid-1920s until being displaced by Disney, namely the Felix the Cat cartoons produced by Pat Sullivan and animated by Otto Messmer.[2] In these terms, neither Felix nor Mickey offer visual regimes which are primarily orientated towards 'realism', but instead present different responses to the technologically informed visual world of urban modernity.

By the mid-1920s, the popularity of Felix the Cat rivalled that of even Charlie Chaplin, and Sullivan's Felix films were far more successful than the output of the Disney studios prior to Mickey Mouse. In fact, as Crafton notes, Felix's characteristic movements were partly modelled on Chaplin, as well as drawing on the conven-tions of racial stereotyping prevalent in popular iconography and commercial art, and a comparison between the two is revealing. Felix's idiosyncratic persona was registered both by a series of repeated gestures (pacing back and forth, slapping his fist into the palm of his hand) and by the plasticity and detachable nature of his body: like

---

[2] Oswald was a rabbit who closely resembled Felix but with long ears, and was the main forerunner of Mickey Mouse. The Oswald series were made by the Disney studio in 1927 and 1928 and were distributed by Universal.

Chaplin tipping his hat, Felix tips his scalp and ears, or twirls his detached tail which has become a walking cane. Felix's debt to Chaplin's gestural lexicon also extends to his basic disposition to the world: like the tramp, Felix is in perennial conflict with his social and physical environment, suffering social discrimination in films like *Felix Revolts* (1924) and *Flim Flam Films* (1927), while more generally battling a myriad range of objects, instruments, animals, and humans. However, according to Crafton, the crucial feature of the Felix series is that Felix's plasticity is extended not simply to particular objects or instruments but to his environment as a whole. Not only objects, but space itself is hyperkinetic in the Felix films, and constantly shifts, folds, and mutates. In *Whys and Otherwise*, probably made in the second half of the 1920s, city blocks rush past the inebriated Felix at frightening speed, while the lock on his front door runs from his key. In *Felix the Cat Woos Whoopee* (1930), buildings sway and neon signs blink rhythmically, a clock tower transforms into an alarm clock when striking the hour, a fish turns into a saxophone and then a monster, and a street light turns first into a coy 'oriental' maiden and then a dragon; in *Oceanantics* (1930) a dancing door turns into Felix, while in *Sure-locked Homes* (1928), a threatening shadow becomes a gorilla, and shirts transform into ghosts that chase Felix across a moving landscape. This extended plasticity was often used to render subjective states such as hallucinations, intoxication, and dream sequences which, as Crafton notes, often employed 'pyrotechnic alternating positive–negative frames, dizzying spiral tunnel effects, and strange distortions of space' (*ibid.*, p. 332). In *Flim Flam Films* such techniques were used to render the image-world of the film camera itself, so that we see a bathing beauty distorted as through a fish-eye lens, soldiers parading upside down, and a balloon 'ascending' from the top of the frame to the bottom.

According to Crafton, what is distinctive about the visual dynamism and mutability of the Felix cartoons is that that it has no limits: there are no dream-framing devices or clear boundaries that distinguish the unstable and constantly mutating spacetime of these hallucinatory worlds from a 'rational' or 'normal' world that might be inhabited outside them. Citing the contemporary French critic Marcel Brion, who described Felix in 1927 as a '*sur-chat*', Crafton aligns the visual world of the Felix cartoons with Surrealism and with the work of the pioneering French animator Emile Cohl (*ibid.*, p. 349). In this visual world, Crafton observes, 'grotesque monsters, exotic landscapes, and impossible disjunctions of space and time are "normal" recurring motifs . . . and [Felix] accepts them with aplomb'; and because 'Felix's world is already in excess of anything one might find in a dream', then 'to show him awakening would be superfluous' (*ibid.*, pp. 341–2). This visual matrix in turn inflects the nature of Felix's perennial struggle with his social and physical world; for if Felix battles his environment, his aim is not to bring it to order, but to survive and pursue his desires through a cunning that employs a similarly mutable and transformative logic. Thus, when the keyhole dodges Felix's proffered key in *Whys and Otherwise*, the exclamation mark that springs from his head is quickly put to use as an alternative keyhole; in *Non-stop Fright* (1927) the numerals on a road sign provide Felix with spectacles, a pipe, and a chair; and in *Flim Flam Films* Felix and his offspring gain entry to the segregated cinema ('No Cats') by pouring themselves into the incoming electric wires, emerging inside within a light fitting. Felix's own body thus proves as adjustable and multi-functional as his environment, and it suffers the same kinds of transformation, detachment, and refunctioning. And because Felix's struggle with his environment occurs within and by means of its disjunctive and unstable space and time, he is subject to its laws of transformation and recombination, and so does not feel pain. The detachable nature of his limbs is accepted as an inevitable facet of animation's logic and, as Crafton observes, 'acknowledges that these parts actually exist separately as sheets, cels and cutouts', just as his environment does (*ibid.*, p. 343). Mishap and physical upset are therefore always grasped as an opportunity within the unpredictable spacetime of animation, rather than as an occasion for suffering; so in *Non-stop Fright* the swirling stars that appear above Felix's head after a fall serve as a handy propeller for his aeroplane.

Through the 1920s, Disney films reflected the commercial dominance of the Felix cartoons, with characters such as Julius and Oswald more or less modelled on Felix's distinctive appearance.[3] However,

---

[3] Julius was the animated cat in the Alice films, the earliest of Disney's regular cartoon series which for financial reasons combined live action and animation.

for Crafton, such similarities mask the development of a very different visual regime, which becomes increasingly recognizable first in the Oswald and then the Mickey Mouse cartoons. Crafton stakes out this divergence by identifying the different affinities of these respective image-worlds with contemporary live-action film, although as we shall see, this comparison involves a wider frame of visual reference: 'if Felix's balletic movements and victimization by the environment are seen to be derived from Chaplin's screen character', Crafton argues, 'then Oswald may be viewed as closer to [Buster] Keaton and his ability to transform the absurd mechanical environment of the modern world into something useful and humane' (*ibid.*, p. 295). This contrast has been developed by Merrit and Kaufman in terms which address increasing simulation of live-action techniques by Disney films, but without at the same time reducing its stylistic development to the pursuit of a kind of 'realism'. The central dynamic identified by Merritt and Kaufman is Disney's attempt to incorporate the mutable or Surrealistic image-world of the Felix cartoons, but within the terms of his own 'gamut of romantic styles'. By the late 1920s, Merritt and Kaufman argue, 'Disney, the least surreal of animators, figured out how to absorb this alien, uncongenial style into his work . . . by incorporating it into character design and behaviour, *not through environmental distortion*' (1993, p. 26; emphasis added).

Merritt and Kaufman identify two complementary elements involved in this process of assimilation: first, the deliberate and consistent approximation of live action protocols of framing, camera movement, and match cutting; and second, the withdrawal of plasticity and hyperkineticism from the environment and its concentration within discrete objects and characters. Disney was not the first animation studio to simulate the visual syntax of live-action film, though previously they tended to be used sporadically; in contrast, from the Oswald cartoons of 1927 onwards, Disney films were marked by an increasingly consistent simulation of the camera set-ups and cutting patterns of contemporary silent features, resulting in a visual style that established a stable and coherent environment within which action takes place. According to Merritt and Kaufman, the corollary of this shift was the localization of plasticity and hyperkineticism within particular bodies, whether of characters or things, which allowed for the sexualization of inanimate objects, the infantilization of the central characters, and the mechanization of animals and things. In the case of the protagonists – first Oswald, then Mickey and Minnie – the concentration on facial gesture and the application of 'squash and stretch' principles to their bodies designates them as sites of sensation and pain; like infants, their responsive bodies demand to be stroked and touched, while also allowing the spectator the voyeuristic pleasure of watching pain. In contrast, the plasticity of the inanimate object or animal which the protagonist uses or struggles against is figured as mechanical, so that they are either 'exploited as a helpless puppet' – as most famously is the case with the musical goat in *Steamboat Willie* (1928) – or regarded 'as a domineering tyrant' to be battled and overcome (*ibid.*, p. 28).

The comparative analysis proposed by Crafton, and developed by Merritt and Kaufman, can be extended in order to understand the Felix series and the Disney cartoons as offering alternative articulations of the relationship between technology and form, rather than seeing them as progressive steps towards an approximation of cinematic 'realism', with its implicit equation of technology and form. Each of these articulations can be understood as proposing different ways of responding to or assimilating the dynamic and unstable space and time of urban modernity; and each exploits the technical capacities of film animation to register a situation in which form becomes mobile and subject to dissolution, reversal, and transformation. However, in the case of the emergent Disney style, the dynamism and mutability of contemporary experience is not figured as the condition of vision, but is rather absorbed within discrete objects and bodies, whose plastic character figures alternatively as sensory responsiveness and as a mechanical transformability. The result is a visual register that at once utilizes the technical resources of animation while at the same time restricting them in ways amenable to traditional semantic and narrative forms. Centrally, the dissolution of visual form is subordinated to a closed economy of pain and pleasure, in which the plasticity of form is orientated towards the finality of the protagonist's wish, regardless of whether it is fulfilled or remains comically unfulfilled. So, in *Plane Crazy* (1928), while an old motor chassis can be stretched and pulled by Mickey into an aeroplane in order to grant his wish for flight, it remains recalcitrant and cantankerous, and sends him finally crashing back to the earth. The film thus exploits the mutability of form with considerable verve, both by the animation and transformation of objects, and by the multiplicity of viewpoints accessed through flight. However, if this is true, the pain figured in Mickey's final dazed state works to subordinate this mutability to the narrative of fulfilment or unfulfilment. By locating the plasticity of objects and bodies within a coherent and stable visual frame, animation's technical capacity to figure the temporal instability of form is circumscribed within a restricted semantic field, organized around the desire for a future in which form is finally fixed. The visual dynamism made technically possible by animation is therefore simultaneously celebrated and subordinated to the traditional narrative of the wish, in which the tension of stored-up anticipation strains irresistibly towards the moment of final release.[4]

In the case of the Felix cartoons, the technical capacities of animation are also played out or framed within inherited forms. However, the diegetic unity increasingly pursued by live-action film is not privileged, but rather takes its place alongside the flattened image space of the newspaper cartoon strip and the multiple planes of commercial art and advertising, observable on a single page of an illustrated magazine or in a glance down a city street. As a result, animation's capacity to render the mutability and dissolution of form is matched by the permeability and interpenetration of different spatial matrices. So in *Oceantics*, Felix gains access to provisions by reaching across into the middle distance and plucking a door from the front of a house; because the door's dimensions are proportionally reduced due to perspectival recession, it serves admirably within the enlarged foreground as a hatch through which to lay hold of the desired cheese. In turn, the cheese transforms into a music roll and is inserted into the pianola displayed on an adjacent advertising hoarding, producing music which animates the shirts in the nearby laundry (cf. Crafton, 1993, p. 343).

---

[4] In the case of *Plane Crazy*, the ease with which the narrative lends itself to pithy summary – say, 'never meddle' or 'pride comes before a fall' – prefigures the moralism that predominates in Disney's later films, when it was increasingly called upon to mitigate the sadistic implications of their economy of pain and pleasure.

Here, animation's technical propensity to reveal the temporal instability of form is not framed within a stable spatial matrix as in Disney, but is echoed or reproduced by the simultaneity of heterogeneous formal frames or visual registers. The plasticity of Felix's world is not 'formless', but emerges from the interplay between the different spatial matrices available within urban American culture. This interplay works in two different directions, producing tears or distortions within individual spatial matrices, while at the same time generating associations and resemblances between them. Thus, in reaching to pluck the miniaturized door, Felix 'tears' the perspectival arrangement of space implied by the scene's proportional recession, so that its three-dimensional space instantly flattens and assumes two dimensions. However, this action also appeals to another, simultaneous mode of recognition; for although we may understand that receding objects are bigger than they appear, we also perceive them within the plane as corresponding to the dimensions of smaller objects in the foreground. In disrupting one regime of vision, this distortion also reveals modes of correspondence or patterning that cut across such apparently immutable distinctions. Equally, when Felix inserts the tubular cheese into the perspectivally rendered but flat space of the advertising hoarding, the flat image instantly fills out to assume three dimensions. Here, the visual correlation between two three-dimensional images reveals that they nonetheless inhabit different spatial matrices. The collisions between different spaces and planes produced by the inter-penetration of incompatible formal registers therefore proceed along two different axes. On the one hand, they serve to reveal the 'edges' or limits of different spatial matrices, which when viewed in their own terms remain invisible; on the other, they discover resemblances which align what are otherwise heterogeneous spatial configurations. And because this shifting milieu provides the visual condition for these cartoons in their entirety, rather than being absorbed within discrete objects or bodies, the protagonist cannot be separated out and opposed to it. Felix himself inhabits, and is subject to, the collisions and mutations of space that comprise this visual environment, which is why it makes no sense for his body to register pain. Felix's body cannot become the central site for marking disfigurement and physical distortion, because this condition has itself become generalized.

Consequently, although Felix's desires motivate his immediate engagements with his environment, they do not provide a temporal organization which would orientate the dissolution of forms towards a final moment of equilibrium and stasis. It is not simply that Felix begins afresh in each weekly episode – as does, of course, Mickey – but rather that his desires and actions are always contingent and tactical, perennially pursuing and exploiting the permeability and mutability of form, rather than seeking to bring the visual environment to order. In contrast to the developing Disney style, animation's temporal dissolution of forms is not made so easily amenable to conventional semantic frames, but instead works precisely by cutting across visual and narrative expectations.

Within the terms of this analysis, the emergence of the dominant Disney style is not so much a matter of the progressive approximation of filmic realism, as the success of one response to contemporary visual experience within a broader set of circumstances. The Disney films managed the visual environment of the day through a particular combination of voyeurism, empathy, and wish, and crucially, were quick to enlist ongoing technological developments in sound and colour in order to achieve the high-production values of the Silly Symphonies of the early 1930s. In contrast, Messmer's black-and-white Felix films lacked the tonal range, sound quality, and lustrous colour displayed by Disney's Oscar-winning *Three Little Pigs* (1933); but nor could they offer the particular combination of empathy and sadism offered by the stretch-and-pull animation developed by Iwerks, or the narrative articulation of wish that in the early Mickey Mouse films is still free of explicit moralism. As a result, the Felix cartoons soon lost their commercial dominance, and increasingly appeared outmoded and dull.[5] Yet, in retrospect, these cartoons can be seen to involve another kind of visual inventiveness and complexity, even though they are largely composed of bare black lines and squiggles. The humour of these

[5] Animation history does not of course stop here. While the onset of Disney's dominance saw the widespread approximation of a consistent, three-dimensional diegetic space, much of the humour of the animated shorts of the 1940s depended on the mutability and elasticity of its co-ordinates. So Tom chases Jerry within an interior space that at first sight recalls live-action film, but the chase covers distances that cannot be accommodated within its dimensions, which we soon realize are variable and capable of being extended or contracted.

cartoons lies in their ability to utilize the technical resources of film animation in order to reveal the limits of the different visual regimes that are brought to bear in their viewing. They exploit the visual dynamism and mutability made possible by film technology in order to overlay and conflate incompatible formal paradigms, setting in motion the different visual regimes that crowd contemporary urban culture. The distortions and correspondences produced serve to reveal the limits of these inherited formal registers, but at the same time they also point to modes of seeing that cannot be articulated within them. In their stark black-and-white depiction, these cartoons are able to gesture from *within* the two- and three-dimensional world of forms to configurations of visual experience which exceed these parameters. In these terms, early animation anticipates some of the central insights offered by Benjamin in his analysis of the technical reproducibility of images. Benjamin's approach is wagered on the radical historicity of the space and time of experience, in contrast to the accounts of contemporary visual culture examined in chapter two, which either fail to address the spatio-temporal implications of technical reproducibility, or fix their analysis around a point of origin now lost. Benjamin's reassessment of the nature of visual experience requires a far-reaching reformulation of the terms of modern philosophy and its thinking of vision, and this chapter attempts to identify the broader conceptual commitments that inform his approach. Yet at the same time, the distinctiveness of this approach can be identified in a more straight-forward fashion: for while Debord, Baudrillard, Virilio, and Jameson all address vision primarily in terms of the perception of form, Benjamin's approach starts with the experience of colour.

THE COLOUR OF EXPERIENCE

If it is possible to find continuities between the philosophical tradition that stretches from Descartes to Husserl on the one hand, and the accounts of technological culture provided by Debord, Baudrillard, Virilio, and Jameson on the other, then one point on which they all agree is the priority of form in addressing vision. Within this context, Howard Caygill's recent reinterpretation of Benjamin's work in terms of 'the colour of experience' locates it as a significant resource for rethinking vision within the conditions of technological modernity. Caygill is able to identify the relevance of Benjamin's thought for contemporary debates over visual culture and technology because his reading departs from the concentrated focus on Benjamin's philosophy of language which has tended to guide his reception. Rather than reading Benjamin in terms of a linguistic metacritique of Kant, Caygill relates Benjamin's disparate engagements – with Kant, with the philosophy of language, with literature, with critical history and the historicity of interpretation, with urban culture, and with the new technologies of reproduction – to his early and abiding interest in visual experience. Caygill's approach is not designed to reduce the complexity and range of these engagements to a central philosophical 'core', but to articulate the philosophical implications of their disparate nature. Indeed, he argues that Benjamin's thought is best understood 'as an attempt to extend the limits of experience treated within philosophy to the point where the identity of philosophy is jeopardized'. For Caygill, one of the central ways in which Benjamin 'makes philosophy vulnerable' is his insistence that the 'paradigm of experience is not linguistic signification but chromatic differentiation' (1998, p. xiv). Benjamin's consideration of colour is therefore understood as allowing him to extend the concept of experience beyond the perception of form, while at the same time locating this excess *within* the terms of formal perception. Caygill argues that by reconceptualizing visual experience in this way, Benjamin is able to address the impact of technology without conceiving it in terms of a fixed and immutable fate.

A sense of Benjamin's developing understanding of the relationship between colour and form can be gained from his early reflections on imagination and colour. In a short, unpublished fragment from 1916 entitled 'A Child's View of Colour', Benjamin contrasts two ways of viewing colour: one that emerges from children's toys, games, and drawings, and from the books produced for them; and one proper to the world of adults (1996, vol. 1, pp. 50–1). The contrast Benjamin develops here draws on the fascination of young children with the transparency and mobility of colour 'as in soap bubbles', a fascination easily lost in the transition to adult life and maturity. According to this fragment, adults 'abstract from colour, regarding it as a deceptive cloak for individual objects existing in time and space'. However, to the child's eyes colour 'is not a layer of something superimposed on matter'; rather, 'where colour provides the contours', Benjamin writes, 'objects are not reduced to things but are constituted by an order consisting of an infinite range of nuances' (*ibid.*, vol. 1, p. 50). Consequently, children's drawings are not concerned with representation but, according to Benjamin, 'take colourfulness as their point of departure'. Consequently, they are not organized in three-dimensional space, nor are they concerned with rendering opaque surfaces or planes which can be synthesized to construct objects; 'there is no reference to form, area or concentration in a single space', Benjamin writes, since 'their goal is colour in its greatest possible transparency' (*ibid.*, vol. 1, p. 51). While these observations may seem excessively anecdotal, they in fact draw on Benjamin's developing dissatisfaction with the academic neo-Kantianism which dominated his university studies; and when the terms of this contrast are read through Benjamin's earlier 'Aphorisms on Imagination and Colour' (1914/15), this comparison can be seen as recognizably addressing this context *(ibid.*, vol. 1, pp. 48–9). The central problem with existing philosophical approaches to perception for Benjamin is that they presuppose the unity and adequacy of form; or, in Kantian terms, they proceed by way of the application of law or the 'canon' to a sensory manifold arranged in three-dimensional space. The adult perspective described in 'A Child's View of Colour' embodies the formal orientation of such a conception of vision, whose 'task is to provide a world order'. Within such 'law-given circumstances', colour is reduced to a purely passive 'content' which simply renders 'the blotchy skin of things'. In these terms, the activity of consciousness is reserved to the law-giving understanding, while the receptivity of the imagination casts the objects of experience as passive data. Benjamin looks to rearticulate this approach by animating or energizing the receptivity of perception. He does this by extending his analysis of visual experience to include colour, a move which has considerable consequences. As Benjamin explains, while the imagination is not to be equated with perception's organization of the sensible world through form – 'which is the concern of law' – it does nonetheless engage with the world through colour, which 'can never be single and pure' but is instead 'full of light and shade, full of movement, arbitrary and always beautiful' (*ibid.*, vol. 1, p. 51).

Two central points emerge here which are crucial to understanding Benjamin's developing approach. First, colour provides Benjamin with a way of extending his conception of visual experience that supplements the traditional concentration on form, or the application of law. In 'Aphorisms on Imagination and Colour', Benjamin describes the perception of form in terms of 'a theory of harmony' that depends on the single 'transition from light to shade', within which 'an infinite range of possibilities' are 'systematically assembled'. Thus, while there are an infinite range of possible forms, this infinity is bounded or contained within the co-ordinates of three-dimensional space, of which the variety of forms are simply permutations (*ibid.*, vol. 1, p. 48). The perception of form reduces visual experience to a geometrical arrangement of planes in space, and so fixes the sensory manifold as the 'symptom' of a single, monochromatic configuration of experience. In contrast, Benjamin argues that colour cannot be thought in terms of such a theory of harmony, because it 'is fluid, the medium of all changes, and not a symptom' (*ibid.*, vol. 1, p. 50). Whereas the linear geometry of three-dimensional space is ordered by the single opposition between light and shade, the value of colours emerges in their changing relation to surrounding colours. As Benjamin notes, 'colour does not relate to optics the way the line relates to geometry', and therefore is not to be thought of in terms of a series of opaque planes whose value is fixed within a static spatial arrangement (*ibid.*, vol. 1, p. 49). Rather, colour is to be understood as a shifting 'medium' or continuum, wherein the mixing of transparent colours produces infinitely varying nuances, and not simply permutations of a single, monochromatic contrast. The second point to emerge here is one that is easily lost sight of given Benjamin's comparative approach in 'A Child's View of Colour', but which is stated emphatically at the beginning of his 'Aphorisms on Imagination and Colour'. Here Benjamin insists that 'the gaze of the imagination is a gaze *within the canon*', although it does not proceed 'in accordance with it' (*ibid.*, vol. 1, p. 48; emphasis added) That is, for Benjamin there is *no pure seeing of colour*, since colour can only be perceived through 'the canon' of form. His analytical comparison between colour and form is therefore artificial, in the sense that it extrapolates or separates out what cannot be so distinguished in experience. As Benjamin observes, colour is always 'distorted by its existence in space', and indeed 'this is the origin of light and shade' (*ibid.*). The seeing of forms, or of objects in space, is itself a mode of the experience of colour, but one in which the infinite nuances of colour are reduced to the monochromatic contrast of light and shade, and so are distorted.

The extension of the concept of experience through colour lies at the heart of Caygill's reinterpretation of Benjamin. Caygill's reading traces the complex interconnections between Benjamin's reflections on colour and his avowed project of 'recasting' Kant's transcendental philosophy as a 'transcendental but speculative philosophy'.[6] In so doing, Caygill indicates how Benjamin's revaluation of visual experience opens it to new configurations and futures. The central terms of this interpretation are established by charting Benjamin's elucidation of Kant's critical philosophy through his reflections on space and colour. As Caygill observes, Benjamin's account of the perception of form corresponds to Kant's transcendental viewpoint: form is understood as inscription upon a plane or surface which provides its conditions of legibility, or the conditions of experience. But 'what is not Kantian', according to Caygill, is the way that Benjamin 'situates the particularity of the transcendental condition of experience within the speculative context of the infinite configuration of surfaces'. Benjamin's conception of colour – as paradoxically existing only *within* the parameters of form, while at the same time *exceeding* them – is thus understood by Caygill as allowing Benjamin to conceive of experience as a 'double infinity', wherein 'the "transcendental" is made up of the conditions of legibility afforded by a particular surface, while the "speculative" comprises the set of such possible surfaces of legibility'. Kant's recognition that an infinite range of perceptions or 'readings' is possible within a given set of conditions of experience, is therefore 'supplemented by the speculative claim that these conditions are themselves but one of an infinite set of possible surfaces or conditions of experience' (1998, p. 4).

Benjamin's understanding of visual experience as a 'double infinity' provides an approach that is not exclusively focused on the perception

---

[6] Caygill, 1998, pp. 2–3; this phrase is taken from 'On Perception' in Benjamin, 1996, vol. 1, p. 95.

of form, setting it apart from the other accounts we have considered. Crucially, such an approach is able to engage both with the elements of legibility and coherence encountered in visual experience, and the elements of incoherence or distortion which it involves. This capacity is emphasized by Caygill in his reading of Benjamin's early consideration of colour in 'The Rainbow: A Dialogue on Phantasy' (1915/16).[7] Here the colours of painting are described by Benjamin as being a 'reflection' of the infinite configuration of colour, which are framed or articulated through the parameters of form. The reflected colours of painting therefore mark a reduction of infinite configuration to the bounded infinity of inscription, which is ordered according to the single contrast between light and shade. As Caygill argues, Benjamin's central concern here is to identify how 'in painting the being-there of things is not configured chromatically through the medium of colour but inscribed upon space as an infinitely extended surface'. This articulation, Caygill explains, 'severely distorts the colour of experience since it translates the chromatic configuration of the *Dasein* of things into events inscribed upon a defined spatial surface', so 'limiting and distorting their appearance' (1998, p. 11). However, for Benjamin, such distortions are neither to be dismissed nor teleologically overcome, for there is no access to the infinity of configuration except through particular surfaces of inscription. As such, distortion offers an intimation of infinite configuration from within the restricted surface of inscription, an idea which, as we shall see, Benjamin develops more fully through the concept of 'similarity'. Caygill illustrates Benjamin's novel attitude to visual distortion through an analogy with the projection of the spherical dimensions of the globe onto the two-dimensional surface of a map: here, the information lost in the process of projection is nonetheless registered in the distortion and warping manifest in the two-dimensional image. Equally, we might understand this conception of experience through the terms of our analysis of early animation: for it is precisely in the moments of distortion and incompatibility that the Felix cartoons gesture from within the world of forms to different modes of experience.

---

[7] This fragment was rediscovered in 1977 and is not currently available in English translation; see Caygill, 1998, pp. 9–10 for a summary.

However, if Benjamin's recasting of Kant retains the framework of transcendental form, or transcendental inscription, it is important to realize the extent to which the speculative supplement of colour reformulates its terms. Centrally, the extension of the concept of experience through colour allows Benjamin to conceive of vision in terms which exceed the opposition of subject and object. As Benjamin argues in 'On the Programme of the Coming Philosophy' (1918), Kant's conception of experience is essentially that of Newtonian physics, a 'concept of naked, primitive, self-evident experience' which is 'unique and temporally limited' (1996, vol. 1, pp. 100–10). That is, the terms of experience are given by the mechanical causality of discrete objects seen by an uninvolved or ideal observer, and is therefore inevitably understood 'as a relation of some sort of subjects and objects or subject and object'. As a consequence, Benjamin argues, experience is inextricably tied to 'the subject nature of the cognizing consciousness', which is itself modelled on 'empirical consciousness, which of course has objects confronting it'. Thus, a restricted conception of empirical perception has come to structure the philosophical co-ordinates of transcendental philosophy, which in turn limits its conception of possible experience; such a perspective, Benjamin complains, implies a notion of experience that is 'virtually reduced to a nadir, to a minimum of significance' (*ibid.*, vol. 1, p. 101). The essay understands phenomenology's significance in terms of its identification of the problems inherent in this restriction of experience, but sees it as unable to free itself from its subordination to the cognizing ego. Benjamin's own response rejects Kant's restriction of experience to the opposition of subject and object, and in turn allows him to avoid a concept of vision centring on subjective intention. As we shall see, Benjamin regards visual experience as the interplay or negotiation of configured patterns of experience, and not as the seeing of external objects by the pure interiority of an isolated consciousness. However, to appreciate fully Benjamin's reformulation of the terms of modern vision, it is necessary to outline briefly the wider conceptual context identified by Caygill in his reading of Benjamin's 'transcendental but speculative philosophy'.

Benjamin's dissatisfaction with Kant ultimately revolves around his separation of the ideas of reason from spatio-temporal experience. For

Kant, to have the kind of experience that we as humans have, we must posit certain regulative 'ideas' – of God, the World and the Soul – in order for that experience to be coherent and consistent, and indeed to be possible at all. However, Kant insists that such 'ideas of reason' are merely regulatory principles and cannot be known or located within experience, which he describes as the relationship between intuition and the understanding. According to Kant, we must posit these ideas and proceed *as if* they existed, but we cannot claim to establish their existence or to know them. The problem that a host of Kant's subsequent critics found with this approach is that its identification of the ideas of reason seems arbitrary, and appears to presuppose the framework of its own possibility. Caygill argues that Benjamin's extension of the concept of experience sought to rearticulate the relationship between intuition, understanding and reason, so that the 'absolute' – or what Kant had identified as the ideas of reason – 'manifests itself in spatio-temporal experience, but indirectly in complex, tortuous and even violent forms' (1998, p. 2). In order to escape the restriction of experience to the relationship between subject and object, Benjamin rejects Kant's confinement of totality to the regulative projection of the rational subject, and seeks instead to find intimations of categorical universality and rational totality within spatio-temporal experience. Caygill identifies a fundamental instability in this approach, in that it involves a tendency to 'dissolve space and time into totality', and so 'threatens to collapse the complexity of spatio-temporal patterning into a closed "redemptive" immanence' (*ibid.*, p. 6). At the same time, he observes that Benjamin's thinking also offers a powerful 'forensic or diacritical principle' if, instead of assuming the terms of the absolute, it focuses on the complexity of spatio-temporal experience in order to discover intimations of the different possibilities that are latent there (*ibid.*, p. 7). From this perspective, Benjamin's work would not offer a 'redemptive criticism' – as, for example, Habermas has argued – but instead seeks 'to recognize or bear witness to the distorted forms of the future in the present' (*ibid.*, p. 9; Habermas, 1979). The present study looks to Benjamin's thought for such a forensic principle, which supplements the traditional concentration on the perception of form with an understanding of the distorted appearance of the 'colour of experience'. Yet, this is not to dismiss the

perception (*ibid.*, vol. 2, p. 695). And in 'On the Mimetic Faculty' (1933), effectively a reduced version of the same essay, Benjamin emphasizes the non-intentional nature of this concept of perception by identifying it with the capacity 'To read what was never written' (*ibid.*, vol. 2, p. 720–2).

Benjamin's invocation of 'reading' here is worth dwelling on, since it raises the important question of the relationship between visual experience and language. Because the concept of 'nonsensuous similarity' operates at the level of apperception rather than perception, it can be extended to language: individual languages are understood by Benjamin as constituting bounded infinities of linguistic possibility which imply or allow for particular modes of experience. Benjamin therefore describes language as an 'archive of nonsensuous similarities' (*ibid.*, vol. 2, p. 697). However, this is not to say that visual experience and discursive conceptuality are made identical or equivalent – indeed, it is axiomatic for Benjamin that they are not. What it does mean is that Benjamin can establish a relationship between them, without having to posit the self-identical transmission of 'sense' to 'meaning' which Husserl tried to secure in the silent monologue of the inner voice. Instead, Benjamin envisages this relationship in terms of his notion of 'translation', as the echoing within one medium of a structuring in a quite distinct and irreducibly different medium, a mode of interaction in which no entity as such is transmitted (see 1996, vol. 1, pp. 253–63). This conception of the relationship between intuition and discursive conceptuality is elaborated in an early, unpublished essay 'Painting, or Signs and Marks' ([1917] *ibid.*, vol. 1, pp. 83–6). Here, Benjamin observes that while visible marks are irreducible to the linguistic sign, their visual character is nonetheless perceived in relation to discursive meaningfulness. In effect, this is a restatement of his earlier insistence that there is no perception of colour outside the 'canon' of form. However, Benjamin insists that visual composition and meaning are not identical, but that their relationship is one of non-identity or externality, in which 'the picture may be connected with *something that it is not*', a process which 'happens by naming the picture' (*ibid.*, vol. 1, p. 85). In naming a picture, a particular linguistic structuring is related to its spatio-temporal composition, a relationship that occurs through temporally specific nonsensuous similarities, and not through any 'natural', exact or immutable connection. This point is stressed by Benjamin's description of naming as the 'entry of a higher power into the medium of the mark', namely, the entry of 'the linguistic word, which lodges in the medium of the language of painting' and 'makes its home there without destroying it' (*ibid.*, vol. 1, p. 85–6).

The contrast with Husserl here is useful in drawing out the different conception of temporality implicit in Benjamin's approach, a difference which is crucial in understanding Benjamin's analysis of technical reproducibility. As Benjamin observes in 'Doctrine of the Similar', vision demands 'a measure of time in which similarities flash up fleetingly out of the stream of things only in order to sink down once more' (1999A, vol. 2, p. 698). This understanding of perception cannot be articulated within the successive temporality of cause and effect which, according to Benjamin, modern philosophy borrowed from Newtonian mechanics, and which can be seen as underlying the linear trajectory from sense to meaning in Husserl. For Benjamin, perception can never occur as 'complete givenness', and so visual experience cannot be converted into linguistic meaning without some kind of residue or excess. The correspondence between meaning and intuition is never identical, complete or absolute, for as a moment of similarity it is always temporally specific, and open to renegotiation and reformulation. Perception can therefore never be fully present 'in the blink of an eye', since the eye-blink itself involves the interplay between heterogeneous modes of experience, whose points of relation or correspondence are contingent and time-bound, and therefore remain open to different possible futures. Such an understanding of vision implies a 'convoluted' rather than a linear temporality, a temporality which for Benjamin underlies both visual experience and discursive meaning (*ibid.*, vol. 2, pp. 237–47). This 'convoluted temporality' is examined most extensively through Benjamin's analysis of the radical historicity of literary interpretation, and can be illustrated through the central terms developed there. However, it must be remembered that this elaboration does not imply the identity of language and vision.

In an important essay, 'Goethe's *Elective Affinities*' (1922), Benjamin describes the historicity of interpretation through the relationship between 'material content' (*Sachgehalt*) and 'truth content' (*Wahrheits-gehalt*), terms which, confusingly, do not in fact describe any 'content' at all (1996, vol. 1, pp. 297–360). The former designates the linguistic configuration of the work – or what gives the terms of 'form' and 'content' – while the latter alludes to the intimation of absolute configuration made possible in the work's reception history, or 'afterlife'. The concept of the afterlife of the literary work develops out of Benjamin's understanding of language in terms of nonsensuous similarity, where reading occurs as the temporally specific overlaying of patterns of meaningfulness, namely those encoded in the linguistic configuration of the work and those informing its reading. While the gap between the two may be relatively narrow in a text's initial reception, it necessarily grows over time, so that the structuring of intention embedded in the work – its 'material content' – appears increasingly strange and alien to subsequent readers. Benjamin develops this idea in his study of the baroque *Trauerspiel*, or 'mourning play', where the initial meaningfulness of a text is understood to decay with the passage of time, so that it becomes increasingly strange and incoherent within the terms of its later reception. In its afterlife, Benjamin writes, 'the attraction of earlier charms diminishes decade by decade' so that 'all ephemeral beauty is completely stripped off, and the work stands as ruin' (1977, p. 182). However, such decay is not to be understood as the loss of the privileged state of meaningfulness or 'origin', as it would be for phenomenology.[8] Rather, the ruin of the work is precisely what reveals something of the terms that configure its own meaningfulness, an insight which is dependent on the element of non-identity or disfigurement in its transmission. As such, ruin reveals elements of a text's futurity, since the disintegration of its initial coherence allows new resonances or similarities to emerge, generating interpretative possibilities unavailable to earlier readings; thus, the process of decay retrospectively discovers hidden anticipations of future possible modes of meaningfulness. Benjamin's claim in his

[8] In the *Trauerspiel* study, Benjamin famously distinguishes his own conception of 'origin' from such a notion: 'The term origin is not intended to describe the process by which the existent came into being, but rather to describe what emerges from the process of becoming and disappearance. Origin is an eddy in the stream of becoming, and in its current it swallows the material involved in the process of genesis' (Benjamin, 1977, p. 45).

essay on *Elective Affinities*, that 'the history of works prepares for their critique', therefore has nothing to do with the retrieval of an integral meaning that is to be made present once again; for what the ruin of the work reveals is something that emerges *only in its afterlife*. Or, as Benjamin describes this process in the *Trauerspiel* study, the 'mortification of works' is not, as for the Romantics, the 'awakening of the consciousness in living works, but the settlement of knowledge in dead ones'; and as such, it is paradoxically the condition for their 'rebirth' (*ibid.*, p. 182).

The implications of this convoluted temporality for visual experience can be understood by identifying how they reformulate the terms of Husserlian perception. From the perspective of such a convoluted temporality, the perceptual nexus is no longer conceived as fixed once and for all in the isolated spontaneity of an integral perceiving consciousness. Rather, as a heterogeneous complex of temporally orientated impressions, it remains open to different possible arrangements of perceptibility within each new regime of intention. Benjamin's approach to visual culture does not therefore imply a closed redemption or circular return to origin, or what Husserl terms a 'return enquiry' (*Rückfrage*). Instead, it aims to 'retrieve' the futurity of 'past' moments of visual experience encoded in the image, moments which, paradoxically, are *yet to appear*. From this perspective, visual experience has folded within it intimations of future configurations of experience, intimations that are not already there, but whose becoming is a facet of, or possibility within, the structuring of the image. In the Goethe essay, Benjamin designates the yet-to-emerge futurity latent in the artwork as 'hope'.[9] 'That most paradoxical, most fleeting hope', writes Benjamin, emerges only afterwards, in the shifting rhythms and patterns of the work's afterlife, 'just as, at twilight, as the sun is extinguished, rises the evening star which outlasts the night' (1996, vol. 1, p. 355). Each moment of perception is inhabited by past histories which themselves have futurity, and so contain anticipations of different possible future modes of perceptibility.

This conception of temporality distinguishes Benjamin's analysis of

[9] For a consideration of Benjamin's notion of hope, see Benjamin, A., 1997.

the technical reproducibility of images from the positions of Debord, Baudrillard, Virilio, and Jameson, and is therefore misrecognized when assimilated to their terms. Indeed, many of the criticisms levelled at Benjamin's supposedly over-optimistic assessment of the technologies of reproduction simply misunderstand the temporal orientation of his analysis, assuming either that he is offering only a description of things as they 'are', or – much worse from Benjamin's perspective – an account of how they will necessarily unfold.[10] It is a mistake to confuse Benjamin's articulation of the futurity of visual experience with notions of technological progress or even optimism, a point that becomes clearer when it is remembered that the concept of 'hope' is itself set within the topography of 'sadness' (*Trauer*).[11] Benjamin offers an early elaboration of his lexicon of sadness in his famous essay on language of 1916, 'On Language as Such and on the Language of Man', which, despite its biblical terminology, effectively translates Benjamin's recasting of Kant into a philosophical account of language (1996, vol. 1, pp. 62–74). The essay describes the relationship between perceptual experience and discursive conceptuality in terms of the doubleness of nature's mourning. In its first sense, the description of nature as 'mourning' articulates the difference between human language and the 'speechlessness' of appearances, while at the same time maintaining their relationship in 'translation' (*ibid.*, p. 72). As such, it anticipates the discussion of naming in 'Painting, or Signs and Marks', written the following year, where the linguistic word 'lodges' in the medium of the visual mark, a medium that is fundamentally external and different to it. In saying that 'nature laments' on being named by Adam before the Fall, Benjamin is restating in biblical terms his conception of the necessary distortion of absolute configuration in its projection within a transcendental surface of inscription. In being perceived, appearances

---

[10] Thus Benjamin insists in *One Way Street* ([1928] 1996, vol. 1, p. 482) that 'he who asks fortune-tellers the future unwittingly forfeits an inner intimation of coming events that is a thousand times more powerful than anything they may say . . . For presence of mind is an extract of the future, and precise awareness of the present moment is more decisive than foreknowledge of the most distant events.'

[11] Such a 'technocratic' notion is inimical to Benamin thinking on two levels, both because it implies a homogenous and empty time, and because it implies the enslavement of nature and technology; see Benjamin, 1973, pp. 260–1.

are structured according to the co-ordinates of human intuition, so that the *Dasein* of things is distorted, a distortion which Benjamin figures as the source of sorrow and lament.

However, according to Benjamin, there is a second sense in which nature mourns, a sense he associates with the Tower of Babel, and which he calls 'the deepest linguistic reason for all melancholy' (*ibid.*, vol. 1, p. 73). This second sense is designated in the essay as 'overnaming', and identifies a particular relationship between discursive conceptuality and things which is structured according to a temporally restricted and non-reciprocal economy of translation. In Adamic naming, human language's translation of the being there of things involves its own reformulation, just as, in the later essay on painting, the linguistic word 'lodges' in the medium of visual mark, so that their relationship remains open to change. However, in 'overnaming' human language regards itself not as one bounded surface of meaning, but as comprising the absolute infinity of configuration underlying the meaningfulness of creation. The process of naming is no longer reciprocal and open to change, but involves the subordination of nature to a static conceptual frame. This frame is organized around the polarity of the 'nameless' or abstract entities of 'good' and 'evil', a single polarity into which all things are translated. Language becomes instrumental and orientated towards the abstract oppositions of judgement, rather than the reciprocity and speculative non-identity of naming. Consequently, language is reduced to 'prattle', a term which designates a restricted *technic* or organization of experience; thus, Benjamin writes, 'the enslavement of language in prattle is joined by the enslavement of things' (*ibid.*, vol. 1, p. 72). To appreciate Benjamin's analysis of the technical reproducibility of images, it is important to understand that it assumes the condition of modern experience to be one of destitution or 'sadness'. While his consideration of technical reproducibility seeks to identify different possible responses to this situation, the attempt to overcome this destitution by fixing the terms of modern experience is not an option for Benjamin. Indeed, attempts to do so are understood as 'auratic', and are seen as leading ineluctably to violence.

LOOKING BACK: THE EXPERIENCE OF MODERNITY

Benjamin's approach to technology aims to draw out its social and political implications by examining the prospects for 'hope' and 'sadness' within modern experience. However, if Benjamin brings a complex conception of temporality to his analyses of the new technologies of modern visual culture, he does not cast them as simply playing out a theoretical master-discourse that is already in place. For Benjamin, 'technology' (*Technik*) is not a term that can simply be slotted into a fixed conceptual framework. Indeed, technology takes on a particular significance within Benjamin's conception of the discontinuity of historical time, because it reformulates the terrain of experience in which the perception of different possible futures might occur. While the ritual image and the work of art both suffer ruin and decay over relatively long periods of time, in photography and film the integrity of the image decays or is ruined *in an instant*. Yet, if this is the case, Benjamin's methodology poses considerable problems for later readers, not so much because it employs an intractable jargon, but because it juxtaposes a number of familiar yet ostensibly incompatible registers. His talk of 'magic' and 'ritual' appears to sit oddly alongside his discussion of the unprecedented nature of modern technology, while his examination of modern politics through the terms of art may seem bizarrely disproportionate and even naïve. However, if Benjamin's terminology is idiosyncratic, it is neither capricious nor haphazard, but attempts to respond to the very character of modern experience which it examines. Benjamin's writing seeks to exploit the 'nonsensuous similarities' embedded in language, which emerge as echoes and disjunctions in the overlaying of heterogenous temporalities involved in reading. This point reminds us of the radically historical nature of Benjamin's own conceptual lexicon, a feature which our presentation has until now tended to neglect. Benjamin's understanding of technology, visual experience, modern philosophy, and modern politics are framed within a historically determinate conception of modernity within which the nature of critique is itself reformulated.[12] In order to

---

[12] In *One Way Street* Benjamin makes clear the relationship between modernity and the decay of Kant's critical philosophy: 'Fools lament the decay of criticism. For its day is long passed.

elaborate Benjamin's understanding of these issues it is therefore
necessary first to identify the broader conceptual role of the aesthetic
within modern thought, and then to attend to the historically variable
character of familiar terms such as 'technology' (*Technik*) and 'experience' (*Erfahrung/Erlebnis*), and borrowed terms such as 'near-sight and
'far-sight' (*Nahsicht*, *Fernsicht*).

The importance of art for Benjamin lies in the historical role of the
aesthetic in the articulation of modern thought and its conception of
experience, and therefore exceeds the consideration of artworks. As
we saw in chapter one, beauty describes the terms of modern
experience through the return of the gaze. For Kant, beauty obtains
when what is seen anticipates the terms of its seeing, so confirming
the compatibility of the forms of intuition – space and time – with the
categorical organization of the understanding, a compatibility that
underlies the transcendental unity of apperception. Beauty therefore
has a significance for Kant that extends beyond what we have
subsequently come to designate as the 'aesthetic', since it attests to the
structure of experience underlying both pure and practical reason –
that is, knowledge and morality. This conception of experience is
structured as the circular return of the gaze: in beauty things 'look
back', or offer a configuration of appearances which matches those
implied by the structure of transcendental consciousness. For Kant,
the corollary of beauty is the sublime, in which nature exceeds the
terms of human intuition, and so no longer 'looks back'.[13] These two
terms have proved remarkably durable, although they have taken on
meanings that Kant did not intend. Thus, for Baudrillard, the blank
return of the simulacrum figured by *trompe l'oeil* rehearses the
aesthetic return of the gaze, although now its return is empty and
worthless. Jameson, on the other hand, follows Jean-François Lyotard,
who sees the failure of such a return identified in the sublime as the
central characteristic of postmodern experience: this idea informs
Jameson's conception of the 'technological sublime' and the perceptual

---

It was at home in a world where perspectives counted and where it was still possible to adopt
a standpoint. Now things press too urgently on human society'. Benjamin, 1996, vol. 1,
p. 476.

[13] See the 'Analytic of the Sublime' in Kant's *Critique of Judgement*.

disorientation of the subject.[14] For Benjamin, Kant's conception of beauty is neither to be accepted – albeit ironically – nor rejected in favour of its opposite, but must first of all be understood historically as a response to the 'sorrowfulness' or decay of modern experience. While there is much of value in Kant's critical philosophy for Benjamin, its conception of beauty remains bound up in a restricted conception of experience, providing a focus for its 'nostalgic' or temporally restrictive tendencies, whose more threatening aspect becomes manifest in Kant's practical philosophy. By emphasizing the historicity of the terms of Kant's transcendental philosophy, and thereby identifying them as particular responses to modern experience, Benjamin is able to reject the single, 'monochromatic' polarity of beauty and the sublime. Instead, he seeks to enumerate a range of different possible modes of the return of the gaze within modern experience, within which he identifies Kant's conception of beauty as potentially 'auratic'.

Benjamin's understanding of Kant's critical philosophy as one possible transcendental surface of inscription can therefore be seen as necessarily viewing it as a historically determinate response to the conditions of modern experience. However, Benjamin rejects any continuous or developmental historical frame within which to set his conception of modernity, and instead seeks to characterize its historical specificity through a set of mobile terms: thus, he describes modernity as the decay of experience (*Erfahrung*) and its dissolution into 'lived experience' (*Erlebnis*), and as the shattering of tradition. The concept of *Erfahrung*, which might be termed 'experience proper', stands behind much of Benjamin's cultural analysis, although Benjamin remains wary of giving it a full or fixed definition. In his essay on Leskov, 'The Storyteller' ([1936] 1973, pp. 83–109), the term can be seen to allude to modes of shared, collective experience that are embedded in the '*physis*' of nature, or the disposition of the phenomenal world. Such modes of experience are characterized by their transmissibility, understood not so much as the endurance of discrete 'contents' or particular social forms, but as the reproduction of their own structuring. Benjamin describes both the transmission and the

[14] See, for example, 'Answering the Question: What is Postmodernism?' in Lyotard, 1984, and Jameson's foreword in the same volume.

transmissibility of particular modes of experience as 'tradition', although this tradition can never in fact be absolute or integral, but always involves elements of destruction and non-identity. The complexities involved in the term *Erfahrung* emerge in part through this conception of tradition; for, at one level, the transmissibility of experience is necessarily also its passing away and reformulation; while at another level, modernity is understood as the shattering of the transmissibility of *Erfahrung*, which is consequently inaccessible and can no longer appear.[15] In contrast to traditional societies, modernity is characterized by the 'lived experience' (*Erlebnis*) of isolated and atomized subjects which regard the *physis* of nature as inert exteriority. Such 'lived experience' is given philosophical expression in, among other places, Kant's transcendental philosophy and in Husserl's phenomenological analysis of the conscious ego. According to Benjamin, the character of *Erfahrung* is therefore only available for modern subjects in distorted and fragmentary forms: important examples which he identifies are Proust's individualized – and hence compensatory – *mémoire involontaire*, and Baudelaire's auratic *correspondances* (1983, pp. 107–54). The invocation of literature here is significant, since the decay of experience is understood in similar terms to the ruin or decay of the artwork examined above. Thus, *Erfahrung* is not to be conceived as a static point of genesis to be recovered or returned to, while decay is not to be mistaken for 'decline'. Indeed, Benjamin identifies past societies that have historically been associated with such an experience as mythic, or as orientated to the closed repetition of tradition through ritual and cult (1973, esp. pp. 225–7). Thus, Benjamin's concept of experience itself functions within his notion of convoluted temporality, and involves the kind of futurity or 'hope' whose future possibilities are yet to be discovered.

Benjamin's concept of technology (*Technik*) is intimately related to his understanding of the role of the aesthetic in modern thought and to his conception of the decay of experience. As we saw in chapter one, despite Baudelaire's recognition of the destruction of tradition in

---

[15] For a fuller consideration of Benjamin's conception of tradition, see McCole, 1993 and Caygill, 'Benjamin, Heidegger and the Destruction of Tradition' in Benjamin, A. and Osborne, P. (eds), 1994.

urban modernity, his understanding of visual experience is restricted by its oppositional structure, in which the pure interiority of the subject confronts a world of exteriority. This bifurcated view is articulated in the opposition between aesthetic 'technique' and 'technology', an opposition that underlies Baudelaire's hostility to photography. The inevitable element of contingency in technology is counterposed to the transcendent character of technique, a transcendence which rejects the mutability of the space and time of experience, and so ultimately demands the subordination of the phenomenal world. Baudelaire's conceptual opposition is reflected in English, which distinguishes linguistically between 'technique' and 'technology'; however, there is no equivalent distinction in German, where 'Technik' can cover both English meanings. As Julian Roberts argues, Benjamin exploits what might seem an unfortunate semantic ambiguity, and it is crucial to his usage that the elements of interiority and exteriority in Baudelaire's opposition are shown linguistically to inhere in one another (1982, pp. 157–62). For Benjamin, Technik designates historical modes of the organization of experience, or the relationship between humanity and the phenomenal world. In these terms, all experience is 'technological', including, for example, aesthetic perception; while visual art is understood as a historically specific set of image technologies.

However, Benjamin's usage does not flatten out the unprecedented character of modern technology, but rather identifies its specificity in terms of the reformulation of the very conditions in which humanity and the phenomenal world find their relation. This usage is evident in his essay on photography, 'A Little History of Photography' (1931), when Benjamin writes that the photographic image makes 'the difference between technology and magic visible as a thoroughly historical variable' (1999A, vol. 2, p. 512). For Benjamin, both magic and photography are technologies, or particular ways of organizing the relationship between humanity and 'nature'; what distinguishes them is modern technology's reformulation of the very condition of this relationship. In early societies, magic is deployed in order to negotiate a nature that exceeds human direction, but the technology of magic itself is understood as being subordinate to human intention. In modernity, however, Benjamin identifies an unprecedented shift within which modern technology reformulates the condition of experience. Following Lukács, he sees 'nature' as itself transformed into the 'second nature' of technology, which can no longer be seen as subordinate to human intention. Therefore, now that technology comes to negotiate with a 'nature' that is itself technological, this relationship cannot be conceived as the opposition between human 'interiority' and the 'exteriority' of nature. In the *Arcades Project*, Benjamin charts the unprecedented character of modern technology by contrasting it with the situation of art, where a notion of aesthetic technique is still separated from the 'externality' of nature. Here Benjamin notes that in pre-modern European societies, the rate of technological development could be assimilated to the changing organization of human experience, figured in art by the priority of 'aesthetic technique'. However, 'the transformation of things that set in around 1800', writes Benjamin, 'dictated the tempo to art', a tempo that became increasing 'breathtaking'. That is, the emergence of technological modernity undermines the sovereignty of the subject and its subordination of the *physis* of nature to its own terms through 'technique'. 'Finally', Benjamin observes, 'we arrive at the present state of things', where 'the possibility now arises' that human experience 'will no longer find time to adapt . . . to technological processes' (1999B, p. 171).

Benjamin's response to this situation was to look to technology itself – primarily the new technologies of image-perception, especially film – in order to identify ways of renegotiating this relationship with the technological 'second nature' of the modern metropolis. This approach demanded a rearticulation of the circular return of the gaze which structures modern aesthetics, a project which Benjamin articulates through a language of 'nearness' and 'distance'. These terms are borrowed from the art historian Alois Riegl, although Benjamin's employment of them is his own, and rejects the notion of the '*Kunstwollen*' for which Riegl is now best known.[16] In his *Late Roman Art Industry* (1901), Riegl sought to break with the prejudices of nineteenth-century art history, which viewed the Renaissance as the

---

[16] Benjamin's critique of the category of 'culture' in his essay on Fuchs clearly indicates his distance from the notion of *Kunstwollen*; yet, having said this, Benjamin sometimes mentions the term approvingly, for example in 'Some Remarks on Folk Art' discussed below.

restoration of Classical perfection lost in the late Roman or Byzantine period (1985). In doing so, Riegl constructs a historical typology of perception within the Mediterranean cultures of antiquity, which he differentiates from the new perceptual matrix underlying Renaissance art. For Riegl, modern, post-Renaissance perception is characterized by the location of discrete objects within a uniform and universal 'deep space', or 'infinite, free space'. That is, it implies an infinite space which is shared simultaneously by all objects, even those not immediately available to perception. Such an organization of perception requires the subject to posit a uniform and universal spacetime as the condition for perceptual experience, allotting each object a fixed location within a consistent and invariable spatio-temporal framework. In contrast, such an abstract, infinite spacetime was unavailable for the cultures of antiquity, according to Riegl. Instead, the different perceptual matrices of these pre-modern cultures emerge from an engagement with the plane, and the earliest such matrix, identified by Riegl with ancient Egyptian art, is characterized by the greatest dependence on the immediacy of sense perception through the interplay of vision and touch.

The mode of perception peculiar to Egyptian art is understood by Riegl as seeking to secure the 'material individuality' of objects by assimilating them to the tactile 'impenetrability' of the plane; but he insists that this is not 'the optical plane, imagined by our eye at a distance from objects, but the tactile plane suggested by the sense of touch'. This is why, according to Riegl, ancient Egyptian art avoids foreshortening and shadow, which imply deep space, and employs flat silhouettes within a symmetrical arrangement that emphasizes the dimensions of the plane. 'From the optical point of view', he writes, 'this is the plane which the eye perceives when it comes so close to the surface of an object that . . . all the shadows, which otherwise could disclose an alteration in depth, disappear' (Riegl, 1985, p. 24). Consequently, he identifies this organization of perception as *Nahsicht* or 'near-sight', which he also terms 'tactile' or 'haptic' vision. The subsequent history of perception in antiquity is understood to involve an increasing tendency towards the development of three-dimensionality within the confines of the plane; that is, a tendency towards *Fernsicht* or 'far-sight'. However, the historical advent of Renaissance art, which in chapter one we identified with the paradigm of representation, marks a new departure in 'far-seeing': objects are released from the plane and disposed in free, infinite space, while the eye withdraws from the contingency of spatio-temporal experience, adopting an unlocated or ideal position from which to survey objects.

Benjamin rearticulates Riegl's history of perception so as to identify the historical character of the conditions of perceptibility, while at the same time hoping to avoid a developmental or progressive historical frame. The short, unpublished fragment, 'Some Remarks on Folk Art' (1929), gives a useful insight into Benjamin's thinking here (1999A, vol. 2, pp. 278–9). In this fragment, Benjamin translates the notion of 'near-seeing' into the terms of his wider conception of visual experience, which we have identified with the seeing of similarities. The structuring of perceptual experience in early societies is dramatized through the visual scenario of looking through a mask: 'wearing a mask', Benjamin writes, 'man looks out on the [world] and builds his figures within it', seeing a world that is itself 'full of masks' (ibid., vol. 2, p. 279). Benjamin's image can be understood in terms of Nietzsche's account of pre-Homeric Greek folk religion: for Nietzsche, the early Greek gods do not represent or 'stand for' abstract concepts or qualities, but directly designate natural forces.[17] Similarly for Benjamin, the organization of perception within traditional folk cultures does not function in terms of the modern paradigm of representation, which extracts a static and universal apperceptive frame from spatio-temporal experience to apply from without. Rather, such cultures 'see through' the natural world; that is, perception is organized directly by the contingency of experience and the culture's cumulative interaction with the phenomenal world. This mode of perception functions in terms of similarity, and not in terms of the seeing of discrete and substantial objects by an isolated and self-identical subject. In looking through the experiential configuration of the mask, the world is perceived as an array of configured surfaces, or 'masks', so that perception occurs as the flashing up of resonances and nonsensuous similarities.

---

[17] This understanding stands behind Nietzsche's discussion of the relationship between the Dionysiac and pre-Homeric folk religion in *The Birth of Tragedy*. However, while *The Birth of Tragedy* looks for the unity of myth in tragedy, Benjamin looks to its decay in the *Traverspiel*.

The central contrast developed by the fragment is between the 'near-sight' figured by the image of looking through a mask, and the 'far-sight' of modern rationality. In the former, the apperceptive eye 'sees through' or is organized by the contingent disposition of things; while in the latter, a static and universal transcendental vantage-point is abstracted from the contingency of spatio-temporal experience. For Benjamin, early societies set this 'near-seeing' within the circular temporality of myth, or the return of the same; however, despite this very real limitation, he argues that this organization of experience nonetheless offers a valuable optic for examining modernity. In particular, such a 'near-sight' challenges the notion of intentional meaning implied by the modern subject, whose isolated interiority claims always to be fully conscious of its 'own' experience. Instead, within the terms of 'near-sight', visual experience involves the coming to be conscious of the different futures hidden within the moment of perception; or, as Benjamin writes, it allows us to realize that 'we have experienced infinitely more than we know about' (1999A, vol. 2, p. 278). In 'Some Remarks on Folk Art' this insight is developed through a comparison between aesthetic perception – as the paradig-matic structuring of experience for transcendental philosophy – and folk art and contemporary popular culture, or 'kitsch'. 'Art teaches us to look into objects', Benjamin claims, describing a gaze whose distanced and static transcendental viewpoint demands that appearances return its terms absolutely and completely. In contrast, folk art and contemporary popular culture 'allow us to look outward from within objects', describing a visual relationship that does not adopt an external vantage point, but instead sees 'through' the disposition of objects. That is, the apperceptive categories of such a vision are immersed *within* the contingency of spatio-temporal experience, which provides the frame through which things are apprehended. Although the polarities of the aesthetic gaze have been dissolved, there is a kind of 'return' here, in the sense of a certain productivity or yield. The shifting overlay of temporally heterogeneous patterns of experience produce moments of similarity or disjunction which 'illuminat[e] in a flash the dark corners of the self, of our dark or light features' (*ibid.*, vol. 2, p. 279).

THE OPTIC OF TECHNOLOGY

Benjamin's rearticulation of Riegl's 'near-sight' provides a crucial conceptual language for his analyses of mass society and the technical reproducibility of images, which together 'bring things "closer"'. Equally, its corollary in 'far-sight' underlies his account of the 'aura' of an object, as 'the unique phenomenon of a distance, however close it may be', although Benjamin will argue that such 'far-seeing' in fact marks the recurrence of myth in modernity. Yet, Benjamin's tactical alignment of folk art and popular culture in 'Some Remarks on Folk Art' needs to be understood in terms of his own methodology of the retrospective perception of futurity: as the perception of 'similarities', and not as some kind of return to a punctual and self-identical 'origin'. Thus, while Benjamin looks back to folk art and magic as a way of developing alternative perspectives on modern experience, he understands modernity as marking a fundamental change in the nature of experience. Benjamin's work of the 1930s, from the voluminous study of Paris known as the *Arcades Project* to the analyses of technical reproducibility which emerged out of it, sought to identify the unprecedented character of modernity, while at the same time identifying the differential return of the archaic. The deployment of the language of 'nearness' and 'distance' in Benjamin's analyses of modern visual culture operates within the broader conception of the decay of experience in modernity. The visual implications of this understanding of modernity are traced by Benjamin through baroque allegory, and its transformation with the generalization of commodity production in the nineteenth century.

Benjamin develops his analysis of allegory in the *Trauerspiel* study, which describes the reformulation of the relationship between word and image – or the *technics* of cognitive and perceptual experience – in early modern Europe. The central features of this realignment are the withdrawal of the appearance of divine meaningfulness from the modern world, and the compensatory development of interiority. Once creaturely things are seen as bereft of any intrinsic significance or connection, the soul withdraws into the spiritual inwardness of Protestantism, a conjunction which Benjamin identifies as 'the triumph of subjectivity and the onset of an arbitrary rule over things' (1977,

p. 233). Baroque allegory is thus understood as clearing the way for the modern conception of vision structured by the aesthetic gaze, in which the subject's apperceptive framework is removed from its imbrication within spatio-temporal experience. This withdrawal renders the world as objectivity, and circumscribes experience as the repetition of the subject's own, fixed transcendental co-ordinates. For Benjamin, the attachment of the linguistic legend to the visual emblem in allegory is not an expression of the inherent meaning of things, a way in which they articulate their inner significance. Rather, the allegorical gaze is a projection of the subject, which reduces the appearance of things to its own co-ordinates; therefore, what is returned or rebounded by 'exteriority' back to the subject is in fact only an image of itself. From this perspective, 'the pre-eminent emblematic property', or allegorical object, is the 'corpse', since what is seen in the world of things is simply an image of the human (*ibid.*, p. 218). But as a consequence, the 'human' is itself dismembered and hollowed out, so that the 'conventional, conscious *physis*' of the integral human body is scattered, and allegory images the absolute abandonment of traditional, organic conceptions of meaningfulness, (*ibid.*, p. 217).

The *Trauerspiel* study's analysis of allegory is extended both historically and conceptually in Benjamin's writing of the 1930s, a process illustrated in concentrated form in 'Central Park' (1938–9), a collection of working notes associated with the *Arcades Project*. In 'Central Park', Benjamin links the development of the mass societies of commodity production to his conception of allegory, arguing that 'the commodity has taken the place of the allegorical way of seeing' (1985, p. 52). However, if Benjamin claims that 'allegory is the armature of the modern', and that 'the emblems recur as commodities', he understands the generalization of allegory in the commodity form as involving its transformation (*ibid.*, p. 49). As we saw in chapter one, nineteenth-century Paris saw an unprecedented reformulation of the traditional co-ordinates of urban appearance, from the new image-landscapes of commercial display and advertising through to Haussmann's reorganization of the topography of the city. Like the illuminated images of the café in Baudelaire's 'The Eyes of the Poor', the commodities that thronged the arcades and the new department stores exhibit a relationship between the image and discursive meaning that recalls the terms of allegory. Just as in allegory, where emblems are plucked from their traditional contexts of meaning, so in commodity production appearances are set free from tradition. Their contingent arrangements and juxtapositions generate new configurations of appearance, making them available for interpretation within different conditions of meaningfulness. However, the technological condition of nineteenth-century Paris sets it apart from the world of early modern Europe, so that both the condition of allegory, and the range of responses to it, are new and unprecedented. Benjamin identifies these responses in terms of two main tendencies, although his particular analyses see their combination giving rise to numerous permutations. The first tendency looks to intensify the transformation of allegorical seeing in technological modernity, while the second looks to technology in an attempt to freeze the relationship of image and meaning, and so 'restore' the image's 'aura'.

That allegory is open to transformation in technological modernity is indicated by the closing pages of the *Trauerspiel* book, where its discussion takes a sudden and unexpected turn. The text had established that the arbitrariness of allegorical meaning signifies 'the desolation of human existence', so that allegory itself comes to be understood as an emblem of the transitoriness of experience and the contingency of earthly meaning. However, the study does not conclude here, but spins this insight around, as it were, and views it from an alternative perspective. The very experience of historical contingency in allegorical perception is now identified as itself revealing or making visible the temporally specific conditions of meaning and experience. As Benjamin writes, from this perspective 'transitoriness is not signified or allegorically presented, so much as, in its own significance, displayed *as allegory*', a turnabout in which 'the final phantasmagoria of the objective' is 'cleared away', and allegory 're-discovers itself' (1977, p. 232). While this alternative perspective is conceived in baroque culture as figuring a renewed belief in divine salvation, in technological modernity Benjamin sees its potential transformation into a new kind of 'near-sight'. This understanding stems from Benjamin's rejection of a progressive view of history, in which the Protestant inwardness of early modern Europe leads ineluctably to the ethical subject of Enlightenment and then the flowering of Romantic interiority. Instead, from Benjamin's vantage point, baroque melancholy can be seen to presage the dissolution of interiority in the welter of 'lived experiences', a situation which he dramatizes through a comparison of the different objects of investment and memory in the baroque and in nineteenth-century Paris.[18] The 'relic', or fragment of the dead saint's body, derives from the pre-eminent emblematic object of the baroque, the corpse, and continues to signify the belief in divine salvation; but its equivalent in the society of commodity production, the mass-produced souvenir, derives 'from deceased experience [*Erfahrung*] which calls itself euphemistically "*Erlebnis*"'. The souvenir thus marks the atrophy of inwardness in 'the person who inventories his past as dead possession'. But for Benjamin, this atrophy is not to be understood as 'decline', but instead reformulates the circular return of the gaze described by aesthetic perception: 'in the nineteenth century', Benjamin explains, 'allegory left the surrounding world, in order to settle in the inner world' (1985, p. 49).

In 'Central Park' Benjamin describes the transformation of the allegorical way of seeing through an account of Baudelaire's poetic practice, which is understood as linguistically encoding this transformation. While 'baroque allegory sees the corpse' – or the world of dead objects – 'from the outside', Benjamin maintains that in his poetry, 'Baudelaire sees it also from the inside' (*ibid.*, p. 51). That is, despite Baudelaire's best intentions, his poetry does not in fact exemplify the sovereign subject's ability to imbue the disconsolate scene of modernity with meaning; for it also illustrates how the terms of subjective meaning are themselves reorganized by the very world of things which are considered as inert and exterior. Lived experience is thus shown to be structured by the world of technologically animated objects, or commodities, thereby undermining the opposition of

---

[18] Benjamin's conception of the after-history of allegory is illuminated by Gillian Rose's essay 'Walter Benjamin – Out of the Sources of Modern Judaism' in Marcus and Nead (eds), 1998. Rose argues that, like Max Weber, Benjamin sees the Protestant ethic as giving rise to 'hypertrophy of the inner life', which correlates 'with the atrophy of political participation'. 'Eventually', Rose writes, 'the interest in salvation itself atrophies, but the inner anxiety of salvation persists and is combined with worldly opportunism and ruthlessness; this combination of anxiety and ruthlessness amounts to the combination of inner and outer violence' (1978, p. 87).

interiority and exteriority, and the restriction of experience to subjective intention which it implies. Appearances are not empty and
worthless, but are involved in articulating and reformulating the
apperceptive categories through which experience is possible. Or, as
Benjamin writes in 'Central Park', 'the buried corpse' – the very
world of things once construed as dead 'exteriority' – can be
recognized as 'the "transcendental Subject" of historical consciousness',
in that the apperceptive frameworks of perception are embedded in
spatio-temporal experience (*ibid.*, p. 35). Vision is no longer to be
understood as the aesthetic return of the gaze, since the absolute
separation or distance between transcendental consciousness and the
world has been breached. Yet nor is it locked into the endless
repetition of the same, as in more recent accounts of visual culture,
which cast the subject's perception as 'commodified' or as directly
colonized by technology. As we have seen, such accounts conceive of
vision as the simultaneous apprehension of objects by a subject,
whether through a frame that is already 'pre-formed' by technology,
or inherited from an earlier structuring of experience. In contrast,
Benjamin understands perception as the overlaying of temporally
heterogeneous patterns of experience, which are open to new configurations of appearing and non-appearing. As such, there is always a
return or yield in visual experience, although it is one that emerges
not in the return of the same, but in the non-identity of similarity.
Thus in 'Central Park', Benjamin argues that in contrast to that of the
baroque, Baudelaire's allegory 'break[s] into [the] world . . . to leave
its harmonious structures in ruins', so marking a site where 'the
commodity attempts to look itself in the face' (*ibid.*, p. 42). In the
surrealism essay of 1929, he identifies this new condition as describing
a situation where 'action puts forth its own image and exists, absorbing
and consuming it', and 'where nearness looks with its own eyes'
(1999A, vol. 2, p. 217). And in the essay on Proust written the same
year, he talks of 'the world distorted in the state of similarity, a world
in which the true surrealist face of existence breaks through' (*ibid.*,
vol. 2, p. 240).

Yet if Benjamin identifies the conditions for a new kind of 'near-
sight', it is not the return of an earlier mode of perception 'as it once
was', but rather involves a differential or inauthentic return. The

character of this return can be understood by setting the transformation of allegorical seeing alongside the associated concept of 'aura'. On various occasions Benjamin draws out different aspects of this term, including its institution of apperceptive distance, its accumulation of involuntary memory, its indebtedness to the transmissibility of tradition, and its contribution to the notion of authenticity. However, a useful starting point for addressing the concept of aura is provided by 'A Little History of Photography', where it is described as 'a strange weave of space and time' ibid., vol. 2, p. 518). In 'Some Motifs in Baudelaire' (1939), Benjamin elaborates this conception of aura by locating it within the terms of the Kantian structuring of experience through aesthetic perception. As the essay explains, when we look at someone we have an expectation that they will return our gaze: therefore, 'to perceive the aura of an object we look at means to invest it with the ability to look at us in return'. Noting that this return 'in the case of thought processes, can apply equally to the look of the eye of the mind and to the glance pure and simple', Benjamin writes that 'where this expectation is met', then 'there is an experience of the aura to its fullest extent' (1983, pp. 148, 147). That is, aura implies the static spatio-temporal matrix of aesthetic perception, wherein the scene rebounds back to the subject an image arranged according to its own fixed transcendental co-ordinates. Or, in Husserlian terms, the perceptual object is conceived as 'complete givenness', as comprising a rigid impressional complex that implies a uniform temporality in which the perceived image is always returned, or 'presentified', as the same. As a response to the dynamic condition of modern technology, auratic perception attempts, in the words of 'Central Park', 'to turn technically determined forms, that is, dependent variables, into constants' (1985, p. 50). Paradoxically, then, although aura is understood by Benjamin as a specifically modern phenomenon, it has its roots in ritual and myth; but as such, it marks the difference between modern allegory and the perceptual conditions of early societies. Unlike the allegorical vision of technological modernity, the 'near-sight' of early, premodern societies implied the eternal return of the same, since the conditions of experience which provided the frame, or 'mask', for perception were relatively static. In modernity, however, the space and time of experience is dynamic and changes rapidly, so that the establishment of a fixed framework of perception is no longer possible in 'near-sight'; instead the achievement of such a static viewpoint requires the withdrawal of the transcendental co-ordinates of vision from spatio-temporal experience. In a sense, then, the 'distanced' perception of aura as much marks the return of the spatio-temporal conditions of myth, as it does the progressive emergence of the modern subject from dogma and superstition.

For Benjamin, both allegory and aura are fundamentally modern conditions of perception which, paradoxically, also involve the differential return of the archaic. Their complex and unstable character means that a range of possible modes of perception are available within their terms. Thus, as Benjamin notes in 'Central Park', while Baudelaire's poetry embodies 'the renunciation of the magic of distance' in allegorical seeing, at the same time it freezes the patterns of similarity that emerge as 'correspondences' (*ibid.*, p. 41). The temporal stasis of Baudelaire's correspondences makes it possible to crystallize out meanings from the swirl of modern experience, but in doing so it holds them rigid and imbues them with aura. Equally, while the commodity form at one level presages the decay of aura, at another level, commodity fetishism embodies the very terms of aura, which Benjamin describes in 'Some Motifs in Baudelaire' as 'the transposition of a response common in human relationships to the relationship between inanimate or natural objects and man' (1976, p. 148). If commodity production sweeps away the fixed perceptual conditions of tradition, 'at the same time', Benjamin observes in 'Central Park', 'advertising seeks to veil the commodity character of things' (1985, p. 42). The destruction of experience (*Erfahrung*) in the generalization of commodity production both withdraws the conditions for aura in the transmissibility of tradition, while at the same time providing new opportunities for auratic perception: for the disconnected moments of lived experience, now free from tradition, lie available for new and potentially restrictive modes of recombination. In 'Central Park', Benjamin articulates this potential in the image of the kaleidoscope, which 'with each turn, collapses everything ordered into a new order'. In the kaleidoscope, technology arranges the dynamic and fragmentary image landscape of lived experience into patterns that constantly move and recombine. But for all its dazzling colours and ceaseless movement, visual experience remains bound by the parameters of a formal symmetry that never changes. For Benjamin, modern technology cannot be opposed to aura, for like allegory, aura is itself a function of modern technology; yet equally, vision is not ineluctably auratic, since the futures of technology are not fixed. However, to realize the different possibilities in technology is to move beyond the limits of art, and to reinvent the larger social and political topography that structures modern experience. 'The concepts of the rulers', writes Benjamin, 'have always been the mirror by means of whose image an "order" was established'; but modernity demands a new relationship between humanity and technology, a relationship in which 'this kaleidoscope must be smashed' (*ibid.*, p. 34).

FUTURES OF TECHNOLOGY

In his writing of the 1920s and 1930s, Benjamin's reformulation of vision and his extension of the modern concept of experience through colour were increasingly brought to bear on the question of technology. His expanded concept of '*Technik*' sought to avoid the oppositions of exteriority and interiority, and of base and superstructure, through which technology had come to be addressed; but it does so not by positing their identity, which for Benjamin is the route pursued by aesthetic perception, a response he describes by the term aura.[19] In fact, Benjamin's understanding of *Technik* envisages the increasingly violent disjunction and non-identity of technique and technology in modernity. Benjamin's attitude was informed by the events of the First World War, which provides a crucial context both for the *Arcades Project* and for his writing on contemporary technical reproduction. For Benjamin, the war manifested the violent consequences of nineteenth-century Europe's failure to come to terms with the new space and time of global technology. Instead of responding to the new, global organization of the phenomenal world, Europe sought refuge in the spatial integrity and temporal self-identity of the nation-

[19] For an account of Benjamin's idiosyncratic deployment of the opposition of base and superstructure see Hannah Arendt's essay 'Walter Benjamin: 1892–1940', included as the introduction to *Illuminations*, 1973, pp. 1–55.

state. In 'The Storyteller', Benjamin writes that 'with the World War a process began to become apparent which has not halted since':

> For never has experience been contradicted more thoroughly than strategic experience by tactical warfare, economic experience by inflation, bodily experience by mechanical warfare, moral experience by those in power. A generation that had gone to school on the horse-drawn streetcar now stood under the open sky in a countryside in which nothing remained unchanged but the clouds, and beneath these clouds, in a field of force of destructive torrents and explosions, was the tiny, fragile human body (1973, p. 84).

In his review essay of 1930, 'Theories of German Fascism', Benjamin sees the war as 'the slave revolt of technology'; that is, as the upsurge of a new configuration of space and time that can no longer be bound within the Enlightenment's restricted notion of experience (1979, pp. 120–8). The attempt by the contemporary mass movement of Fascism to reimpose the inherited co-ordinates of experience, and so subordinate the phenomenal world as 'nature', is understood by Benjamin as creating the conditions for an unprecedented upsurge of violence. 'In the parallelogram of forces formed by these two – nature and nation', Benjamin observes, 'war is the diagonal' (*ibid.*, p. 127). The essay argues that if Europe fails to recognize the new conditions of global society, or what it terms 'technology's right of co-determination in the social order', then 'millions of human bodies will indeed . . . be chopped to pieces and chewed up by iron and gas' (*ibid.*, pp. 120, 128).

If Benjamin's thinking was increasingly focused on the violent prospects of European modernity, in the *Arcades Project* he attempted to unearth the different possible futures that might lie entombed in the forgotten objects of nineteenth-century Paris. For if the character of the present is given by what in the past was successful, then what was unsuccessful may offer alternative perspectives when returned into a present in which its possibilities were not realized. The co-ordinates guiding Benjamin's methodology are themselves set out in the *Arcades Project*, when Benjamin rejects the attempts by intellectuals like Ludwig Klages to erect an opposition 'between the symbol-space of nature and that of technology'. In contrast, Benjamin argues that 'to every new configuration of nature – and at bottom, technology is just such a configuration – there correspond new "images"', or *technics* of perception and apperception (1999B, p. 390). For Benjamin, the very difficulty which the nineteenth century found in assimilating technology meant that it generated a dizzying array of different responses, of which only a restricted range became immediately successful and so were pursued. In the case of the *technics* of architecture, most prominent for Benjamin were the arcades, which he describes as 'glass before its time, premature iron'. With the success of the department store, the arcades quickly became outmoded, and were soon perceived as 'dirty and sad' (*ibid.*, p. 150). But for Benjamin, the arcades are not simply to be considered as outmoded or past, since 'everything past . . . can acquire a higher grade of actuality than it had in the moment of its existing'; however, the emergence of this 'higher actuality is determined by the image as which and in which it is comprehended'. Just as in his understanding of the convoluted temporality of visual experience, so Benjamin understands the prospects of technology in terms of 'the actualization of former contexts', which transforms the appearance of the familiar through unexpected resonances and similarites, and so 'puts the truth of all present action to the test'. Thus, writes Benjamin, 'it serves to ignite the explosive materials that are latent in what has been' (*ibid.*, p. 392).

If Benjamin saw in the disfigured landscape of the front the failure of modernity to negotiate the new organization of the phenomenal world, he saw more durable and survivable configurations of experience emerging in modern cities. In particular, in the essay on Naples he co-authored with Asja Lacis in 1924, Benjamin saw the architectural arrangement of this southern European city as anticipating central elements of modern experience, which are described through the spatial category of 'porosity' and the temporal category of 'transitivity'. 'Porosity', the essay remarks, 'is the inexhaustible law of life in this city, reappearing everywhere' (1999A, vol. 2, p. 417). However, these categories are not in themselves benign, and the responses they give rise to include poverty, violence, and crime. In a later essay, 'Experience and Poverty' (1933), Benjamin draws out a number of different responses to the porosity and transitivity of modern experience (*ibid.*, vol. 2, pp. 731–6). These include a new propensity to mysticism and superstition, and the increasing attraction of the fantasy of technological control exemplified by the cartoons of Mickey Mouse, in which 'nature and technology have completely merged' and 'everything is solved in the simplest and most comfortable way' (*ibid.*, vol. 2, p. 735). As we have seen in our earlier comparison of Mickey Mouse and Felix, such fantasies recognize the unprecedented nature of modern technology, but restrict its futures to subjective intention, or the fulfilment of the nostalgic wish. While for Benjamin such fantasies are not to be dismissed, they pale into the background beside two further responses, both of which are described as forms of barbarism. The first is described as 'a new, positive concept of barbarism', which attempts to address the unprecedented condition of global technology by 'starting from the very beginning' and shedding the traditional structures of interiority and the 'human' (*ibid.*, vol. 2, p. 733). The second form of barbarism is identified with the 'holding on to things' which 'has become the monopoly of a few powerful people'; that is, with the attempt to re-impose traditional structures of experience upon conditions with which they are violently incompatible (*ibid.*, vol. 2, p. 735). For Howard Caygill, these two conceptions of barbarism can be understood in terms of Nietzsche's distinction between 'active' and 'passive' nihilism: 'one takes destruction as the opportunity to establish a new configuration of experience, the other intensifies destruction' (1998, p. 32).

For Benjamin, the *technics* of cultural production are understood as offering ways of negotiating and assimilating the new condition of modern experience: as he writes in 'Experience and Poverty', through 'its buildings, pictures, and stories, mankind is preparing to outlive culture', adding 'the main thing is that it does so with a laugh' (1999A, vol. 2, p. 735). In contrast, Baron Haussmann's rebuilding of Paris illustrates the attempt to re-impose traditional structures of experience upon the transitivity and porosity of the modern metropolis: as Benjamin observes in the *Arcades Project*, 'Haussmann's predilection for perspectives [and] for long open vistas represents an attempt to dictate art forms to technology', in this case the 'technology of city planning' (1999B, p. 126). For Benjamin, the monumentalism of Haussmann's Paris rehearses the closed perceptual economy of aesthetic vision, which demands that the world of objects reflects back its own fixed transcendental co-ordinates; thus, Benjamin notes, 'under the bourgeoisie, cities . . . retain the character of fortifications' (*ibid.*, p. 215). While for Benjamin architecture and urban planning are in many ways the pre-eminent site for the negotiation of human experience and the 'second nature' of technology – not least because architecture has always resisted the categories of art – famously he ascribes a particular role in this process to film. Benjamin argues that the expanded 'spectrum of optical, and now acoustical, perception' in film also makes possible 'a similar deepening of apperception' (1973, p. 237). Just as in his analysis of the arcades, Benjamin attempts to identify different possible futures for perception and apperception in film, rather than describing how things stand, or how they will inevitably turn out.

Benjamin's analysis of film is prepared for by his reflections on photography in 'A Little History of Photography' (1931), and in particular by the notion of the 'optical unconscious' which he develops there (1999A, vol. 2, pp. 507–30). Benjamin's concept of the 'optical unconscious' draws on an analogy with the Freudian unconscious, but is quite distinct from it. Both terms are designed to undermine radically the supremacy of subjective intention, but as Benjamin notes, Freud's is concerned with an 'instinctual unconscious', while his own operates at the level of apperception (*ibid.*, p. 512). Echoing Baudelaire's account of the irreducible contingency of the photograph – although not his evaluation of its significance – the essay stresses the fact that the image-world captured by the camera never entirely coincides with the parameters of human intuition. Before the photograph, 'the beholder feels an irresistible urge to search . . . for the tiniest spark of contingency, of the here and now, with which reality has (so to speak) seared the subject'. Because the photographic image is organized according to the parameters of the technological apparatus, it does not conform to the co-ordinates of aesthetic technique, or subjective intention. Therefore, as Benjamin writes, 'it is another nature which speaks to the camera rather than to the eye', an image-world which is '"other" above all in the sense that a space informed by human consciousness gives way to a space informed by the unconscious'. For Benjamin, the significance of this difference emerges in retrospect, since the co-ordinates of human perception are under-stood as variable and constantly changing. While such moments appear initially as distortion or incoherence because they fail to return the gaze, they may subsequently become meaningful or coherent within new regimes of perception. Within this expanded temporal perspective the element of contingency introduced by the camera is not blank or worthless, but can be recognized as 'the inconspicuous spot where in the immediacy of that long-forgotten moment the future nests so eloquently that we, looking back, may rediscover it' (*ibid.*, vol. 2, p. 510). According to the essay, the photograph's capturing of contin-gency has two important consequences, although subsequent critical accounts have tended to identify only the first of these. By revealing the historically variable nature of visibility, the elements of contingency captured in the photographic image undermine the fixity of the apperceptive conditions of vision claimed by auratic perception: thus, Benjamin writes, photographs 'suck the aura out of reality like water from a sinking ship' (*ibid.*, vol. 2, p. 518). But further, photographs also demand a different apperceptive arrangement; or in Benjamin's terms, they 'bring things *closer* to us'. By 'presenting [things] at face value', the photographic image 'sets the scene for a salutary estrange-ment between man and his surroundings', which are no longer subordinate to the prior parameters of human intuition. Instead, the co-ordinates of perception must negotiate the variable space and time of things, a situation which the essay describes as giving 'free play to the politically educated eye, under whose gaze all intimacies are sacrificed to the illumination of detail' (*ibid.*, vol. 2, p. 519). However, as the essay notes, while this new situation is anticipated by pho-tography, it is realized most emphatically by film, and it is in terms of film that Benjamin subsequently develops his account of the new possibilities for visual experience in modernity.

The importance of film for Benjamin lies in its joining together of individual images, an aspect of film technology which provides a constructive principle that reinvents the parameters of Kantian judge-ment. A useful context for reading Benjamin's analysis of film in these terms is provided by the comparison made between the picture puzzle and the kaleidoscope in the *Arcades Project*. As we have seen, for Benjamin the kaleidoscope presents a technical arrangement that restricts the futures of visual experience, offering only the eternal return of the same. Or to put it another way, while the kaleidoscope allows for different rules of arrangement or form, the canon of form or the condition of legality always remains the same. Thus the kaleidoscope images the technological re-imposition of aesthetic perception, which Benjamin increasingly describes in terms of the contemplation demanded by works of art. In the *Arcades Project* the kaleidoscope is compared to the picture puzzles that became popular at about the same time, and which were composed of a mêlée of juxtaposed images and text, all arranged according to different axes of orientation on the page. The comparison presents these picture puzzles as constituting a different visual matrix to that of the kaleidoscope, one which anticipates the commodity, the captioned photograph, photomontage, the chaotic visual scene of contemporary city streets, and film – but which also looks back to allegory. For Benjamin, the picture puzzle describes a way of relating visual experience and discursive meaning – or what Kant had termed the 'schematizing' of intuition and concept – that is not circumscribed by the imposition of a fixed transcendental canon or condition of legality, but which is open to new possible configurations of arrangement, and so reinvents the canon of law or form. Thus, the picture puzzle is described as the 'schemata of dreamwork', although if this description alludes to Freud, Benjamin makes clear that 'we, however . . . are less on the trail of the psyche than on the track of things' (1999B, p. 212). Benjamin illustrates this reformulation of Kantian schematism through the figure of the allegorist:

> Through the disorderly fund which his knowledge places at his disposal, the allegorist rummages here and there for a particular piece, holds it next to some other piece, and tests if they fit together – that meaning with this image or this image with that meaning. The result *can never be known beforehand*, for there is no natural mediation between the two . . . At no point is it written in the stars that the allegorist's profundity will lead it to one meaning rather than another. And though it may once have acquired such a meaning, this can always be withdrawn in favour of a different meaning (*ibid.*, pp. 368–9; emphasis added).

In the picture puzzle, the relationship between visual experience and meaning is not fixed within a prior transcendental frame, in which the forms of intuition (space and time) and the categorical structure of discursive meaning are given. Rather, the frame itself emerges from the contingent juxtapositions of meaning and image which occur in the distracted gaze of the allegorist, who 'tests' different meanings against ever new visual arrangements.

Benjamin extends this description of 'distracted testing' to the medium of film in his seminal essay, 'The Work of Art in the Epoch of its Technical Reproducibility'.[20] Significantly, Benjamin's analysis considers film as a medium and is not simply directed towards avant-garde film practices, an orientation that stems from his broader understanding of visual experience (cf. 1999B, pp. 395–6). Because vision is understood in terms of the seeing of similarities as opposed to the seeing of objects by a subject, the essay does not assume a fixed 'reality' lying 'behind' technological appearance, which would alternatively be 'hidden' or brought to light by particular aesthetic techniques or formal innovations. Indeed, as the essay points out, within technological modernity the perception of a 'reality' that would be 'equipment-free' is itself the 'height of artifice' (1973, p. 235). Rather, the central issue for Benjamin is that the medium of film offers a perceptual matrix that is able to match the transitivity and porosity of the 'second nature' of modern technology, and as such it implies an entirely new relationship between 'technology' and 'technique'. From the aesthetic viewpoint, 'technique' seeks to arrange dead exteriority – or 'technology' – within the rigid space and time of a fixed transcendental organization; but in film, technique negotiates with technology from *within technology*. That is, film responds to the porosity and transitivity of the phenomenal world by producing an image-world that functions in these same terms, allowing modes of visual experience that respond to the new conditions of experience, rather than seeking to impose fixed parameters. Or, as Benjamin remarks, 'because of its thoroughgoing permeation of reality with mechanical equipment', film

---

[20] 'The Work of Art in the Age of Mechanical Reproduction' in *Illuminations*, 1973, pp. 219–53; in the text I follow the what has become established English translation of the essay's title, rather than Harry Zohn's translation in *Illuminations*.

makes it possible to see 'an aspect of reality which is free of all equipment' (*ibid.*, p. 236). Benjamin is not claiming here that in film we see the 'real', but that film articulates the possibility of a relationship between technique and the 'second nature' of technology which is not one of subordination, but is reciprocal and open to negotiation. This understanding of film is elaborated in the essay in terms of a reformulation of the terms of Kantian judgement, a reformulation in which the law of form is not located prior to perception, but is invented in the moment of perception itself. As the essay explains, in film, images are not subordinated to a prior framework or canon of coherence and meaningfulness, but instead, 'the meaning of each single picture [is] prescribed by the sequence of all the preceding ones' (*ibid.*, p. 228). That is, the spatio-temporal co-ordinates of formal coherence and meaning are themselves produced through the sequencing and interrelation of images, rather than being a function of a fixed transcendental framework. Benjamin illustrates this idea through an analogy between the film camera and the surgeon: like the surgeon, the camera 'penetrates deeply into [the] web' of the phenomenal world, cutting it up into 'fragments' which 'are assembled under a new law' (*ibid.*, p. 236). Or, in the vocabulary of nearness and distance, film immerses the apperceptive frame within the contingent arrangement of appearances, rather than imposing a static transcendental framework from without. In these terms, the law of visibility is not fixed and established prior to experience, but is itself open to renegotiation and reinvention in technology.

For Benjamin, film offers an expansion of perception that reformulates the transcendental structure of the critical philosophy, and which therefore also has important implications for knowledge and for politics. However, just as in the case of Benjamin's description of Naples, this assessment of film is not in and of itself benign. As he notes throughout the 'Work of Art' essay, without a broader reorganization of the social, political, and economic structuring of modernity, 'no other revolutionary merit can be accredited to today's film than the promotion of a revolutionary criticism of the traditional concepts of art' (*ibid.*, p. 233). Indeed, where Benjamin directly addresses the potential of film within existing social structures, he envisages a process of 'selection' before the technologies of image circulation 'from which the star and the dictator emerge victorious' (*ibid.*, p. 249 n. 12). And in the epilogue to the essay, Benjamin sees an increasing disjunction between political organization, or 'technique', and the new space and time of global technology: 'if the natural utilization of productive forces is impeded by the property system, the increase in technical devices, in speed, and in the sources of energy will press for an unnatural utilization, and this is found in war'. From the perspective of the late 1930s, Benjamin saw a stark choice between Fascism – which reimposes the traditional configuration of the nation-state, so rendering politics 'aesthetic' – and communism – which the essay claims 'responds by politicizing art' (*ibid.*, p. 244). However, in *One Way Street* (1928), written nearly a decade earlier, Benjamin had glimpsed different futures for technology which exceed this restricted polarity, and it is here that the significance of Benjamin's approach for our contemporary situation emerges most clearly (1996, vol. 1, pp. 444–88).

In the closing section of *One Way Street*, Benjamin observes that 'in technology, a *physis* is being organized through which mankind's contact with the cosmos takes a new and different form from that which it had in nations and families' (*ibid.*, vol. 1, p. 487). In the same text, Benjamin offers an image which dramatizes these changes in terms that provide a marked contrast with the recent theoretical positions we have considered. Where Debord, Baudrillard, Virilio, and Jameson see technology as withdrawing visual experience from its involvement in the economic, social, and political imperatives of modernity, Benjamin situates vision's fate in technology at the heart of the modern *polis*:

> Just as all things, in a perpetual process of mingling and contamina-tion, are losing their intrinsic character while ambiguity displaces authenticity, so is the city. Great cities – whose incomparably sustaining and reassuring power encloses those at work within them in the peace of the fortress and lifts from them, with the view of the horizon, awareness of the ever vigilant elemental forces – are seen to be breached at all points by the invading countryside. Not by the landscape, but by what in untrammelled nature is most bitter: ploughed land, highways, night sky that the veil of vibrant

redness no longer conceals. The insecurity of the busy areas puts the city dweller in the opaque but truly dreadful situation in which he must assimilate, along with isolated monstrosities from the open country, the abortions of urban architectonics (*ibid.*, vol. 1, p. 454).

In this image, the temporality of modernity is shown to be complex. At one level its co-ordinates are dynamic and constantly changing, and the space and time of social interaction and experience are in a perpetual state of reformulation; but at another, the site of civility continues to be structured by a monumental architecture inherited from the past. The histories of violence through which civility has constituted itself therefore persist in the massive walls of the fortress; yet in their persistence, they are ruined and deformed, and so they describe a topography in which the past returns, although 'inauthentically' and not as it once was. The integrity of the city is breached by a 'second nature' that refuses to be fixed as 'landscape' within the temporal and spatial limits emanating from the metropolis, but which instead proves violently incompatible. Yet if the curtain walls of the fortress have been breached, they still limit the visual scope and range of its inhabitants, and so must be understood to shape the prospects for action and intercourse in new and unexpected ways.

Paradoxically, Benjamin's image presents the fate of vision in modernity as open, yet paradoxically it also locates it in a site that is shaped by the histories that converge there. The image does not necessarily imply the decline of the fortress, since the eruption of zones of violence would not inevitably disrupt its fabric. Instead, these zones might be enlisted to sustain this new, violent configuration, and therefore the organization of vision that emerges within its altered structure would render this situation 'opaque'. Yet, equally, the image does not present the future of modernity as fixed, for the moments of violent eruption also hold the possibility of transformation. The breaches in the city walls, rather than hardening within this new configuration, might open out new prospects and vistas for the inhabitants of the city, enabling organizations of vision that are no longer structured around the monumental self-identity and integrity of the inside. The fate of vision in modernity is neither one of inevitable progress nor decline, yet nor is it caught within a static and perennial condition. But if the futures of vision remain in a sense open, they are located in a site defined by the paradoxical combination of persistence and change presented by the image of the decaying fortress. For Benjamin the complexities of this situation cannot be addressed by a keener vision that 'sees through' the illusions of urban modernity, nor by a new vantage point which claims to survey it from above. Rather, it requires a different conception of the visibile, one that does not simply assume the terms of perception, but which focuses on the distortions and incoherence of visual experience in order to glimpse the changing configuration of the site which gives the law of visibility.

Afterword: Recognizing Modernity

> But one *pictures* being to oneself, perhaps in the image of
> pure light as the clarity of undimmed seeing, and then
> nothing as pure night – and this distinction is linked with
> this very familiar sensuous difference. But, as a matter of
> fact, if this very seeing is more exactly imagined, one can
> readily perceive that in absolute clearness there is seen just
> as much, and as little, as in absolute darkness, that the one
> is as good as the other, that pure seeing is a seeing of
> nothing.
>
> G. W. F. Hegel, Science of Logic

The central argument developed in this book is that any investigation of
contemporary visual culture must engage with the invisible conditions
of visual experience while at the same time addressing technology's
animation of the visible world. From this perspective, the particular
problem posed by technology is not that it empties appearances of all
value, but that it constantly reinvents the co-ordinates of visual experience. To recall Husserl's phrase, critical analysis cannot presuppose the
self-presence of the visible 'in the blink of an eye', and therefore it
cannot assume a fixed and universal transcendental architecture or
framework. Without equating the work of two very different thinkers,
this study argues that Benjamin's approach to vision and technology
anticipates important aspects of Derrida's call to rethink the transcendental conditions of perceptual experience. In these terms, Benjamin's
achievement lies in sustaining a double commitment, on the one hand
to tracing the apperceptive conditions of vision, and on the other to
registering the historical specificity of visual experience.

In this light, there is a considerable irony in the claim made by Debord, Baudrillard, Virilio, and Jameson to have broken decisively with the pure visibility of modern thought. For in arguing that there is nothing to see in technological appearances, they repeat the reduction that Benjamin identified in the Enlightenment's Newtonian conception of experience. But there is a further irony here, since one of the central criticisms of modern conceptions of vision has centred on the unacknowledged violence of their universal claims. The positions developed by many contemporary cultural critics are in fact character-ized by a similar universalizing tendency, yet their accounts are modelled on an extremely restricted context of experience, usually associated with the urban centres of the West Coast of the United States. Indeed, as Josh Cohen has argued, Los Angeles has assumed a 'paradigmatic status' within recent analyses of the new condition of visual culture, a role he identifies in the work of Baudrillard, Virilio, and Jameson among others (1998, p. 114). In contrast, the study of nineteenth-century Paris, which occupied much of Benjamin's last decade, refuses to ascribe such a status to the city, endeavouring instead to trace the myriad patterns of experience interred in the wreckage of the nineteenth century, against which moments of similar-ity emerge within the shifting optics of the present. However abstruse Benjamin's thinking of vision may sometimes be, in a very immediate sense it suggests some important lessons for cultural analysis. As indicated by the series of city portraits which criss-cross his writing on modernity – from Naples in the south, to Moscow in the east, Paris in the west, and Berlin, uncomfortably, at the centre – the revaluation of spatio-temporal experience requires an engagement with the specificity of different contexts of experience; not, however, as fixed co-ordinates, but as a network of vantage points through which to view other cities and other modes of experience, and thereby reflect on the limits of each particular condition of seeing. Even though Benjamin's own analyses were limited to the cities of Europe, his methodology implicitly argues that in order to address the cultures of global technology, criticism must explore and overlay different patterns of experience. And in the light of the ever-expanding reach of modern technology, we might add that now more than ever, criticism must look beyond the limits of Europe and the West.

The broader theoretical significance of Benjamin's approach emerges in the context of the widespread suspicion of the role of vision and the visible in modern thought. As we saw in the introduction, this suspicion has been powerfully articulated by Richard Beardsworth in terms of the political blindness of modern conceptions of visibility and recognition. In particular, Beardsworth argues that the central axis of modern political thought, associated with Kant and Hegel, depends on a 'logic' of recognition that 'is cast in terms of light and dark', an oppositional logic which implies a commitment to the presence of what is there before us and is visible (1996, p. 87). By locating violence in a site – and therefore assuming its visibility and presence to consciousness – modern recognition 'ends up being blind because it is unable to see beyond the law of visibility' (*ibid.*, p. 94). The significance of Howard Caygill's reinterpretation of Benjamin's work lies in its identification of a different conception of visibility. Within the terms of Caygill's reading, Benjamin's thinking can be understood as an attempt to address the specificity and locatedness of visual experience without reducing it to conscious intention or casting it as fully present, while at the same time seeking to glimpse intimations of the conditions which give 'the law of visibility' in the shifting patterns of similarity, distortion, and incoherence which necessarily arise there. As such, it describes a way of looking beyond the law of visibility precisely by directing its gaze upon the blurring and distortion that emerges within vision.

By way of a conclusion, however, I would like to suggest that the value of Caygill's rereading of Benjamin lies as much in its identification of his failures as of his achievements. According to Caygill, Benjamin's thinking attempts to sustain a difficult poise between irreconcilable demands. In seeking to revalue spatio-temporal experience, Benjamin understands this project to involve rethinking its relationship with the absolute. In Caygill's terms, his solution seeks to evade 'Kant's exclusion of the absolute from all but moral experience', while at the same time rejecting 'the Hegelian view of a developmental history of spirit, or the continuous process of mediation between the absolute and spatio-temporal experience' (1998, p. 2). Benjamin's 'transcendental but speculative philosophy' is therefore 'an anti-Hegelian speculative philosophy driven by a nihilistic refusal of any attempt to grasp or comprehend the absolute through finite categories' (*ibid.*, p. 1). But as such, it finds itself caught within significant epistemological and political difficulties. In epistemological terms, Caygill argues that Benjamin must 'at once deriv[e] the categories from temporal experience while according them the dignity of being more than a by-product of experience' (*ibid.*, p. 26). Equally, if Benjamin seeks to reinvent the modern concept of freedom as 'a freedom of movement or transitivity rather than the positional freedom of a subject', then the question remains as to how this transitivity is to orientate itself within the complex and uneven spatio-temporal co-ordinates of global technology (*ibid.*, p. 121). Yet if Caygill suggests that Benjamin's work 'may even in the end be judged a cautionary failure', within the context traced here Benjamin's thinking can be seen to retain a particular significance for contemporary theoretical debates precisely in revealing such difficulties (*ibid.*, p. 3). From this perspective, Benjamin's work both offers resources for rethinking spatio-temporal experience, and serves to remind us of the urgency of questions that have slipped from view or which have come to appear redundant.

These broader theoretical questions necessarily lie beyond the scope of the present study, but in closing it is possible to identify aspects of Benjamin's own methodology that might help to frame them. In the face of the unprecedented character of modern technology, contemporary theory has tended to emphasize the inapplicability of earlier paradigms and to identify its own positions as inaugurating a radical and even apocalyptic break with the past. But such a perspective assumes the self-identity of the past, and casts earlier modes of thinking as univocal and fixed. This study has looked to find different ways of negotiating the inheritance bequeathed by modern culture – for example, in our reading of Baudelaire's poem 'The Eyes of the Poor', and in Derrida's reinterpretation of Husserl's *Phenomenology of Internal Time-Consciousness*. Benjamin's own methodology can be seen to explore the temporal complexity of rereading and return, whether at the level of cultural analysis or at the level of his recasting of Kant. In examining both the objects of experience and the intuitive and conceptual frameworks through which they are apprehended, Benjamin's intellectual gaze describes a kind of looking back that seeks to grasp the specificity of the present in relation to the changing actuality of the past. The past – whether as the artefacts or images that survive into the present, or as earlier conceptual configurations which persist within our inherited structures of thought – is subject to ruin and decay while, in modernity, the very condition of the past's transmissibility is shattered. Yet the past is not eradicated, but always returns, even though this return is inescapably inauthentic and distorting, and necessarily involves absence, disfigurement, and loss. Benjamin's thinking suggests that we cannot simply disregard the past, nor dream of escaping it absolutely. But equally, it also demonstrates that retrospection need not be nostalgic, since the moment of looking back is also the moment when we might catch a glimpse of different possible futures.

Bibliography

Altieri, C. 1979. *Enlarging the Temple*. Lewisburg: Bucknell University Press.

Arendt, H. 1989. *The Human Condition*. Chicago: University of Chicago Press.

Aumont, J. 1994. *The Image*, trans. C. Pajackowska. London: B.F.I.

Barthes, R. 1973. *Mythologies*, trans. A. Lavers. London: Granada.

Baudelaire, C. 1972. *Selected Writings on Art and Literature*, trans. P. E. Charvet. Harmondsworth: Penguin.

—— 1989. *The Poems in Prose*, vol. 2, trans. F. Scarfe. London: Anvil.

—— 1993. *Flowers of Evil*, trans. J. McGowan, Oxford: O.U.P.

Baudrillard, J. 1981. *For a Critique of the Political Economy of the Sign*, trans. C. Levin. n.p.: Telos.

—— 1988A. *America*, trans. C. Turner. London: Verso.

—— 1988B. *Selected Writings*, ed. M. Poster. Cambridge: Polity.

—— 1990. *Seduction*, trans. B. Singer. London: Macmillan.

—— [1976] 1993. *Symbolic Exchange and Death*, trans. I. Grant. London: Sage.

—— [1968] 1996. *The System of Objects*, trans. J. Benedict. London: Verso.

—— [1970] 1998 *Consumer Society*, trans. C. Turner. London: Sage.

Baudry, J.-L. 1974–5. 'Ideological effects of the basic cinematographic apparatus'. *Film Quarterly*, 27:2.

Beardsworth, R. 1996. *Derrida and the Political*. London: Routledge.

Benjamin, A. 1997. *Present Hope. Philosophy, Architecture, Judaism*. London: Routledge.

—— and P. Osborne, eds. 1994. *Walter Benjamin's Philosophy. Destruction and Experience*. London: Routledge.

Benjamin, W. 1973. *Illuminations*, trans. H. Zohn. London: Fontana.

—— 1977. *The Origin of German Tragic Drama*, trans. J. Osborne. London: Verso.

—— 1979. 'Theories of German Fascism'. *New German Critique*, 17.

—— 1983. *Charles Baudelaire*, trans. H. Zohn. London: Verso.

— 1985. 'Central Park', trans. L. Spencer. *New German Critique*, 34.

— 1996. *Selected Writings*, vol. 1, trans. R. Livingstone *et al*. Cambridge, M.A.: Belknap-Harvard University Press.

— 1999A. *Selected Writings*, vol. 2. Cambridge, M. A.: Belknap-Harvard University Press.

— 1999B. *The Arcades Project*, trans. H. Eiland and K. McLaughlin. Cambridge, M.A.: Belknap-Harvard University Press.

Berman, M. 1983. *All that Is Solid Melts into Air. The Experience of Modernity*. London: Verso.

Bernstein, J. 1984. *The Philosophy of the Novel. Lukács, Marxism and the Dialectics of Form*. Brighton: Harvester.

Bürger, P. 1984. *Theory of the Avant-garde*, trans. M. Shaw. Minneapolis: University of Minnesota Press.

Cassirer, E. 1981. *Kant's Life and Thought*, trans. J. Haden. New Haven: Yale University Press.

Caygill, H. 1998. *Walter Benjamin. The colour of experience*. London: Routledge.

Clark, T. J. 1973. *The Absolute Bourgeois. Artists and Politics in France 1848–1851*. London: Thames & Hudson.

Cohen, J. 1998. *Spectacular Allegories. Postmodern American Writing and the Politics of Seeing*. London: Pluto.

Crafton, D. 1993. *Before Mickey. The Animated Film 1898–1928*. Chicago: University of Chicago Press.

Crary, J. 1999. *Suspensions of Perception. Attention, Spectacle, and Modern Culture*. Cambridge, M.A.: M.I.T. Press.

Debord, G. 1983. *Society of the Spectacle*. Detroit: Black & Red.

Derrida, J. 1973. *Speech and Phenomena. And Other Essays on Husserl's Theory of Signs*, trans. D. B. Allison. Evanston: Northwestern University Press.

— 1978. *Edmund Husserl's Origin of Geometry: An Introduction*, trans. J. P. Leavey. Stony Brook: Nicolas Hays.

Descartes, R. 1988. *Selected Philosophical Writings*, trans. J. Cottingham *et al*. Cambridge: C.U.P.

— 1998. *The World and Other Writings*, trans. S. Gaukroger. Cambridge: C.U.P.

Descombes, V. 1980. *Modern French Philosophy*, trans. L. Scott-Fox and J. M. Harding. Cambridge: C.U.P.

Foucault, M. 1970. *The Order of Things*. London: Routledge.

Freund, G. 1980. *Photography and Society*. London: Gordon Fraser.

Galassi, P. 1981. *Before Photography*. New York: Museum of Modern Art.

Garber, D. 2001. *Descartes Embodied. Reading Cartesian Philosophy through Cartesian Science*. Cambridge: C.U.P.

Habermas, J. 1979. 'Conscious-raising or redemptive criticism: the contemporaneity of Walter Benjamin', trans. P. Brewster and C. H. Buchner. *New German Critique*, 17.

Hegel, G. W. F. 1969. *Science of Logic*, trans. A. V. Miller. London: George Allen & Unwin.

Heidegger, M. 1975. *Poetry, Language, Thought*, trans. A. Hofstadter. New York: Harper & Row.

Husserl, E. 1964. *The Phenomenology of Internal Time-Consciousness*, trans. J. S. Churchill. Bloomington: Indiana University Press.

Jameson, F. 1991. *Postmodernism or, the Cultural Logic of Late Capitalism*. London: Verso.

Jay, M. 1993. *Downcast Eyes. The Denigration of Vision in Twentieth Century French Thought*. Berkeley: University of California Press.

Kant, I. 1929. *Critique of Pure Reason*, trans. N. K. Smith. London: Macmillan.

— 1987. *Critique of Judgement*, trans. W. S. Pluhar. Indianapolis: Hackett.

Levin, D. M., ed. 1993. *Modernity and the Hegemony of Vision*, Berkeley: University of California Press.

Levinas, E. 1998. *Discovering Existence with Husserl*, trans. R. A. Cohen and M. B. Smith, Evanston: Northwestern University Press.

Lowney, J. 1991. 'The "Post-anti-Aesthetic" poetics of Frank O'Hara'. *Contemporary Literature*, 32:2.

Lukács, G. 1971. *History and Class Consciousness*, trans. R. Livingstone. London: Merlin.

Lyotard, J.-F. 1984. *The Postmodern Condition: A Report on Knowledge*, trans. G. Bennington and B. Massumi. Manchester: Manchester University Press.

Maltin, L. 1987. *Of Mice and Magic: A History of American Animated Cartoons*. New York: Plume.

Marcus, L. and L. Nead, eds. 1998. *The Actuality of Walter Benjamin*. London: Lawrence and Wishart.

McCole, J. 1993. *Walter Benjamin and the Antinomies of Tradition*. Ithaca: Cornell University Press.

Merleau-Ponty, M. 1964A. *The Primacy of Perception*, trans. W. Cobb *et al*. Evanston: Northwestern University Press.

— 1964B. *Sense and Non-sense*, trans. H. L. Dreyfus and P. A. Dreyfus. Evanston: Northwestern University Press.

Merritt, R. and J. B. Kaufman. 1993. *Walt in Wonderland. The Silent Films of Walt Disney*. Pordenone: La Giornate del Cinema Muto.

Metz, C. 1986. *The Imaginary Signifier: Psychoanalysis and Cinema*, trans. C. Britton *et al*. Bloomington: Indiana University Press.

Neale, S. 1985. *Cinema and Technology*. London: Macmillan.

Nietzsche, F. 1993. *The Birth of Tragedy*, trans. S. Whiteside. Harmondsworth: Penguin.

O'Hara, F. 1995. *The Collected Poems of Frank O'Hara*. Berkeley: University of California Press.

Owen, D. 1995. *Nietzsche, Politics and Modernity*. London: Sage.

Park, D. 1997. *The Fire within the Eye. A Historical Essay on the Nature and Meaning of Light*. Princeton: Princeton University Press.

Perloff, M. 1977. *Frank O'Hara. Poet among Painters*. New York: Braziller.

Pippin, R. B. 1991. *Modernism as a Philosophical Problem*. Oxford: Blackwell.

Riegl, A. 1985. *Late Roman Art Industry*, trans. R. Winkes. n.p: Giorgio Bretschneider.

Roberts, J. 1982. *Walter Benjamin*. London: Macmillan.

Rose, G. 1978. *The Melancholy Science. An Introduction to the Thought of T. W. Adorno*. London: Macmillan.

— 1979. *Hegel contra Sociology*. London: Athlone.

Ross. A. 1990. 'The Death of Lady Day'. In *Frank O'Hara*, ed. J. Elledge. Ann Arbor: University of Michigan Press.

Scharf, A. 1974. *Art and Photography*. Harmondsworth: Penguin.

Virilio, P. 1989. *War and Cinema*, trans. P. Camiller. London: Verso.

— 1994. *The Vision Machine*, trans. J. Rose. London: B.F.I.

Zaborowska, M., ed. 1998. *Other Americans, Other Americas*. Aarhus: Aarhus University Press.

Index